SAT® Subject Test:

PHYSICS

2015–2016

RELATED KAPLAN TITLES FOR COLLEGE-BOUND STUDENTS

AP Biology
AP Calculus AB & BC
AP Chemistry
AP English Language & Composition
AP English Literature & Composition
AP Environmental Science
AP European History
AP Human Geography
AP Macroeconomics/Microeconomics
AP Physics B & C
AP Psychology
AP Statistics
AP U.S. Government & Politics
AP U.S. History
AP World History

ACT Strategies, Practice, and Personalized Feedback
ACT 6 Practice Tests with 12 Expert Video Tutorials

SAT Strategies, Practice, and Review
SAT Premier
12 Practice Tests for the SAT
SAT Critical Reading Workbook
SAT Math Workbook
SAT Writing Workbook

Frankenstein: A Kaplan Score-Raising Classic
The Tales of Edgar Allan Poe: A Kaplan Score-Raising Classic
Dr. Jekyll and Mr. Hyde: A Kaplan Score-Raising Classic
The Scarlet Letter: A Kaplan Score-Raising Classic
The War of the Worlds: A Kaplan Score-Raising Classic
Wuthering Heights: A Kaplan Score-Raising Classic

SAT Subject Test: Biology E/M
SAT Subject Test: Chemistry
SAT Subject Test: Literature
SAT Subject Test: Mathematics Level 1
SAT Subject Test: Mathematics Level 2
SAT Subject Test: U.S. History

SAT® Subject Test:

PHYSICS

2015–2016

Hugh Henderson

KAPLAN PUBLISHING

New York

This publication is designed to provide accurate and authoritative information in regard to the subject matter covered. It is sold with the understanding that the publisher is not engaged in rendering legal, accounting, or other professional service. If legal advice or other expert assistance is required, the services of a competent professional should be sought.

© 2015 Grace Freedson's Publishing Network, LLC.

Published by Kaplan Publishing, a division of Kaplan, Inc.
395 Hudson Street
New York, NY 10014

Printed in the United States of America

10 9 8 7 6 5 4 3 2 1

ISBN-13: 978-1-61865-847-0

Kaplan Publishing books are available at special quantity discounts to use for sales promotions, employee premiums, or educational purposes. For more information or to purchase books, please call the Simon & Schuster special sales department at 866-506-1949.

Table of Contents

ABOUT THE AUTHOR

Hugh Henderson received his bachelor of science degree in physics from Stephen F. Austin State University, and earned a master's degree in physics and teaching from the University of Texas at Dallas in 1991. He is a former member of the Physics Test Development Committee for the Advanced Placement Program® and has led numerous workshops in the United States and abroad for teachers and students in science curriculum and test preparation. He has authored several articles on science education and has taught physics at Plano Senior High School in Plano, Texas, since 1985.

The author would like to give special thanks to Connie Wells for her invaluable suggestions in the preparation of this book, and to his wife Rachel, "the evidence of God's grace in my life."

AVAILABLE ONLINE

FOR ANY TEST CHANGES OR LATE-BREAKING DEVELOPMENTS
kaptest.com/publishing

The material in this book is up-to-date at the time of publication. However, the College Board and Educational Testing Service (ETS) may have instituted changes in the test after this book was published. Be sure to read the materials you receive when you register for the test.

If there are any important late-breaking developments—or any changes or corrections to the Kaplan test preparation materials in this book—we will post that information online at **kaptest.com/publishing**.

For customer service, please contact us at **booksupport@kaplan.com**.

Part One

The Basics

Chapter 1: **About the SAT Subject Tests**

- Common Questions About the SAT Subject Tests
- SAT Subject Test Mastery

You're serious about going to the college of your choice. You wouldn't have opened this book otherwise. You've made a wise choice, because this book can help you to achieve your college admissions goal. It'll show you how to score your best on the SAT Subject Test: Physics. But before you begin to prepare for the SAT Subject Test: Physics, you need some general information about the SAT Subject Tests and how this book will help you prep.

COMMON QUESTIONS ABOUT THE SAT SUBJECT TESTS

The following background information about the SAT Subject Tests is important to keep in mind as you get ready to prep for the SAT Subject Test: Physics. Remember, though, that sometimes the test makers change the test policies after a book has gone to press. The information here is accurate at the time of publication, but it's a good idea to check the test information on the College Board website at **collegeboard.com**.

What Are the SAT Subject Tests?

The SAT Subject Tests consist of more than 20 different Subject Tests. These tests are designed to measure what you have learned in such subjects as literature, American history and social studies, biology, and Spanish. Each test lasts one hour and consists entirely of multiple-choice questions. On any one test date, you can take up to three Subject Tests.

How Do the SAT Subject Tests Differ from the SAT?

The SAT is largely a test of verbal and math skills. True, you need to know some vocabulary and some formulas for the SAT; but it's designed to measure how well you read and think rather than how much you remember. The SAT Subject Tests are very different. They're designed to measure what you know about specific disciplines. Sure, critical reading and thinking skills play a part on these tests, but their main purpose is to determine exactly what you know about math, history, physics, and so on.

How Do Colleges Use the SAT Subject Tests?

> Colleges use your SAT Subject Test scores in both admissions and placement decisions.

Many people will tell you that the SAT and the Subject Tests measure only your ability to perform on standardized exams—that they measure neither your reading and thinking skills nor your level of knowledge. Maybe they're right. But these people don't work for colleges. Those schools that require SAT scores feel that these scores are an important indicator of your ability to succeed in college. Specifically, they use your scores in one or both of two ways: to help them make admissions and/or placement decisions.

Like the SAT, the SAT Subject Tests provide schools with a standard measure of academic aptitude, which they use to compare you with applicants from different high schools and different educational backgrounds. This information helps them to decide whether you're ready to handle their curriculum.

SAT Subject Test scores may also be used to decide what course of study is appropriate for you once you've been admitted. A low score on the SAT Subject Test: Literature, for example, might mean that you have to take a remedial English course. Conversely, a high score on the SAT Subject Test: Mathematics might mean that you'll be exempted from an introductory math course.

Which SAT Subject Tests Should I Take?

> Many colleges require you to take certain SAT Subject Tests. Check with all of the schools you're interested in applying to before deciding which tests to take.

The simple answer is: Those that you'll do well on. High scores, after all, can only help your chances for admission. Unfortunately, many colleges demand that you take particular tests, usually one of the mathematics tests. Some schools will give you a degree of choice in the matter, especially if they want you to take a total of three tests. Before you register to take any tests, therefore, check with the colleges you're interested in to find out exactly which tests they require. Don't rely on high school guidance counselors or admissions handbooks for this information. They might not give you accurate or current information.

When Can I Take the SAT Subject Tests?

Most of the SAT Subject Tests, including physics, are administered six times a year: in October, November, December, January, May, and June. A few of the tests are offered less frequently. Due to admissions deadlines, many colleges insist that you take the SAT Subject Tests no later than December or January of your senior year in high school. You may even have to take them sooner if you're interested in applying for "early admission" to a school.

Those schools that use scores only for placement decisions may allow you to take the SAT Subject Tests as late as May or June of your senior year. You should check with colleges to find out which test dates are most appropriate for you.

How Do I Register for the SAT Subject Tests?

The College Board administers the SAT Subject Tests, so you must sign up for the tests with them. The easiest way to register is online. Visit the College Board's website at www.collegeboard.com and click on "Register for the SAT" for registration information. If you register online, you immediately get to choose your test date and test center, and you have 24-hour access to print your admission ticket. You'll need access to a credit card to complete online registration.

If you would prefer to register by mail, you must obtain a copy of the *SAT Paper Registration Guide*. This publication contains all of the necessary information, including current test dates and fees. It can be obtained at any high school guidance office or directly from the College Board.

If you have previously registered for an SAT or SAT Subject Test, you can reregister by telephone for an additional fee ($15 at the time of this printing). If you choose this option, you should still read the College Board publications carefully before you make any decisions.

> Want to register for the SAT Subject Tests or get more info? Go to www.collegeboard.com or ask your school counselor's office for the *SAT Paper Registration Guide*, which contains a registration form, test dates, fees, and instructions.
>
> **By mail:** Mail in the registration form to the College Board.
>
> **Online:** With a credit card, you can register online at www. collegeboard.com.

How Are the SAT Subject Tests Scored?

Like the SAT, the SAT Subject Tests are scored on a 200–800 scale.

What's a "Good" Score?

That's tricky. The obvious answer is: The score that the colleges of your choice demand. Keep in mind, though, that SAT Subject Test scores are just one piece of information that colleges will use to evaluate you. The decision to accept or reject you will be based on many criteria, including your high school transcript, your SAT scores, your recommendations, your personal statement, your interview (where applicable), your extracurricular activities, and the like. So, failure to achieve the necessary score doesn't automatically mean that your chances of getting in have been damaged.

What Should I Bring to the SAT Subject Tests?

It's a good idea to get your test materials together the day before the tests. You'll need an admission ticket; a form of identification (check the *Registration Guide* or College Board website to find out what is permissible); a few sharpened No. 2 pencils; and a good eraser. (Note that calculators are not allowed on any of the SAT Subject Tests except for Math Level 1 and Math Level 2.) If you'll be registering as a standby, collect

> Gather your test materials the day before the test. You'll need
> - Your admission ticket
> - A proper form of I.D.
> - Some sharpened No. 2 pencils
> - A good eraser

the appropriate forms beforehand. Also, make sure that you know how to get to the test center.

SAT SUBJECT TEST MASTERY

Now that you know a little about the SAT Subject Tests, it's time to let you in on a few basic test-taking skills and strategies that can improve your performance on them. You should practice these skills and strategies as you prepare for the SAT Subject Tests.

Use the Test Structure to Your Advantage

The SAT Subject Tests are different from the tests that you're used to taking. On your high school tests, you probably go through the questions in order. You probably spend more time on hard questions than on easy ones, since hard questions are generally worth more points. And you often show your work, since your teachers tell you that how you approach questions is as important as getting the right answers.

None of this applies to the SAT Subject Tests. You can benefit from moving around within the tests, hard questions are worth the same as easy ones, and it doesn't matter how you answer the questions—only what your answers are.

The SAT Subject Tests are highly predictable. Because the format and directions of the SAT Subject Tests remain unchanged from test to test, you can learn the setup of each test in advance. On test day, the various question types on each test shouldn't be new to you.

One of the easiest things you can do to help your performance on an SAT Subject Test is to understand the directions before taking the test. Since the instructions are always the same, there's no reason to waste a lot of time on test day reading them. Learn them beforehand as you work through this book and the College Board publications.

> Learn SAT Subject Test directions as you prepare for the tests. That way, you'll have more time to spend answering the questions on test day.

Not all of the questions on the SAT Subject Tests are equally difficult. The questions often get harder as you work through different parts of a test. This pattern can work to your benefit. Try to be aware of where you are in a test.

When working on more basic problems, you can generally trust your first impulse—the obvious answer is likely to be correct. As you get to the end of a test section, you need to be a bit more suspicious. Now the answers probably won't come as quickly and easily; if they do, look again because the obvious answers may be wrong. Watch out for answers that just "look right." They may be *distracters*: wrong answer choices deliberately meant to entice you.

There's no mandatory order to the questions on the SAT Subject Tests. You're allowed to skip around on the SAT Subject Tests. High scorers know this fact. They move through the tests efficiently. They don't dwell on any one question, even a hard one, until they've tried every question at least once.

When you run into questions that look tough, circle them in your test booklet and skip them for the time being. Go back and try again after you've answered the easier ones if you've got time. After a second look, troublesome questions can turn out to be remarkably simple.

If you've started to answer a question but get confused, quit and go on to the next question. Persistence might pay off in high school classes, but it usually hurts your SAT Subject Test scores. Don't spend so much time answering one hard question that you use up three or four questions' worth of time. That'll cost you points, especially if you don't even get the hard question right.

> Do the questions in the order that's best for you. Skip hard questions until you've gone through every question once. Don't pass up the opportunity to score easy points by wasting time on hard questions. Come back to them later.

You can use the so-called guessing penalty to your advantage. You might have heard it said that the SAT Subject Tests have a "guessing penalty." That's a misnomer. It's really a *wrong-answer penalty*. If you guess wrong, you get a small penalty. If you guess right, you get full credit.

The fact is, if you can eliminate one or more answer choices as definitely wrong, you'll turn the odds in your favor and actually come out ahead by guessing. The fractional points that you lose are meant to offset the points you might get "accidentally" by guessing the correct answer. With practice, however, you'll see that it's often easy to eliminate *several* answer choices on some of the questions.

> Don't guess, unless you can eliminate at least one answer choice. Don't leave a question blank unless you have absolutely no idea how to answer it.

The answer grid has no heart. It sounds simple, but it's extremely important: Don't make mistakes filling out your answer grid. When time is short, it's easy to get confused going back and forth between your test booklet and your grid. If you know the answers, but misgrid them, you won't get the points. Here's how to avoid mistakes.

Always circle the questions you skip. Put a big circle in your test booklet around any question numbers that you skip. When you go back, these questions will be easy to relocate. Also, if you accidentally skip a box on the grid, you'll be able to check your grid against your booklet to see where you went wrong.

> A common mistake is filling in all of the questions with the right answers—in the wrong spots. Whenever you skip a question, circle it in your test booklet and make doubly sure that you skip it on the answer grid as well.

Always circle the answers you choose. Circling your answers in the test booklet makes it easier to check your grid against your booklet.

Grid five or more answers at once. Don't transfer your answers to the grid after every question. Transfer them after every five questions. That way, you won't keep breaking your concentration to mark the grid. You'll save time and gain accuracy.

A Strategic Approach to SAT Subject Test Questions

Apart from knowing the setup of the SAT Subject Tests that you'll be taking, you've got to have a system for attacking the questions. You wouldn't travel around an unfamiliar city without a map, and you shouldn't approach the SAT Subject Tests without a plan. What follows is the best method for approaching SAT Subject Test questions systematically.

Think about the questions before you look at the answers. The test makers love to put distracters among the answer choices. Distracters are answers that look like they're correct, but aren't. If you jump right into the answer choices without thinking first about what you're looking for, you're much more likely to fall for one of these traps.

> Try to think of the answer to a question before you shop among the answer choices. If you've got some idea of what you're looking for, you'll be less likely to be fooled by "trap" choices.

Guess—when you can eliminate at least one answer choice. You already know that the "guessing penalty" can work in your favor. Don't simply skip questions that you can't answer. Spend some time with them in order to see whether you can eliminate any of the answer choices. If you can, it pays for you to guess.

Pace yourself. The SAT Subject Tests give you a lot of questions in a short period of time. To get through the tests, you can't spend too much time on any single question. Keep moving through the tests at a good speed. If you run into a hard question, circle it in your test booklet, skip it, and come back to it later if you have time.

> Work quickly on easier questions to leave more time for harder questions, but not so quickly that you make careless errors. And it's okay to leave a few questions blank if you have to—you can still get a high score.

You don't have to spend the same amount of time on every question. Ideally, you should be able to work through the easier questions at a brisk, steady clip, and use a little more time on the harder questions. One caution: Don't rush through basic questions just to save time for the harder ones. The basic questions are points in your pocket, and you're better off not getting to some harder questions if it means losing easy points because of careless mistakes. Remember, you don't earn any extra credit for answering hard questions.

Locate quick points if you're running out of time. Some questions can be done more quickly than others because they require less work or because choices can be eliminated more easily. If you start to run out of time, look for these quicker questions.

When you take the SAT Subject Tests, you have one clear objective in mind: to score as many points as you can. It's that simple. The rest of this book is dedicated to helping you to do that on the SAT Subject Test: Physics.

Chapter 2: **Getting Ready for the SAT Subject Test: Physics**

- Content
- Scoring Information
- Question Types
- Kaplan Strategies
- Stress Management
- Tips for Just Before the Test

CONTENT

The SAT Subject Test: Physics expects you to have a mastery of the concepts and principles covered in a one-year, college-prep physics class. This one-hour exam consists of 75 multiple-choice questions covering the topics in the outline that follows. The questions will require you to recall and understand the terms, principles, and concepts listed in Table 2.1 and apply these to solve specific physics problems. You will also need to show your understanding of simple algebraic, trigonometric, and graphical relationships, such as equations, sine, cosine, tangent, slope, and area under a curve, as well as ratios and proportions.

You will not be allowed to use a calculator on this exam, but don't worry; the math should be nothing more than simple calculations—nothing more difficult than multiplication or division. You will be provided with any physical constants you may need, along with the values of relevant trigonometric relationships such as sine, cosine, and tangent.

Occasionally, you will be given some laboratory data and asked to draw conclusions about the data or the analysis of the data—for example, you may have to interpret a graph. Of course, the SAT Subject Test: Physics is limited in the amount of lab skills it can test, since the format of the test includes only multiple-choice questions.

Table 2.1: Topics on the SAT Subject Test: Physics

Topic	Percent of Test
Mechanics	**36–42%**
Kinematics velocity, acceleration, one-dimensional motion, projectile motion	
Dynamics force, Newton's laws, statics	
Energy and Momentum potential and kinetic energy, work, power, impulse, conservation laws	
Circular Motion and Rotation uniform circular motion, centripetal force, torque, angular momentum	
Vibrations simple harmonic motion, mass on a spring, simple pendulum	
Gravity law of gravitation and orbits	
Electricity and Magnetism	**18–24%**
Electric Fields, Forces, and Potentials Coulomb's law, induced charge, field and potential of groups of point charges, charged particles in electric fields	
Magnetic Fields and Forces permanent magnets, fields caused by currents, particles in magnetic fields	
Electromagnetic Induction induced currents and fields	
Circuits and Circuit Elements capacitance, resistance, Ohm's law, Joule's law, DC circuits with resistance and capacitance	
Waves	**15–19%**
General Wave Properties speed, frequency, wavelength, Doppler effect	
Reflection and Refraction Snell's law, changes in wavelength and speed	
Interference, Diffraction, and Polarization single-slit diffraction, double-slit interference, standing wave patterns	
Ray Optics image formation in lenses and mirrors	

(Continued on next page)

Topic	Percent of Test
Heat, Kinetic Theory, and Thermodynamics	**6–11%**
Thermal Properties mechanical equivalent of heat, temperature, specific and latent heats, thermal expansion, heat transfer	
Gases and Kinetic Theory ideal gas law from molecular properties	
Laws of Thermodynamics first and second laws, internal energy, heat engine efficiency	
Modern Physics	**6–11%**
Quantum Phenomena photons, photoelectric effect, the uncertainty principle	
Atomic Physics Rutherford and Bohr models, atomic energy levels, atomic spectra	
Nuclear and Particle Physics radioactivity, nuclear or particle reactions	
Special Relativity mass-energy equivalence, limiting velocity	
Contemporary Physics astrophysics, biophysics, superconductivity	
Miscellaneous	**4–9%**
Measurement	
Math Skills	
Laboratory Skills	
History of Physics	
Questions of a General Nature That Overlap Several Topics	

The review chapters in this book follow these topics closely. As you can see, the SAT Subject Test: Physics covers a broad range of topics. It requires you to think about these topics in ways you may not have done before. As a result, it's likely that some test questions will involve topics that you did not cover in your physics class. Don't be alarmed; there is so much to physics that you cannot possibly cover everything in a year. If, while taking the diagnostic test in this book, you discover that there are areas you haven't covered in school, plan to spend a little extra time on those chapters that cover your areas of weakness.

There are three levels of concept application used throughout the SAT Subject Test: Physics. *Recall questions*, comprising 20 to 33 percent of the test (15–25 questions), require you to simply remember a definition or concept. *Single-concept questions* require you to apply a single concept to a question in order to arrive at the answer. These questions typically comprise 40 to 53 percent of the test (30–40 questions). *Multiple-concept questions* require you to think through and relate (synthesize) several concepts together to arrive at an answer to a question. These are often the most difficult of the three levels of concept application, and comprise 20 to 33 percent of the test (15–25 questions).

Three basic skills are tested on the SAT Subject Test: Physics:
1. Recalling information
2. Applying knowledge
3. Synthesizing information

SCORING INFORMATION

This exam is scored in a range from 200 to 800 (in multiples of 10), just like a section of the SAT. Your raw score is calculated by subtracting ¼ of the number of questions you got wrong from the number of questions you got right. If you answered 55 questions correctly and 17 questions incorrectly, having skipped 3 questions, then your raw score would be:

Number correct	55
$\frac{1}{4} \times$ Number incorrect:	– 4.25
Raw score:	50.75 (rounded to 51)

This raw score is then compared to all the other test takers' scores to come up with a scaled score. This scaling takes into account any slight variations between test administrations. On a recent administration, it was possible to miss 12 questions and still receive a scaled score of 800. So basically, you can miss a few questions and still receive a competitive score.

Our test strategies won't make up for a weakness in a given area, but they will help you to manage your time effectively and maximize points.

QUESTION TYPES

The multiple-choice questions on the SAT Subject Test: Physics are divided up into two types: *classification questions* and *five-choice completion questions*. Make sure you feel comfortable with all question types and their directions before test day. Don't waste time rereading familiar directions when you are being timed!

Classification Questions

On test day, do classification questions first; they require less reading and will give you the most points for your time invested.

Classification questions consist of five lettered choices, typically ideas, physical laws, graphs, or some other type of data presentation. Following the five choices will be three to five statements or questions. One of the five choices will be the best answer for each question or the best fit for each statement. Any of the five choices may be used more than once, so do not eliminate an answer just because you have used it.

Read through the directions and attempt to answer questions 1–3. Check your answers against the explanations that follow the question set.

Directions: Each set of lettered choices below refers to the numbered questions or statements immediately following it. Select the one lettered choice that best answers each question or best fits each statement, and then fill in the corresponding oval on the answer sheet. A choice may be used once, more than once, or not at all in each set.

Sample Questions 1–3 relate to the following.

(A)   mass

(B)   amplitude

(C)   length

(D)   equilibrium position

(E)   restoring force

> Don't eliminate an answer choice just because you've used it. Answer choices on classification questions can be used more than once.

1. For a pendulum swinging at a small angle, which of the above affects the period of the pendulum?

2. Which of the above is the point at which the potential energy of the pendulum is maximum?

3. Which of the above is the point at which the kinetic energy of the pendulum is maximum?

As a pendulum swings at a small angle, its period depends only upon the length of the pendulum. The mass of the pendulum bob and the amplitude of swing (assuming small angles) do not change the time for one complete swing. The potential energy of the pendulum is maximum when the pendulum is the highest distance above its equilibrium position, which corresponds to its amplitude, or maximum displacement from its equilibrium position. The kinetic energy of the pendulum is maximum as it swings through the equilibrium position, since the pendulum speeds up as it moves toward the equilibrium position and slows down after it passes the equilibrium position. Thus, the correct answers for this question set are: 1 (C); 2 (B); 3 (D).

Five-Choice Completion Questions

There are three types of these questions, all of which use the same set of directions.

Directions: Each of the incomplete statements or questions below is followed by five suggested completions or answers. In each case, select the one that is best and fill in the corresponding oval on the answer sheet.

Type 1 Questions

These have a unique solution, often the only correct answer or the best answer. Sometimes, however, the most inappropriate answer will be correct; these question types will have the words NOT, EXCEPT, or LEAST somewhere in the stimulus.

Sample Questions 4–5.

4. An object released from rest at time $t = 0$ falls freely under the influence of gravity.

   What is the speed of the object at $t = 2$ seconds?

   (A) 2 m/s
   (B) 5 m/s
   (C) 10 m/s
   (D) 20 m/s
   (E) 40 m/s

5. Which of the following is NOT an example of a vector?

   (A) force
   (B) velocity
   (C) displacement
   (D) mass
   (E) momentum

Question 4 tests your understanding of the velocity and acceleration of a falling object. As an object falls freely, it gains 10 m/s of speed for each second it falls. Thus, after two seconds, its speed is 20 m/s. You could also use the equation $v = gt$, where $g = 10$ m/s^2 and $t = 2$ s. Thus, answer (D) is correct.

Question 5 distinguishes between a vector and a scalar. A vector is a quantity having both magnitude and direction, such as force, velocity, displacement, and momentum. Mass is a scalar, having no direction. Therefore, answer (D) is correct.

Type 2 Questions

These typically have three to five Roman numeral statements following each question. One or more of these statements may be the correct answer. Following each statement, there are five lettered choices with various combinations of the Roman numerals. You must select the combination that includes all of the correct answers and excludes all of the incorrect answers.

Sample Question 6.

6. A candle may be placed on the principal axis at the following distances from the center of a convex lens:

   I. at the focal length

   II. at 3/2 the focal length

   III. less than the focal length

   IV. greater than twice the focal length

   Which of the above will produce an image that is larger than the actual candle?

(A) I only

(B) I, II, and III only

(C) II and III only

(D) II, III, and IV only

(E) I, II, III, and IV

A convex lens produces a real image when the candle is placed at a distance greater than the focal length, and an enlarged virtual image when it is placed at a distance less than the focal length. No image is produced when the candle is placed at the focal length; thus, statement I is not correct. If the candle is placed between the focal length and twice the focal length, the image is also enlarged, but the image is smaller if the candle is placed at a distance greater than twice the focal length. Therefore, statements II and III will produce an image larger than the candle, and the correct answer is (C).

Type 3 Questions

These questions are also organized in sets, but they center on an experiment, chart, graph, or other experimental data presentation. They assess how well you apply science to unfamiliar situations. Each question is independent of the others; in addition, these questions are typically found in the latter part of the test. Most students find them to be the most difficult questions on the test.

Type 3 questions test your ability to identify a problem; evaluate experimental situations; suggest hypotheses; interpret data such as graphs or mathematical expressions; make inferences and draw conclusions; check the logical consistency of hypotheses based on your observations; convert information to graphical form; apply mathematical relationships; and select the appropriate procedure for further study.

Sample Questions 7–9 are based on the radioactive decay equation shown below.

$$^{226}_{88}\text{Ra} \rightarrow {}^{A}_{Z}\text{X} + {}^{4}_{2}\text{He}$$

7. The type of radiation emitted in the above decay is

(A) alpha.

(B) beta.

(C) gamma.

(D) neutrino.

(E) electron.

8. The atomic number of the daughter atom that correctly completes the equation is

(A) 226.

(B) 224.

(C) 222.

(D) 86.

(E) 84.

9. The mass number of the daughter atom that correctly completes the equation is

   (A) 226.
   (B) 224.
   (C) 222.
   (D) 86.
   (E) 84.

In this radioactive decay, the element radium emits a helium nucleus, which is also known as an alpha particle. Because an alpha particle consists of 2 protons and 2 neutrons, it has an atomic number of 2 (number of protons) and a mass number of 4 (number of protons and neutrons). Thus, a radium atom undergoing alpha decay loses two atomic numbers, leaving 86, and four mass numbers, leaving 222. The correct answers are: 7 (A); 8 (D); 9 (C).

KAPLAN STRATEGIES

There are ways to approach this test that will allow you to maximize your score. Read through these strategies before you begin your diagnostic practice test. Try to internalize each of them so that on test day they will be second nature to you. If you accomplish this, you will be rewarded with a higher score on your SAT Subject Test: Physics.

1. Do classification questions first; they require less reading, so you'll get the most points for your time invested.

2. Next, do the Type 1 and Type 2 five-choice completion questions. Again, you will get more points with less time invested.

3. This test emphasizes general trends and basic physics concepts, so you probably won't see a question/graph that would take a rocket scientist 30 minutes to figure out. Look for trends and wide variations in graphs. If a value or a plot is vastly different from the others, it is likely that there will be a question about it. Also be prepared to use the slope of a graph or area under a curve to determine quantities.

4. Look for opposing answers in the answer selections. If two answers are close in wording or if they contain opposite ideas, there is a strong possibility that one of them is the right answer.

5. By the same token, if two answers mean basically the same thing, then they both cannot be correct and you can eliminate both answer choices.

6. Use the structure of a Type 3 Roman numeral question to your advantage. Eliminate choices as soon as you find them to be inconsistent with what is asked in the question. Similarly, consider only those choices that include a statement that you've already determined to be true.

7. Predict your answer before you go to the answer choices so you don't get persuaded by the wrong answers. This helps protect you from persuasive or tricky incorrect choices. Most wrong answer choices are logical twists on the correct choice.

8. Eliminate answers and guess.

9. Think, don't compute!

STRESS MANAGEMENT

The countdown has begun. Your date with THE TEST is looming on the horizon. Anxiety is on the rise. The butterflies in your stomach have gone ballistic. Perhaps you feel as if the last thing you ate has turned into a lead ball. Your thinking is getting cloudy. Maybe you think you won't be ready. Maybe you already know your stuff, but you're going into panic mode anyway. Worst of all, you're not sure of what to do about it.

Don't freak! It is possible to tame that anxiety and stress—before and during the test. We'll show you how. You won't believe how quickly and easily you can deal with that killer anxiety.

Make the Most of Your Prep Time

Lack of control is one of the prime causes of stress. A ton of research shows that if you don't have a sense of control over what's happening in your life you can easily end up feeling helpless and hopeless. So, just having concrete things to do and to think about—taking control—will help reduce your stress. This section shows you how to take control during the days leading up to taking the test.

Identify the Sources of Stress

In the space provided, jot down (in pencil) anything you identify as a source of your test-related stress. The idea is to pin down that free-floating anxiety so you can take control of it. Here are some common examples to get you started:

- I always freeze up on tests.
- I'm nervous about the math (or the vocabulary or reading, etc.).
- I need a good/great score to go to Acme College.
- My older brother/sister/best friend/girlfriend/boyfriend did really well. I must match their scores or do better.
- My parents, who are paying for school, will be really disappointed if I don't test well.
- I'm afraid of losing my focus and concentration.

- I'm afraid I'm not spending enough time preparing.
- I study like crazy but nothing seems to stick in my mind.
- I always run out of time and get panicky.
- I feel as though thinking is becoming like wading through thick mud.

Sources of Stress

_____   _____

_____   _____

_____   _____

_____

Take a few minutes to think about the things you've just written down. Then rewrite them in some sort of order. List the statements you most associate with your stress and anxiety first, and put the least disturbing items last. Chances are, the top of the list is a fairly accurate description of exactly how you react to test anxiety, both physically and mentally. The later items usually describe your fears (disappointing Mom and Dad, looking bad, etc.). As you write the list, you're forming a hierarchy of items so you can deal first with the anxiety provokers that bug you most. Very often, taking care of the major items from the top of the list goes a long way toward relieving overall testing anxiety. You probably won't have to bother with the stuff you placed last.

Use Your Strengths and Weaknesses

Take one minute to list the areas of the test that you are good at. They can be general ("electricity") or specific ("using Ohm's law to calculate voltage"). Put down as many as you can think of, and, if possible, time yourself. Write for the entire time; don't stop writing until you've reached the one-minute stopping point.

Strong Test Subjects

_____   _____

_____   _____

_____   _____

Next, take one minute to list the areas of the test you're not so good at, just plain bad at, have failed at, or keep failing at. Again, keep it to one minute, and continue writing until you reach the cutoff. Don't be afraid to identify and write down your weak spots!

In all probability, as you do both lists, you'll find you are strong in some areas and not so strong in others. Taking stock of your assets and liabilities lets you know which areas you don't have to worry about, and which ones will demand extra attention and effort.

Weak Test Subjects

_____   _____

_____   _____

_____   _____

_____   _____

Facing your weak spots gives you some distinct advantages. It helps a lot to find out where you need to spend extra effort. Increased exposure to tough material makes it more familiar and less intimidating. (After all, we mostly fear what we don't know and are probably afraid to face.) You'll feel better about yourself because you're dealing directly with areas of the test that bring on your anxiety. You can't help feeling more confident when you know you're actively strengthening your chances of earning a higher overall test score.

Now, go back to the "good" list, and expand it for two minutes. Take the general items on that first list and make them more specific; take the specific items and expand them into more general conclusions. Naturally, if anything new comes to mind, jot it down. Focus all of your attention and effort on your strengths. Don't underestimate yourself or your abilities. Give yourself full credit. At the same time, don't list strengths you don't really have; you'll only be fooling yourself.

Whatever you know comfortably (that is, almost as well as you know the back of your hand) goes on your "good" list. Okay. You've got the picture. Now, get ready, check your starting time, and start writing down items on your expanded "good" list.

Strong Test Subjects: An Expanded List

_____   _____

_____   _____

_____   _____

_____   _____

After you've stopped, check your time. Did you find yourself going beyond the two minutes allotted? Did you write down more things than you thought you knew? Is it possible you know more than you've given yourself credit for? Could that mean you've found a number of areas in which you feel strong?

You just took an active step toward helping yourself. Notice any increased feelings of confidence? Enjoy them.

Here's another way to think about your writing exercise. Every area of strength and confidence you can identify is much like having a reserve of solid gold at Fort Knox. You'll be able to draw on your reserves as you need them. You can use your reserves to solve difficult questions, maintain confidence, and keep test stress and anxiety at a distance. The encouraging thing is that every time you recognize another area of strength, succeed at coming up with a solution, or get a good score on a test, you increase your reserves. And, there is absolutely no limit to how much self-confidence you can have or how good you can feel about yourself.

Imagine Yourself Succeeding

This next little group of exercises is both physical and mental. It's a natural follow-up to what you've just accomplished with your lists.

First, get yourself into a comfortable sitting position in a quiet setting. Wear loose clothes. If you wear glasses, take them off. Then, close your eyes and breathe in a deep, satisfying breath of air. Really fill your lungs until your rib cage is fully expanded and you can't take in any more. Then, exhale the air completely. Imagine you're blowing out a candle with your last little puff of air. Do this two or three more times, filling your lungs to their maximum and emptying them totally. Keep your eyes closed, comfortably but not tightly. Let your body sink deeper into the chair as you become even more comfortable.

With your eyes shut, you can notice something very interesting: You're no longer dealing with the worrisome stuff going on in the world outside of you. Now you can concentrate on what happens inside of you. The more you recognize your own physical reactions to stress and anxiety, the more you can control them. You may not realize it, but you've begun to regain a sense of being in control.

Let images begin to form on the "viewing screens" on the back of your eyelids. You're experiencing visualizations from the place in your mind that makes pictures. Allow the images to come easily and naturally; don't force them. Imagine yourself in a relaxing situation. It might be in a special place you've visited before or one you've read about. It can be a fictional location that you create in your imagination, but a real-life memory of a place or situation you know is usually better. Make it as detailed as possible and notice as much as you can.

Stay focused on the images as you sink farther back into your chair. Breathe easily and naturally. You might have the sensation of stress or tension draining from your muscles and flowing downward, out of your feet and away from you.

Take a moment to check how you're feeling. Notice how comfortable you've become. Imagine how much easier it would be if you could take the test feeling this relaxed and at ease. You've coupled the images of your special place with sensations of comfort and relaxation. You've also found a way to become relaxed simply by visualizing your own safe, special place.

Now close your eyes and start remembering a real-life situation in which you did well on a test. If you can't come up with one, remember a situation in which you did something (academic or otherwise) that you were really proud of—a genuine accomplishment. Make the memory as detailed as possible. Think about the sights, the sounds, the smells, even the tastes associated with this memorable experience. Remember how confident you felt as you accomplished your goal. Now start thinking about the upcoming test. Keep your thoughts and feelings in line with that successful experience. Don't make comparisons between them. Just imagine taking the upcoming test with the same feelings of confidence and relaxed control.

This exercise is a great way to bring the test down to earth. You should practice this exercise often, especially when the prospect of taking the exam starts to bum you out. The more you practice it, the more effective the exercise will be for you.

Exercise Your Frustrations Away

Whether it is jogging, walking, biking, mild aerobics, pushups, or a pickup basketball game, physical exercise is a very effective way to stimulate both your mind and body and to improve your ability to think and concentrate. A surprising number of students get out of the habit of regular exercise, ironically because they're spending so much time prepping for exams. Also, sedentary people—this is a medical fact—get less oxygen to the blood and hence to the head than active people. You can live fine with a little less oxygen; you just can't think as well.

Any big test is a bit like a race. Thinking clearly at the end is just as important as having a quick mind early on. If you can't sustain your energy level in the last sections of the exam, there's too good a chance you could blow it. You need a fit body that can weather the demands any big exam puts on you. Along with a good diet and adequate sleep, exercise is an important part of keeping yourself in fighting shape and thinking clearly for the long haul.

There's another thing that happens when students don't make exercise an integral part of their test preparation. Like any organism in nature, you operate best if all your "energy systems" are in balance. Studying uses a lot of energy, but it's all mental. When you take a study break, do something active instead of raiding the fridge or vegging out in front of the TV. Take a five- to ten-minute activity break for every 50 or 60 minutes that you study. The physical exertion gets your body into the act, which helps to keep your mind and body in sync. Then, when you finish studying for the night and go to bed, you won't lie there, tense and unable to sleep because your head is overtired and your body wants to pump iron or run a marathon.

One warning about exercise, however: It's not a good idea to exercise vigorously right before you go to bed. This may make it hard to fall asleep. For the same reason, it's also not a good idea to study right up to bedtime. Make time for a "buffer period" before you go to bed: For 30 to 60 minutes, just take a hot shower, meditate, or simply relax.

The Dangers of Drugs

Using drugs (prescription or recreational) specifically to prepare for and take a big test is definitely self-defeating. (And, if they're illegal drugs, you may end up with a bigger problem than the SAT Subject Test: Physics on your hands.) Every drug has major drawbacks—and a false sense of security is only one of them. You may have heard that popping uppers helps you study by keeping you alert. If they're illegal, definitely forget about it. They wouldn't really work anyway, since amphetamines make it hard to retain information. Mild stimulants, such as coffee, cola, or over-the-counter caffeine pills can sometimes help as you study, since they keep you alert. On the down side, they can also lead to agitation, restlessness, and insomnia. Some people can drink a pot of high-octane coffee and sleep like a baby. Others have one cup and start to vibrate. It all depends on your tolerance for caffeine. Remember, a little anxiety is a good thing. The adrenaline that gets pumped into your bloodstream helps you stay alert and think more clearly. But with too much anxiety, you can't think straight at all.

Take a Deep Breath . . .

Here's another natural route to relaxation and invigoration. It's a classic isometric exercise that you can do whenever you get stressed out—just before the test begins, or even during the test. It's very simple and takes just a few minutes.

Close your eyes. Starting with your eyelids—without holding your breath—gradually tighten every muscle in your body (but not to the point of pain) in the following sequence:

1. Close your eyes tightly.

2. Squeeze your nose and mouth together so that your whole face is scrunched up. (If it makes you self-conscious to do this in the test room, skip the face-scrunching part.)

3. Pull your chin into your chest, and pull your shoulders together.

4. Tighten your arms to your body, then clench your hands into tight fists.

5. Pull in your stomach.

6. Squeeze your thighs and buttocks together, and tighten your calves.

7. Stretch your feet, then curl your toes (watch out for cramping in this part).

At this point, every muscle should be tightened. Now, relax your body, one part at a time, in reverse order, starting with your toes. Let the tension drop out of each muscle. The entire process might take five minutes from start to finish (maybe a couple of minutes during the test). This clenching and unclenching exercise should help you to feel very relaxed.

. . . And Keep Breathing

Conscious attention to breathing is an excellent way of managing test stress (or any stress, for that matter). The majority of people who get into trouble during tests take shallow breaths. They breathe using only their upper chests and shoulder muscles, and may even hold their breath for long periods of time. Conversely, the test taker who by accident or design keeps breathing normally and rhythmically is likely to be more relaxed and in better control during the entire test experience.

So, now is the time to get into the habit of relaxed breathing. Do the next exercise to learn to breathe in a natural, easy rhythm. By the way, this is another technique you can use during the test to collect your thoughts and ward off excess stress. The entire exercise should take no more than three to five minutes.

With your eyes still closed, breathe in slowly and deeply through your nose. Hold the breath for a bit, and then release it through your mouth. The key is to breathe slowly and deeply by using your diaphragm (the big band of muscle that spans your body just above your waist) to draw air in and out naturally and effortlessly. Breathing with your diaphragm encourages relaxation and helps minimize tension. Try it and notice how relaxed and comfortable you feel.

Handling Stress During the Test

The biggest stress monster will be the test itself. Fear not; there are methods of quelling your stress during the test.

- Keep moving forward instead of getting bogged down in a difficult question or passage. You don't have to get everything right to achieve a fine score. So, don't linger out of desperation on a question that is going nowhere, even after you've spent considerable time on it. The best test takers skip difficult material temporarily in search of the easier stuff. They mark the ones that require extra time and thought. This strategy buys time and builds confidence so you can handle the tough stuff later.

- Don't be thrown if other test takers seem to be working more busily and furiously than you are. Continue to spend your time patiently but doggedly thinking through your answers; it's going to lead to higher-quality test taking and better results. Don't mistake the other people's sheer activity as a sign of progress or higher scores.

- Keep breathing! Weak test takers tend to share one major trait: They forget to breathe properly as the test proceeds. They start holding their breath without realizing it, or they breathe erratically or arrhythmically. Improper breathing hurts confidence and accuracy, and worse, it interferes with clear thinking.

- Some quick isometrics during the test—especially if concentration is wandering or energy is waning—can help. Try this: Put your palms together and press intensely for a few seconds. Concentrate on the tension you feel through your palms, wrists, forearms, and up into your biceps and shoulders. Then, quickly release the pressure. Feel the difference as you let go. Focus on the warm relaxation that floods through the muscles. Now, you're ready to return to the task.

- Here's another isometric that will relieve tension in both your neck and eye muscles. Slowly rotate your head from side to side, turning your head and eyes to look as far back over each shoulder as you can. Feel the muscles stretch on one side of your neck as they contract on the other. Repeat five times in each direction.

TIPS FOR JUST BEFORE THE TEST

- The best test takers do less and less as the test approaches. Taper off your study schedule and take it easy on yourself. You want to be relaxed and ready on the day of the test. Give yourself time off, especially the evening before the exam. By that time, if you've studied well, everything you need to know is firmly stored in your memory banks.

- Positive self-talk can be extremely liberating and invigorating, especially as the test looms closer. Tell yourself things such as, "I choose to take this test" rather than "I have to"; "I will do well" rather than "I hope things go well"; "I can" rather than "I cannot." Be aware of negative, self-defeating thoughts and images and immediately counter any that you become aware of. Replace them with affirming statements that encourage your self-esteem and confidence. Create and practice visualizations that build on your positive statements.

- Get your act together sooner rather than later. Have everything (including choice of clothing) laid out days in advance. Most important, know where the test will be held and the easiest, quickest way to get there. You will gain great peace of mind if you know that all the little details—gas in the car, directions, etc.—are firmly in your control before the day of the test.

- Experience the test site a few days in advance. This is very helpful if you are especially anxious. If possible, find out what room you will be assigned to, and try to sit there (by yourself) for a while. Better yet, bring some practice material and do at least a section or two, if not an entire practice test, in that room. In this case, familiarity doesn't breed contempt; it generates comfort and confidence.

- Forgo any practice on the day before the test. It's in your best interest to marshal your physical and psychological resources for 24 hours or so. Even racehorses are kept in the paddock and treated like princes the day before a race. Keep the upcoming test out of your consciousness; go to a movie, take a pleasant hike, or just relax. Don't eat junk food or tons of sugar. And—of course—get plenty of rest the night before. Just don't go to bed too early. It's hard to fall asleep earlier than you're used to, and you don't want to lie there thinking about the test.

With what you've just learned here, you're armed and ready to do battle with the test. This book and your studies will give you the information you'll need to answer the questions. It's all firmly planted in your mind. You also know how to deal with any excess tension that might come along, both when you're studying for and when you're taking the exam. You've experienced everything you need to tame your test anxiety and stress. You're going to get a great score.

Part Two

Diagnostic Test

HOW TO TAKE THE DIAGNOSTIC TEST

Before taking this diagnostic test, find a quiet room where you can work uninterrupted for one hour. Make sure you have several No. 2 pencils with erasers.

Use the answer grid provided to record your answers. Guidelines for scoring your test appear on the reverse side of the answer grid. Time yourself. Spend no more than one hour on the 75 questions. Once you start the diagnostic test, don't stop until you've reached the one-hour time limit. You'll find an answer key and complete answer explanations following the test. Be sure to read the explanations for all questions, even those you answered correctly. Finally, you'll learn how the diagnostic test can help you in your review of physics.

Good luck!

HOW TO CALCULATE YOUR SCORE

Step 1: Figure out your raw score. Use the answer key to count the number of questions you answered correctly and the number of questions you answered incorrectly. (Do not count any questions you left blank.) Multiply the number wrong by 0.25 and subtract the result from the number correct. Round the result to the nearest whole number. This is your raw score.

SAT Subject Test: Physics: Diagnostic Test

Number right		Number wrong		Raw score
☐	−	$\left(0.25 \times \right.$ ☐ $\left. \right)$	=	☐

Step 2: Find your scaled score. In the Score Conversion Table below, find your raw score (rounded to the nearest whole number) in one of the columns to the left. The score directly to the right of that number will be your scaled score.

A note on your diagnostic test score: Don't take this score too literally. Practice test conditions cannot precisely mirror real test conditions. Your actual SAT Subject Test: Physics score will almost certainly vary from your diagnostic and practice test scores. However, your scores on the diagnostic and practice tests will give you a rough idea of your range on the actual exam.

Conversion Table

Raw	Scaled	Raw	Scaled	Raw	Scaled	Raw	Scaled	Raw	Scaled	Raw	Scaled
75	800	59	780	43	690	27	590	11	480	−5	380
74	800	58	770	42	680	26	580	10	480	−6	370
73	800	57	770	41	670	25	580	9	470	−7	370
72	800	56	760	40	670	24	570	8	470	−8	360
71	800	55	760	39	660	23	570	7	460	−9	350
70	800	54	750	38	650	22	560	6	450	−10	350
69	800	53	750	37	650	21	550	5	450	−11	340
68	800	52	740	36	640	20	540	4	440	−12	330
67	800	51	730	35	640	19	540	3	430	−13	330
66	800	50	730	34	630	18	530	2	430	−14	320
65	800	49	720	33	630	17	530	1	420	−15	310
64	800	48	720	32	620	16	520	0	410	−16	310
63	800	47	710	31	610	15	510	−1	410	−17	300
62	790	46	700	30	610	14	510	−2	400	−18	290
61	790	45	700	29	600	13	500	−3	390	−19	290
60	780	44	690	28	600	12	490	−4	390		

Diagnostic Test
Answer Grid

1. (A) (B) (C) (D) (E)
2. (A) (B) (C) (D) (E)
3. (A) (B) (C) (D) (E)
4. (A) (B) (C) (D) (E)
5. (A) (B) (C) (D) (E)
6. (A) (B) (C) (D) (E)
7. (A) (B) (C) (D) (E)
8. (A) (B) (C) (D) (E)
9. (A) (B) (C) (D) (E)
10. (A) (B) (C) (D) (E)
11. (A) (B) (C) (D) (E)
12. (A) (B) (C) (D) (E)
13. (A) (B) (C) (D) (E)
14. (A) (B) (C) (D) (E)
15. (A) (B) (C) (D) (E)
16. (A) (B) (C) (D) (E)
17. (A) (B) (C) (D) (E)
18. (A) (B) (C) (D) (E)
19. (A) (B) (C) (D) (E)
20. (A) (B) (C) (D) (E)
21. (A) (B) (C) (D) (E)
22. (A) (B) (C) (D) (E)
23. (A) (B) (C) (D) (E)
24. (A) (B) (C) (D) (E)
25. (A) (B) (C) (D) (E)

26. (A) (B) (C) (D) (E)
27. (A) (B) (C) (D) (E)
28. (A) (B) (C) (D) (E)
29. (A) (B) (C) (D) (E)
30. (A) (B) (C) (D) (E)
31. (A) (B) (C) (D) (E)
32. (A) (B) (C) (D) (E)
33. (A) (B) (C) (D) (E)
34. (A) (B) (C) (D) (E)
35. (A) (B) (C) (D) (E)
36. (A) (B) (C) (D) (E)
37. (A) (B) (C) (D) (E)
38. (A) (B) (C) (D) (E)
39. (A) (B) (C) (D) (E)
40. (A) (B) (C) (D) (E)
41. (A) (B) (C) (D) (E)
42. (A) (B) (C) (D) (E)
43. (A) (B) (C) (D) (E)
44. (A) (B) (C) (D) (E)
45. (A) (B) (C) (D) (E)
46. (A) (B) (C) (D) (E)
47. (A) (B) (C) (D) (E)
48. (A) (B) (C) (D) (E)
49. (A) (B) (C) (D) (E)
50. (A) (B) (C) (D) (E)

51. (A) (B) (C) (D) (E)
52. (A) (B) (C) (D) (E)
53. (A) (B) (C) (D) (E)
54. (A) (B) (C) (D) (E)
55. (A) (B) (C) (D) (E)
56. (A) (B) (C) (D) (E)
57. (A) (B) (C) (D) (E)
58. (A) (B) (C) (D) (E)
59. (A) (B) (C) (D) (E)
60. (A) (B) (C) (D) (E)
61. (A) (B) (C) (D) (E)
62. (A) (B) (C) (D) (E)
63. (A) (B) (C) (D) (E)
64. (A) (B) (C) (D) (E)
65. (A) (B) (C) (D) (E)
66. (A) (B) (C) (D) (E)
67. (A) (B) (C) (D) (E)
68. (A) (B) (C) (D) (E)
69. (A) (B) (C) (D) (E)
70. (A) (B) (C) (D) (E)
71. (A) (B) (C) (D) (E)
72. (A) (B) (C) (D) (E)
73. (A) (B) (C) (D) (E)
74. (A) (B) (C) (D) (E)
75. (A) (B) (C) (D) (E)

Diagnostic Test

Part A

Directions: Each set of lettered choices below relates to the numbered questions immediately following it. Select the one lettered choice that best answers each question. A choice may be used once, more than once, or not at all in each set.

Questions 1–3 relate to the diagram below and the choices that follow.

A projectile is launched at an angle from level ground. Assume air resistance is negligible.

(A) horizontal velocity
(B) vertical velocity
(C) horizontal acceleration
(D) vertical acceleration
(E) angle at which the projectile is launched

1. Which of the above choices is NOT constant throughout the flight of the projectile?

    B

2. Which of the above choices is zero throughout the flight of the projectile?

    C

3. Which of the above choices changes direction during the flight of the projectile?

    B

Questions 4–7 relate to the following equations or physical principles that might be used to solve certain problems.

(A) Newton's first law (law of inertia)
(B) Newton's second law ($F_{net} = ma$)
(C) Newton's third law (For every action there is an equal and opposite reaction.)
(D) Newton's law of universal gravitation
(E) conservation of linear momentum

Select the choice that should be used to provide the best and most direct solution to each of the following problems.

4. Two lead spheres each of mass m are 3 cm apart and are not in contact. What force do they apply to each other?

    D

5. A jar remains <u>at rest</u> on a table when a piece of paper is pulled out from under it.

    A

6. A ball of clay is shot at a block of wood on a table and the two stick together. What was the initial speed of the clay?

    E

7. Two teams pull against each other on a rope that is stretched across a stream. One team pulls with 1,000 N of force. What is the tension in the rope?

    C

GO ON TO THE NEXT PAGE

Questions 8–9 relate to a small particle entering a magnetic field **B**, which is directed out of the page as shown.

(handwritten: Figure B)

(A) proton
(B) electron
(C) neutron
(D) x-ray
(E) photon of red light

8. Which of the above particles would follow the path shown below while moving through the magnetic field?

electron

9. Which of the above particles would follow the path shown below while moving through the magnetic field?

proton

Questions 10–13 relate to the following.

(A) reflection
(B) refraction
(C) diffraction
(D) constructive interference
(E) destructive interference

10. Which of the above occurs when two waves that are in phase with each other meet at the same time in the same medium? *D*

11. Which of the above creates two angles that are equal to each other? *A*

12. Which of the above causes a wave to change its speed and wavelength? *B*

13. Which of the above occurs when a wave passes through a small opening?

C

(handwritten notes:)
Right Hand Rule #1
thumb – current
fingers curl
current carrying wire

#2
thumb — fingers
ILB → force = palm
QVB — fingers
force = palm
thumb

GO ON TO THE NEXT PAGE

Part B

Directions: Each of the questions or incomplete statements below is followed by five answer choices. Select the one that is best in each case.

14. Each of the figures below shows the forces acting on a particle, where each force is the same magnitude. In which figure can the particle's velocity be constant?

(A) (B) (C) (D) (E)

15. The water in a river is running due west. A boy in a boat tries to cross the river by rowing due south. The motion of the boat relative to the shore is

(A) due south.
(B) due north.
(C) due west.
(D) southwest.
(E) northeast.

Questions 16–17 refer to the circuit shown below.

16. The current through the 4 Ω resistor is

(A) 2 A.
(B) 4 A.
(C) 6 A.
(D) 8 A.
(E) 12 A.

17. The voltage across the 4 Ω resistor is

(A) 4 V.
(B) 8 V.
(C) 12 V.
(D) 16 V.
(E) 24 V.

GO ON TO THE NEXT PAGE

18. Two parallel wires are located a distance $2d$ apart. Each wire has a current of 1 A flowing into the page as shown above. The direction of the net magnetic field at point P halfway between the wires is

    (A) →.
    (B) ←.
    (C) ↑.
    (D) ↓.
    (E) zero.

19. A 500 kg car is initially at rest and is pushed by a constant horizontal force for a distance of 30 meters at which point the car has a kinetic energy of 18,000 J. The magnitude of the force is most nearly

    (A) 500 N.
    (B) 600 N.
    (C) 1,500 N.
    (D) 15,000 N.
    (E) 540,000 N.

    $W = F \cdot d$

    $18000 = F \cdot (30)$

20. Two objects collide on a surface with negligible friction. In the absence of external forces, which of the following statements is true?

    (A) The total momentum before the collision is always equal to the total momentum after the collision.
    (B) Both momentum and kinetic energy are conserved in the collision.
    (C) The two objects must stick together.
    (D) The speed of each object must remain the same before and after the collision.
    (E) The momentum of each object must remain the same before and after the collision.

21. A ball with a large mass and a ball with a small mass roll off a horizontal table at exactly the same time with exactly the same velocity. Neglecting air resistance, which of the following is true?

    (A) The larger ball will reach the ground first, since it has more weight.
    (B) The two balls will reach the ground at the same time, but the smaller ball will travel farther horizontally.
    (C) The two balls will reach the ground at the same time and will travel the same horizontal distance.
    (D) The two balls will reach the ground at the same time, but the larger ball will travel farther horizontally.
    (E) The smaller ball will land first, since it has less weight.

22. An electric generator produces current by the process of

    (A) capacitance.
    (B) electromagnetic induction.
    (C) an electric motor.
    (D) a battery.
    (E) resistance.

GO ON TO THE NEXT PAGE

23. A mass is attached to the end of a fixed spring as shown above. The spring is compressed upward and then released. Immediately after the spring is released, which of the following increase?

(A) kinetic energy, gravitational potential energy, elastic potential energy

(B) kinetic energy and gravitational potential energy

(C) kinetic energy only

(D) gravitational potential energy and elastic potential energy

(E) elastic potential energy only

24. Three charges of +1 microcoulomb, +2 microcoulombs, and −2 microcoulombs are fixed at the vertices of an equilateral triangle as shown above. The net force acting on the +1 microcoulomb charge is directed in which direction?

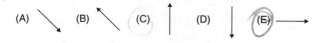

(A)   (B)   (C)   (D)   (E) ⟶

Questions 25–26 refer to the below graph.

Two trains, X and Y, begin moving on parallel tracks from the same starting position at a train station. The graph above shows their respective distances from the starting point as functions of time.

25. At time T,

(A) train X is moving faster than train Y.

(B) train Y is moving faster than train X.

(C) trains X and Y are moving at the same speed.

(D) train X is ahead of train Y.

(E) train Y is ahead of train X.

26. Which of the following statements is true?

(A) Train Y moves faster than train X at all points on the graph.

(B) Train X moves faster than train Y at all points on the graph.

(C) Train X will reach the distance d_2 before train Y.

(D) Train Y will reach the distance d_2 before train X.

(E) The trains will reach the distance d_2 at the same time.

GO ON TO THE NEXT PAGE

27. If a rotating amusement park ride completes 6 revolutions in one minute, its frequency of rotation is

    (A) 360 Hz
    (B) 60 Hz
    (C) 10 Hz
    (D) 1 Hz
    (E) 0.1 Hz

28. Pluto orbits the Sun in an elliptical orbit. Which of the following statements is true of Pluto's orbit?

    (A) The gravitational force acting between Pluto and the Sun must point in the direction of Pluto's velocity.
    (B) The gravitational force between Pluto and the Sun is greater when Pluto is farthest from the Sun.
    (C) The speed of Pluto is greatest when Pluto is closest to the Sun.
    (D) The speed of Pluto is greatest when Pluto is farthest from the Sun.
    (E) The gravitational force between the Sun and Pluto is constant at all points in Pluto's orbit.

29. The pitch of a middle-C sound wave has a frequency of 256 Hz. If the speed of sound in air is 350 m/s, what is the wavelength of middle-C in air?

    (A) 89,600 m
    (B) 350 m
    (C) 94 m
    (D) 1.4 m
    (E) 0.73 m

30. The energy transferred between two bodies due to a temperature difference is called

    (A) potential energy.
    (B) nuclear energy.
    (C) chemical energy.
    (D) heat energy.
    (E) temperature energy.

31. An electron of mass 9.1×10^{-31} kg is orbiting in a circular path of radius 100 meters with a speed of 3×10^7 m/s in a magnetic field. Which of the following is the best estimate of the order of magnitude of the magnetic force needed to maintain this orbit?

    (A) 10^{-22} N
    (B) 10^{-17} N
    (C) 10^{-10} N
    (D) 10^{-6} N
    (E) 10^{-2} N

32. Two blocks A and B are attached to a string that passes over a pulley of negligible mass and friction as shown above. The two blocks do not have equal mass. Which of the following statements is true?

    (A) Block A is more massive than block B.
    (B) Block B is more massive than block A.
    (C) Both blocks will move with the same constant velocity.
    (D) Both blocks will move with the same constant acceleration.
    (E) Block A must have a greater acceleration than block B.

GO ON TO THE NEXT PAGE

$W = \dfrac{J}{S}$

$P = 20 \text{ cm}$
$d_o = 30$
$d_i = 60$

Questions 33–34 relate to the circuit shown below.

33. The current I_1 in the 1 Ω resistor is related to the current I_2 in the 2 Ω resistor by which of the following equations?

(A) $I_1 = \dfrac{1}{2} I_2$ 1 : 2

(B) $I_1 = \dfrac{2}{3} I_2$ $\dfrac{1}{3}$ $\dfrac{2}{3}$

(C) $I_1 = I_2$

(D) $I_1 = \dfrac{3}{2} I_2$ I

(E) $I_1 = 2I_2$

34. The voltage V_1 across the 1 Ω resistor is related to the voltage V_2 across the 2 Ω resistor by which of the following equations?

(A) $V_1 = \dfrac{1}{2} V_2$

(B) $V_1 = \dfrac{2}{3} V_2$

(C) $V_1 = V_2$

(D) $V_1 = \dfrac{3}{2} V_2$

(E) $V_1 = 2V_2$

best in NOT a vacuum

35. Sound has the highest speed in which of the following?

(A) steel

(B) wood

(C) water

(D) air

(E) helium

$c = P\pi$

36. A converging lens has a focal length of 20 cm. A candle is placed at 30 cm from the lens, and an image is formed 60 cm from the lens. The magnification is

(A) 0.5.
(B) 0.67.
(C) 1.5.
(D) 2.0.
(E) 3.0.

37. The image formed by a plane mirror alone is always

(A) real.
(B) virtual.
(C) larger than the object.
(D) smaller than the object.
(E) inverted.

38. Which of the following statements is true of two waves that interfere with each other?

(A) They always create a larger wave than either of the individual waves.
(B) The larger wave always cancels the smaller wave.
(C) The displacements of the individual waves are added at each point.
(D) An antinode is always created.
(E) A node is always created.

39. How much energy does a 2,400-watt micro-wave oven use in 3 minutes?

(A) 432,000 J
(B) 7,200 J
(C) 800 J
(D) 24 J
(E) 13.3 J

   watt / s

$\dfrac{J}{S} \cdot \dfrac{1}{S}$, $\dfrac{J}{S^2}$

$W = \dfrac{J}{S}$

$P = W = \dfrac{J}{S}$ $W = \dfrac{J}{S}$

$2400 = \dfrac{J}{180}$

GO ON TO THE NEXT PAGE

Questions 40–41 refer to the electroscope shown below.

40. A positively charged rod is brought near the knob of an uncharged electroscope and the leaves of the electroscope diverge as shown above. The leaves diverge because

   (A) they are both negatively charged.
   (B) they are both positively charged.
   (C) one is positive and one is negative.
   (D) one leaf is neutral and one is positive.
   (E) both leaves are neutral.

41. As the positively charged rod is held near the knob, the electroscope is grounded with a wire. Then the grounding wire and the positively charged rod are removed. The leaves of the electroscope

   (A) diverge and are negatively charged.
   (B) diverge and are positively charged.
   (C) converge and are negatively charged.
   (D) converge and are positively charged.
   (E) converge and are neutral.

42. As shown above, a positive charge moves through a magnetic field **B** of magnitude 10^{-2} T with a speed of 10^{6} m/s when it experiences a force of 10^{-14} N. The magnitude of the charge is

   (A) 10^{-22} C.
   (B) 10^{-18} C.
   (C) 10^{-10} C.
   (D) 10^{-6} C.
   (E) 10^{-2} C.

Questions 43–44 relate to the standing wave in a string shown below.

A standing wave is produced in a string when a periodic wave is passed through the string and is reflected off the fixed end. The wavelength of the wave in the string shown above is 0.5 m, and the frequency of vibration is 120 Hz.

43. The speed of the wave is

   (A) 240 m/s.
   (B) 120 m/s.
   (C) 60 m/s.
   (D) 30 m/s.
   (E) 20 m/s.

44. The length of the string is

   (A) 2.0 m.
   (B) 1.0 m.
   (C) 0.5 m.
   (D) 0.25 m.
   (E) 0.1 m.

GO ON TO THE NEXT PAGE

Questions 45–46 refer to the following.

The heat of fusion of ice is 3.3×10^5 J/kg and the specific heat of water is 4.2×10^3 J/kg°C. Heat is added to a 3 kg block of ice (initial temperature = 0°), and continues to be added to raise the temperature of the resulting water to 30°C.

45. How much heat is needed to melt the block of ice?

    (A) 1.26×10^4 J
    (B) 4.2×10^5 J
    (C) 3.3×10^5 J
    (D) 6.6×10^5 J
    (E) 9.9×10^5 J

46. How much heat is required to raise the liquid water from 0° C to 30° C?

    (A) 1.26×10^4 J
    (B) 4.2×10^3 J
    (C) 3.8×10^5 J
    (D) 6.6×10^5 J
    (E) 9.9×10^5 J

47. A beam of light is incident on a piece of glass, and most of the beam is refracted through the glass. Which of the following properties of the light does NOT change as it is refracted?

    (A) speed
    (B) frequency
    (C) wavelength
    (D) direction
    (E) intensity

Questions 48–49 refer to the following.

A railroad car of mass 1,000 kg is being pulled on tracks of negligible friction by ropes tied to two horses, causing the car to move along the dashed horizontal line as shown above. The net force acting on the car is 500 N. (sin 45° = cos 45° = 0.7)

48. What is the tension in each rope?

    (A) 1,000 N
    (B) 500 N
    (C) 350 N
    (D) 250 N
    (E) 100 N

49. What is the acceleration of the car?

    (A) 5 m/s²
    (B) 3.5 m/s²
    (C) 2.5 m/s²
    (D) 2.0 m/s²
    (E) 0.5 m/s²

50. The photoelectric effect is best explained by the

    (A) wave model of light.
    (B) photon model of light.
    (C) interference of light waves.
    (D) diffraction of light waves.
    (E) Heisenberg uncertainty principle.

GO ON TO THE NEXT PAGE

51. If the average speed of the molecules of an ideal gas is doubled, the temperature of the gas

   (A) remains the same.
   (B) is doubled.
   (C) is halved.
   (D) is quadrupled.
   (E) is quartered.

Questions 52–53 refer to the following.

A heat engine uses heat to do 50 J of work, and then exhausts 100 J of energy into a cold reservoir.

52. The heat added to the heat engine is

   (A) 150 J.
   (B) 100 J.
   (C) 50 J.
   (D) 2 J.
   (E) zero.

53. The efficiency of the heat engine is

   (A) 25%.
   (B) 33%.
   (C) 50%.
   (D) 75%.
   (E) 100%.

Questions 54–55 refer to the following.

A ball of mass m is thrown horizontally at a vertical wall with a speed v and bounces off elastically and horizontally.

54. What is the magnitude of the change in momentum of the ball?

   (A) mv
   (B) $2mv$
   (C) $\dfrac{mv}{2}$
   (D) $\dfrac{mv}{4}$
   (E) zero

55. Which of the following force vs. time graphs below best represents the force acting on the ball while it is in contact with the wall?

56. A periodic wave is sent through a tight spring. If the tension in the spring is reduced, the wavelength of the wave will

   (A) decrease.
   (B) increase.
   (C) remain the same.
   (D) become zero.
   (E) equal the length of the spring.

GO ON TO THE NEXT PAGE

Questions 57–58 refer to the following.

A child on a skateboard crosses a line on the sidewalk traveling with a speed of 2 m/s when he begins accelerating at a constant rate of 2 m/s².

57. What will be the child's speed after 3 s?

  (A) 8 m/s
  (B) 9 m/s
  (C) 12 m/s
  (D) 15 m/s
  (E) 18 m/s

58. How far past the line on the sidewalk will the child be after 3 s?

  (A) 8 m
  (B) 9 m
  (C) 12 m
  (D) 15 m
  (E) 18 m

59. A series of alternate bright and dark bands of light appear on a screen. What most likely caused this pattern on the screen?

  (A) light passing through a converging lens
  (B) light passing through a diverging lens
  (C) light passing through two very narrow slits
  (D) photons emitted from a metal
  (E) photons in an emission spectrum

60. A constant force acts on a mass. If the mass were tripled but the force remained constant, the acceleration of the mass would be

  (A) nine times as much.
  (B) three times as much.
  (C) unchanged.
  (D) one-third as much.
  (E) one-ninth as much.

Questions 61–62 refer to the diagram below.

The diagram represents a mass on a spring fixed to a wall sliding on a surface of negligible friction. The mass oscillates between points A and C, and B is halfway between A and C.

61. The restoring force acting on the mass is greatest

  (A) at B.
  (B) at A and C.
  (C) between A and B.
  (D) between B and C.
  (E) at A, B, and C.

62. When the mass passes through B, it has

  (A) kinetic energy but no potential energy.
  (B) potential energy but no kinetic energy.
  (C) kinetic energy and potential energy.
  (D) no kinetic or potential energy.
  (E) total energy equal to zero.

63. As the moon orbits the Earth in a circular orbit,

  (A) its velocity is parallel to the gravitational force between the moon and the Earth.
  (B) its speed increases.
  (C) its acceleration increases.
  (D) its acceleration is constant in both magnitude and direction.
  (E) its acceleration is constant in magnitude but variable in direction.

GO ON TO THE NEXT PAGE

64. Neglecting air resistance, all objects fall with the same acceleration because

(A) the gravitational force is the same on each.
(B) their weights are equal.
(C) the ratio of weight to mass for all objects is a constant.
(D) the ratio of force to acceleration for all objects is a constant.
(E) the inertia of all objects is the same.

65. A boy facing forward in a tall bus throws a ball straight up at the same instant the bus begins to accelerate forward. Which of the following best describes the subsequent motion of the ball?

(A) The ball goes up and then straight back down into the boy's hand.
(B) The ball goes up and lands in front of the boy.
(C) The ball goes up and lands behind the boy.
(D) The ball stops in the air as the bus is accelerating and "floats" until the bus stops accelerating.
(E) The ball goes up and to the right of the boy.

66. On a cold morning, a metal floor feels colder to your feet than a wood floor because

(A) metal conducts heat more readily than wood.
(B) wood conducts heat more readily than metal.
(C) metal has a higher specific heat than wood.
(D) the temperature of the wood is higher than the temperature of the metal.
(E) the temperature of the metal is higher than the temperature of the wood.

67. A ray of light is shined from beneath the water to the air above the water as shown above. Which of the following rays is the refracted ray?

(A) AB
(B) BC
(C) BD
(D) BE
(E) BF

Questions 68–69 refer to the choices below.

I.   Sound waves
II. Visible light waves
III. X-rays

68. Which of the above waves can be refracted?

(A) I only
(B) II only
(C) I and II only
(D) I and III only
(E) I, II, and III

69. Which of the above waves CANNOT be polarized?

(A) I only
(B) II only
(C) I and II only
(D) I and III only
(E) I, II, and III

GO ON TO THE NEXT PAGE

70. The amplitude of the wave shown above is

    (A) 0.5 m.
    (B) 1.0 m.
    (C) 2.0 m.
    (D) 4.0 m.
    (E) 8.0 m.

71. The half-life of a particular element is 6 days. What percent of the original sample of the element remains after 24 days?

    (A) 100%
    (B) 50%
    (C) 25%
    (D) 12.5%
    (E) 6.25%

72. Which of the following is NOT an isotope of uranium?

    (A) $^{235}_{92}U$
    (B) $^{236}_{92}U$
    (C) $^{238}_{92}U$
    (D) $^{239}_{92}U$
    (E) $^{235}_{91}U$

Questions 73–74 refer to the following.

A ball on the end of a string is being swung in a *vertical* circle as shown below. Points I, II, and III are labeled on the circle.

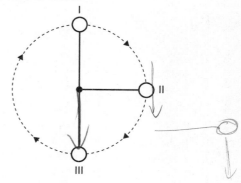

73. Which of the following statements is true?

    (A) The tension in the string is greater at point III than at point I.
    (B) The tension in the string is greater at point I than at point III.
    (C) The tension at point I is equal to the tension at point III.
    (D) The tension in the string is greatest at point II.
    (E) The tension in the string is the same at points I, II, and III.

74. If the string were to break at point II, what would be the path of the ball?

    (A) ⟶ (B) ⟵ (C) ↑ (D) ↓ (E) ⤵

75. A brick is dropped from a high scaffold and strikes the ground 4 seconds later. How high is the scaffold?

    (A) 20 m
    (B) 40 m
    (C) 60 m
    (D) 80 m
    (E) 100 m

STOP!

If you finish before time is up, you may check your work.

Answer Key
Diagnostic Test

1. B	20. A	39. A	58. D
2. C	21. C	40. B	59. C
3. B	22. B	41. A	60. D
4. D	23. C	42. B	61. B
5. A	24. E	43. C	62. A
6. E	25. A	44. B	63. E
7. C	26. C	45. E	64. C
8. B	27. E	46. C	65. C
9. A	28. C	47. B	66. A
10. D	29. D	48. C	67. B
11. A	30. D	49. E	68. E
12. B	31. B	50. B	69. A
13. C	32. D	51. D	70. C
14. C	33. E	52. A	71. E
15. D	34. C	53. B	72. E
16. B	35. A	54. B	73. A
17. D	36. D	55. B	74. D
18. E	37. B	56. A	75. D
19. B	38. C	57. A	

ANSWERS AND EXPLANATIONS

1. B

The vertical velocity decreases on the way up and increases on the way down.

2. C

Since the horizontal velocity is constant throughout the flight, the horizontal acceleration is zero.

3. B

The vertical velocity is directed up during the first half of the flight, and down during the second half of the flight.

4. D

The force between the masses can be calculated by Newton's law of universal gravitation.

5. A

The jar's inertia causes it to stay at rest as the paper is pulled out from under it.

6. E

The momentum of the clay before the collision is equal to the momentum of the clay and wood block after the collision.

7. C

The action force of a team pulling on the rope is equal and opposite to the force the rope pulls on the team, which is equal to the tension in the rope.

8. B

By the second right-hand rule, if you put your thumb in the direction of the velocity of the charge and your fingers in the direction of the magnetic field (outward), your palm will face the direction of the force acting on the charge. In this case, only your left hand will match these vectors, and thus the charge must be negative, an electron.

9. A

By the right-hand rule, the charge must be opposite the charge in question 8. Thus, the charge is positive, a proton.

10. D

When two waves are in phase with each other, the crest of one wave meets the crest of the other wave, and constructive interference occurs.

11. A

The law of reflection states that the angle of incidence is equal to the angle of reflection as measured from the normal line.

12. B

When a wave passes from one medium into another, it refracts, changing both its wavelength and speed.

13. C

When a wave squeezes through a small opening, part of the wave lags behind, and the wave bends or diffracts.

14. C

The net force on the particle is zero, and thus it can be moving with a constant velocity according to the law of inertia.

15. D

As the boy rows south, the river carries his boat to the west, causing his resultant velocity to be southwest.

16. B

The total current in the circuit passes through the 4 Ω resistor. The total resistance in the circuit is the sum of the parallel combination of the 3 Ω and 6 Ω resistors (which is 2 Ω), and the 4 Ω resistor. Since the total resistance is 6 Ω, the total current in the circuit is

$$I = \frac{V}{R_{total}} = \frac{24V}{6\ \Omega} = 4\ A,$$

which is also the current through the 4 Ω resistor.

17. D

By Ohm's law, $V = IR = (4A)(4\ \Omega) = 16\ V.$

18. E

By the right-hand rule, the wire on the left creates a magnetic field that is directed to the top of the page at point P, and the wire on the right creates a magnetic field that is directed down to the bottom of the page, and the two cancel each other out.

19. B

The work done on the car is equal to the change in its kinetic energy, and force, work, and displacement are related to each other by the equation

$$F = \frac{W}{d} = \frac{\Delta KE}{d} = \frac{18,000\ J}{30\ m} = 600\ N.$$

20. A

Since there are no external forces acting on the system, the total momentum of the system must remain constant.

21. C

All masses will fall at the same acceleration and land at the same time, and since the mass also does not affect the horizontal distance traveled, they will land at the same place at the same time.

22. B

In an electric generator, a coil of wire is rotated in a magnetic field, producing a current by electromagnetic induction.

23. C

As the mass falls, its kinetic energy increases initially, but the potential energy decreases until the mass reaches the equilibrium position.

24. E

The +1µC charge is pulled downward and to the right toward the negative charge, and at the same time is pushed upward and to the right by the positive charge, producing a net force on the +1µC charge that is directed to the right.

25. A

The slope of both graphs represents speed, and the slope of train X is greater than the slope of train Y at time T.

26. C

If we extend the lines for trains X and Y, we see that train X reaches d_2 at an earlier time than train Y.

27. E

Frequency in Hertz is equal to the number of revolutions per second. In this case, we have 6 revolutions/60 seconds = 0.1 rev/s or 0.1 Hz.

28. C

The law of conservation of angular momentum states that the closer an orbiting planet is to the Sun, the smaller its orbital radius, and the greater its velocity.

29. D

$$\lambda = \frac{v}{f} = \frac{350\ m/s}{256\ Hz} = 1.4\ m$$

30. D

Heat energy flows from a body of higher temperature to a body of lower temperature.

31. B

The magnetic force needed to keep the electron orbiting in a circle is a centripetal force. The equation for centripetal force is

$$F = \frac{mv^2}{r}.$$

When the given values are substituted into this equation, the force, to the nearest order of magnitude, is 10^{-17} N.

32. D

We don't know which way the two blocks will accelerate since we don't know which block is more massive, but since they are connected to each other by a string, they must have the same acceleration.

33. E

Since the 1 Ω resistor has half the resistance of the 2 Ω resistor in this parallel circuit, twice the current passes through the 1 Ω resistor as the 2 Ω resistor, $I_1 = 2I_2$.

34. C

Since the two resistors are in parallel with each other, they have the same voltage across them.

35. A

Sound tends to travel at the highest speed through more dense material, and steel is the most dense of the choices.

36. D

The magnification is found by the ratio of the image distance to object distance,
$$\frac{60 \text{ cm}}{30 \text{ cm}} = 2.$$

37. B

A plane mirror alone always creates a virtual image that is the same size as the object, but left-right reversed.

38. C

The principle of superposition states that the displacements of the waves that coincide at each point can be added to find the height of the wave created by constructive or destructive interference.

39. A

Energy in Joules = (power in watts)(time in seconds) = (2,400 W)(180 s) = 432,000 J.

40. B

Although the electroscope is neutral, electrons in the metal are attracted to the rod and go to the top of the electroscope, leaving the leaves with a deficiency of electrons and positively charged.

41. A

Electrons are attracted from the ground to the rod, and therefore more electrons deposit themselves on the electroscope giving it a net negative charge. We could also think of the positive charges being repelled from the rod and escaping to the ground through the grounding wire, leaving the electroscope negatively charged.

42. B

$F = qvB$ implies that

$$q = \frac{F}{vB} = \frac{10^{-14} \text{ N}}{(10^6 \text{ m/s}) (10^{-2} \text{ } T)} = 10^{-18} \text{ C}.$$

43. C

$$v = f\lambda = (120 \text{ Hz})(0.5 \text{ m}) = 60 \text{ m/s}$$

44. B

Two "loops" make up one wavelength of 0.5 m, so there are two wavelengths in the string that is 1.0 meter long.

45. E

To melt the ice, it takes heat energy equal to $Q = mH_f$, where H_f is the heat of fusion for ice, giving $Q = (3 \text{ kg})(3.3 \times 10^5 \text{ J/kg}) = 9.9 \times 10^5 \text{ J}$.

46. C

The heat required to raise the temperature by $30°C$ is

$$Q = mc\Delta T,$$
$$= (3 \text{ kg})(4.2 \times 10^3 \text{ J/kg°C})(30°C - 0°C),$$
$$= 3.8 \times 10^5 \text{ J}.$$

47. B

Frequency depends of the source of the light, not on the medium through which it passes.

48. C

The net force is made up of the horizontal component of each tension, each component being equal to $T_x = T\cos 45 = 0.7T$. Since there are two horizontal components making up the net horizontal force of 500 N, we can write $2(0.7)T = 500$ N, and $T = 350$ N (approximately).

49. E

The acceleration of the car can be found by Newton's second law:

$$a = \frac{F_{net}}{m} = \frac{500 \text{ N}}{1,000 \text{ kg}} = 0.5 \text{ m/s}^2$$

50. B

Each photon can give its energy to an electron and give the electron enough energy to escape the metal.

51. D

Temperature is proportional to the average kinetic energy of the molecules, and kinetic energy is proportional to the square of speed. Thus, doubling the speed of the molecules will give us four times the temperature.

52. A

The heat added is equal to the work done by the engine plus any heat exhausted. Thus, the heat added = 50 J + 100 J = 150 J.

53. B

The efficiency is the ratio of the work done to the heat added ($\times$ 100%):

$$\text{Efficiency} = \frac{\text{Work}}{\text{Heat added}} = \frac{50 \text{ J}}{150 \text{ J}} \times 100\% = 33\%$$

54. B

The change in momentum of the ball is $p_f - p_i$ and since the ball reverses direction when it strikes the wall, the change in momentum would be $mv - (-mv) = 2mv$. The change in momentum cannot be zero, since the wall exerts an external force on the ball.

55. B

The force starts out small as the ball first makes contact with the wall, then gets larger as the ball is squashed against the wall, then smaller again as it rebounds from the wall.

56. A

The wave travels at a higher speed in a tight spring, and at a lower speed in a loose spring. With reduced tension in the spring, the wavelength will be smaller since the speed is smaller, and wavelength is proportional to speed by $v = f\lambda$.

57. A

$$v_f = v_i + at = (2 \text{ m/s}) + (2 \text{ m/s}^2)(3 \text{ s}) = 8 \text{ m/s}$$

58. D

$$s = v_i t + = \frac{1}{2} at^2 = (2 \text{ m/s})(3 \text{ s}) + \frac{1}{2}(2 \text{ m/s}^2)(3 \text{ s})^2$$
$$= 15 \text{ m}$$

59. C

The series of bright and dark lines are antinodes and nodes created by the interference of light waves after passing through two narrow slits.

60. D

Newton's second law states that $F_{net} = ma$, so to keep F_{net} constant, if we triple the mass, the acceleration will be reduced to one-third as much. In other words, if force is constant, acceleration is inversely proportional to the mass.

61. B

The restoring force exerted by the spring on the mass is greatest when the stretch of the spring is greatest, at the amplitudes A and C.

62. A

Since point B is the equilibrium position for the mass on the spring, the spring force at B is zero, and the mass has reached its maximum speed, and all of the energy in the system is kinetic energy.

63. E

The magnitude of the acceleration remains constant, but since it must continually adjust its direction to point toward the center of the orbit, it is always changing direction.

64. C

By Newton's second law, the ratio of the weight of an object to its mass is the acceleration due to gravity, and is constant, $W/m = g$.

65. C

As the ball rises, it continues forward at a constant velocity according the law of inertia, but the bus accelerates out from under it, making it appear to the boy that the ball goes over his head and lands behind him.

66. A

The heat from your feet is more readily conducted to the metal because the metal is a good conductor, leaving your feet with a lack of heat and feeling cold.

67. B

As the ray of light exits the water into the air, it bends away from the normal, since the ray is passing from a more dense medium (water) to a less dense medium (air).

68. E

When passing from one medium to another, all three of the choices would refract, changing their speed and wavelength.

69. A

Sound is a longitudinal wave, and only transverse waves can be polarized, that is, made to vibrate in only one plane.

70. C

The amplitude of a wave is the maximum displacement from the baseline to a crest, or from the baseline to a trough, in this case, 2.0 m.

71. E

A time of 24 days represents 4 half-lives, since each half-life is 6 days. If we cut 100% in half four times, we get 6.25% of the sample remaining.

72. E

Isotopes of an element can have various mass numbers (number of protons and neutrons), but must have the same atomic number (number of protons). Thus, there is no uranium with an atomic number of 91.

73. A

At point III, the tension in the string must be enough to support the weight of the ball *and* provide the centripetal force.

74. D

At point II, the ball is instantaneously moving straight downward, and if the string breaks at this point, the ball will move downward.

75. D

$$s = \frac{1}{2}gt^2 = \frac{1}{2}(10 \text{ m/s}^2)(4 \text{ s})^2 = 80 \text{ m}$$

HOW TO USE THE RESULTS OF YOUR DIAGNOSTIC TEST IN YOUR REVIEW

After taking the diagnostic test, you should have an idea of what subjects you are strong in and what topics you need to study more. You can use this information to tailor your approach to the following review chapters. If your time to prepare for the test is limited, skip right to the chapters covering the aspects of physics that you need to review most.

Part Three

Physics Review

Chapter 3: **Measurement, Scalars, and Vectors**

- Exponents
- Graphing
- Trigonometry
- Scalars and Vectors

The purpose of this chapter is to briefly review some of the math skills you will need in order to be successful on the SAT Subject Test: Physics, including exponents, powers of ten, the metric system and SI units, scientific notation, graphs, trigonometry, scalars, and vectors. If you are confident in your math skills in these areas, you may want to skip ahead to the next chapter. Otherwise, let's get warmed up!

EXPONENTS

For any nonzero number a and any integer n:

exponent of zero: $a^0 = 1$

exponent of one: $a^1 = a$

negative exponent: $a^{-n} = \dfrac{1}{a^n}$

If a, b, x, y, and z are all integers:

product of powers: $(a^x)(a^y) = a^{x+y}$

power of powers: $(a^x)^y = a^{xy}$

quotient of powers: $\dfrac{a^x}{a^y} = a^{x-y}$

power of a product: $(ab)^x = a^x b^x$

power of a monomial: $(a^x b^y)^z = a^{xz} b^{yz}$

the nth root of powers: $\sqrt[y]{a^x} = a^{x/y}$

Powers of Ten

The rules for exponents listed above can also be applied when $a = 10$. For example:

$10^0 = 1$

$10^1 = 10$

$10^2 = 100$

$10^3 = 1,000$, and so on. Also:

$10^{-1} = \dfrac{1}{10}$

$10^{-2} = \dfrac{1}{100}$

$10^{-3} = \dfrac{1}{1,000}$, and so on.

Scientific Notation

In physics, very large and very small numbers are often used. It is convenient for us to write these numbers as a number between 1 and 10 (the *mantissa*) times a power of ten. For example, the mass of the Earth is 6,000,000,000,000,000,000,000,000 kg, or a 6 followed by 24 zeroes. We can write this as 6×10^{24} kg in scientific notation, and we refer to 6 as the *mantissa* and 24 as the *power of ten*. By the same token, the mass of an electron in kg is a decimal point followed by 30 zeroes and then 911. In scientific notation, we would write the mass of an electron as 9.11×10^{-31} kg.

The Metric System and Systeme Internationale (SI) Units

The metric system is a system of units of different sizes that are related by powers of ten. The base units of the metric system that are commonly used on the SAT Subject Test: Physics are listed in Table 3.1.

Table 3.1: SI Base Units of the Metric System

Base Quantity	Base Unit	Symbol
Length	meter	m
Mass	kilogram	kg
Time	second	s
Temperature	Kelvin	K
Amount of Substance	mole	mol
Electric Current	ampere	A

All other units used on the SAT Subject Test: Physics are derived from these base units. Several of the powers of ten have been given names in the metric system. These metric prefixes are placed before a unit to indicate the power of ten that is the multiplier of that unit. Common examples of these metric prefixes are listed in Table 3.2 below.

Table 3.2: Common Metric Prefixes

Prefix	Symbol	Power of Ten	Example
nano	n	10^{-9}	nanosecond (ns)
micro	μ	10^{-6}	microfarad (μF)
milli	m	10^{-3}	milligram (mg)
centi	c	10^{-2}	centimeter (cm)
kilo	k	10^{3}	kilogram (kg)
mega	M	10^{6}	megawatt (MW)

GRAPHING

As you prepare for the SAT Subject Test: Physics, you might need to review some of your graphing skills. You will need to be able to interpret linear and parabolic graphs, and find the slope of a line and the area under a curve.

Linear Graphs

A linear graph results when we plot two quantities that are proportional to each other. The change in the quantity on the *y*-axis is called the *rise*, and the change in the quantity on the *x*-axis is called the *run*. The rise divided by the run is a constant for a linear graph, and we call this constant the *slope*, denoted by the letter *m*. We write:

> A linear graph has a constant slope, meaning the two quantities are proportional to each other.

$$\text{slope } m = \frac{rise}{run} = \frac{\Delta y}{\Delta x}$$

The slope of a linear graph is defined as the rate of change of *y* with respect to *x*.

Example: A simple circuit consisting of a power supply, wires of negligible resistance, and a resistor is connected, and several voltages and currents are measured. A graph of voltage (in volts) versus current (in amperes) for a simple circuit is plotted on the following page.

We see that we can draw the best-fit straight line through the data points. Remember, a best-fit line represents the average of the data, so points should be distributed evenly both above and below the line. The slope of the line can be found by choosing two points that are on the line. In this case, we have chosen the points (0.5 A, 2 V) and (2.5 A, 6 V):

$$\text{slope } m = \frac{rise}{run} = \frac{\Delta y}{\Delta x} = \frac{V_2 - V_1}{I_2 - I_1} = \frac{6V - 2V}{2.5A - 0.5A} = 2 \frac{V}{A} \quad \text{or } 2 \, \Omega$$

The ratio of the voltage to the current is the *resistance* of the circuit. We say that voltage and current are proportional to each other, and the resistance is the slope of a voltage vs. current graph. We will return to circuits in chapter 12.

Area Under a Curve

Another common way to analyze a graph is to find the area under the curve. Remember, a curve is a generic word for any line resulting from graphing two quantities, and can mean a curved line or a straight line. The area under a curve is equal to the product of the two quantities on the axes for a particular interval. For example, consider the graph of velocity (in meters per second) vs. time (in seconds) on the following page.

If we consider the time interval from 0 to 8 s, we can find the area under the curve (graph). The area from 0 to 4 s is the area of a triangle with a base of 4 s and a height of 10 m/s. The area from 4 s to 8 s is a rectangle with a base of 4 s and a height of 10 m/s. The total area under the graph is the sum of the area of the triangle and the area of the rectangle:

$$\text{Total area} = \frac{1}{2}(\text{base})(\text{height}) + (\text{base})(\text{height}) = \frac{1}{2}(4 \text{ s})(10 \text{ m/s}) + (4 \text{ s})(10 \text{ m/s}) = 60 \text{ m}$$

Note that the units for the area under the graph is meters, which indicates that the area under a velocity vs. time graph is *displacement*. Motion is discussed further in chapter 4.

> The slope of a graph is the ratio of the change in the quantities, whereas the area under the curve is proportional to the change in the *product* of x and y: $\Delta(xy)$ or $x_2y_2 - x_1y_1$.

Parabolic Graphs

Often, two quantities in physics are not proportional to each other, but one quantity depends on the *square* of the other. For example, for an object falling freely from rest, the total distance fallen is proportional to the square of the time it has been falling. The equation that relates distance fallen to the time of fall is

$$s = \frac{1}{2}gt^2,$$

where g is the acceleration of the falling object due to gravity, about 10 m/s². Since s is proportional to t^2 (and not to t), the graph of s vs. t will be a parabola.

> A *parabola* results when one quantity is proportional to the square of the other.

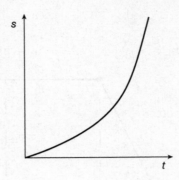

Of course, if we plotted s vs. t^2, we would get a straight line with a slope of $\frac{1}{2}g$. We will review several examples of parabolic relationships in later chapters.

TRIGONOMETRY

Trigonometry is the study of triangles, and often right triangles. The lengths of the sides of a right triangle can be used to define some useful relationships, called the *sine*, *cosine*, and *tangent*, abbreviated *sin*, *cos*, and *tan*, respectively. Take a look at the right triangle below.

The functions *sin, cos,* and *tan* are defined as the following:

$$\sin \theta = \frac{opposite\ side}{hypotenuse} = \frac{a}{c}$$

$$\cos \theta = \frac{adjacent\ side}{hypotenuse} = \frac{b}{c}$$

$$\tan \theta = \frac{opposite\ side}{adjacent\ side} = \frac{a}{b}$$

Also, the three sides are related to each other by the Pythagorean theorem:

$$c^2 = a^2 + b^2$$

Since you will not be allowed to use a calculator on the SAT Subject Test: Physics, trigonometric values will often be given to you with the questions that might use them. The relationships above will be particularly helpful when dealing with vectors.

SCALARS AND VECTORS

A *scalar* is a quantity that has no direction associated with it, such as mass, volume, time, and temperature. We say that scalars have only magnitude, or size. A mass may have a magnitude of 2 kilograms, a volume may have a magnitude of 5 liters, and so on, but a *vector* is a quantity that has both magnitude (size) and direction (angle). For example, if someone tells you that he is going to apply a 10 newton force on you, you would want to know the direction of the force—that is, whether it will be a push or a pull. So, force is a vector, since direction is important in specifying a force. See chapter 5 for more on forces. Other examples of vectors are velocity, acceleration, and momentum.

> A *scalar*, like *mass*, has only size. A *vector*, like *force*, has both size and direction.

Another example of a vector is *displacement*. Displacement **s** is the straight-line distance between two points, and is a vector that points from an object's initial position toward its final position. Let's say a hiker walks 6 km due west, then 8 km due north, then 10 km due east. What is the hiker's displacement from the origin?

A vector can be represented by an arrow whose length gives an indication of its magnitude (size), with the arrow tip pointing in the direction of the vector. We represent a vector by a letter written in bold type. For this example, we list the displacement vectors like this:

$$s_1 = 6 \text{ km west}$$

$$s_2 = 8 \text{ km north}$$

$$s_3 = 10 \text{ km east}$$

We can graphically add vectors to each other by placing the tail of one vector onto the tip of the previous vector. For our hiker displacement example, we can graphically add the second displacement vector to the first, and the third displacement vector to the second as shown in the diagrams.

A *vector* can be added like displacements (that is, tip-to-tail) to get the *resultant*.

The *resultant vector* is the displacement from the origin to the tip of the last vector. In other words, the *resultant* is the *vector sum* of the individual vectors, and can replace the individual vectors to represent the same result. Of course, just adding the lengths of the vectors together will not achieve the same result. Adding 6 km, 8 km, and 10 km gives 24 km, which is the total distance traveled, but not the straight-line displacement from the origin. We see in the diagram below that the resultant displacement is 8.9 km from the origin at an angle of 27° east of the north axis.

We could have added the displacement vectors in any order and achieved the same resultant. Therefore, we say that the addition of vectors is *commutative*.

The *equilibrant* is the vector that can cancel or balance the resultant vector. In this case, the equilibrant displacement is the vector that can bring the hiker back to the origin. Thus, the equilibrant is always equal and opposite to the resultant vector.

Vector Components

We may also work with vectors mathematically by breaking them into their components. A vector component is the projection or shadow of a vector onto the x-axis or y-axis. For example, let's say we have two vectors **A** and **B** as shown below.

 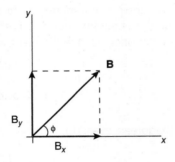

We will call the projection of vector **A** onto the x-axis its x-component, A_x. Similarly, the projection of **A** onto the y-axis is A_y. The vector sum of A_x and A_y is **A**, and, since the magnitude of **A** is the hypotenuse of the triangle formed by legs A_x and A_y, the Pythagorean theorem holds true:

$$|A| = \sqrt{A_x^{\,2} + A_y^{\,2}}$$

From the figures above, we get the following:

$$A_x = A \cos \alpha$$

$$A_y = A \sin \alpha$$

$$\tan \alpha = \frac{A_y}{A_x}$$

We can write the same relationships for vector **B** by simply replacing **A** with **B** and the angles α with ϕ in each of the previous equations.

Adding Vectors Using Components

Earlier we added vectors together graphically to find their resultant. Using the tip-to-tail method of adding vectors, we can find the resultant of **A** and **B**, which we will call **C**.

We can also use their components to find the resultant of vectors **A** and **B**. The x-component of the resultant vector **C** is the sum of the x-components of **A** and **B**. Similarly, the y-component of the resultant vector **C** is the sum of the y-components of **A** and **B**. Thus,

> The algebraic sum of the x-components of two vectors equals the x-component of the resultant; the same is true of the y-components.

$$C_x = A_x + B_x \text{ and, } C_y = A_y + B_y,$$

and by the Pythagorean theorem,

$$|C| = \sqrt{C_x^2 + C_y^2}.$$

Example: Using the diagrams above, let **A** = 4 meters at 30° from the x-axis, and **B** = 3 meters at 45° from the x-axis. Find the magnitude and direction of the resultant vector **C**. (cos 30° = 0.87, sin 30° = 0.50, cos 45° = sin 45° = 0.70)

Solution: First, we need to find A_x, A_y, B_x, and B_y.

$$A_x = A \cos 30° = (4 \text{ m})\cos 30° = (4 \text{ m})(0.87) = 3.5 \text{ m}$$

$$A_y = A \sin 30° = (4 \text{ m})\sin 30° = (4 \text{ m})(0.50) = 2.0 \text{ m}$$

$$B_x = B \cos 45° = (3 \text{ m})\cos 45° = (3 \text{ m})(0.70) = 2.1 \text{ m}$$

$$B_y = B \sin 45° = (3 \text{ m})\sin 45° = (3 \text{ m})(0.70) = 2.1 \text{ m}$$

Now we can find the *x*- and *y*-components of the resultant **C**:

$$C_x = A_x + B_x = 3.5 \text{ m} + 2.1 \text{ m} = 5.6 \text{ m}$$

$$C_y = A_y + B_y = 2.0 \text{ m} + 2.1 \text{ m} = 4.1 \text{ m}$$

The magnitude of the resultant **C** is

$$|C| = \sqrt{C_x^2 + C_y^2} = \sqrt{(5.6 \text{ m})^2 + (4.1 \text{ m})^2} = 6.9 \text{ m},$$

and its angle from the *x*-axis can be found by

$$\tan \theta = \frac{C_y}{C_x},$$

$$\theta = \tan^{-1}\left[\frac{4.1}{5.6}\right] = 36.2°.$$

The properties of vectors we've discussed here can be applied to any vector, including velocity, acceleration, force, and momentum. We will review the vector properties of these quantities in later chapters.

MEASUREMENT, SCALARS, AND VECTORS REVIEW QUESTIONS

1. The number 300,000,000 can be written as

   (A) 3×10^6.
   (B) 3×10^7.
   (C) 3×10^8.
   (D) 3×10^9.
   (E) 3×10^{-9}.

2. The fundamental SI units for mass, length, and time, respectively, are

   (A) newton, meter, minute.
   (B) kilogram, meter, second.
   (C) pound, foot, hour.
   (D) pound, foot, second.
   (E) kilogram, centimeter, hour.

3. A millimeter is

   (A) 10^3 m.
   (B) 10^2 m.
   (C) 10^1 m.
   (D) 10^{-3} m.
   (E) 10^{-6} m.

4. How many nanometers are in a kilometer?

   (A) 10^{-9}
   (B) 10^9
   (C) 10^{-12}
   (D) 10^{12}
   (E) 10^{27}

5. The data plotted on a graph of distance on the y-axis vs. time on the x-axis yields a linear graph. The slope of the graph is

   (A) $\dfrac{\Delta d}{\Delta t}$.
   (B) $(\Delta d)(\Delta t)$.
   (C) $\dfrac{\Delta t}{\Delta d}$.
   (D) $(\Delta d) + (\Delta t)$.
   (E) $(\Delta d) - (\Delta t)$.

6. Consider the velocity vs. time graph shown.

   The area under the graph from 2 s to 6 s is most nearly

   (A) 8.
   (B) 16.
   (C) 24.
   (D) 32.
   (E) 36.

7. Data from an experiment shows that kinetic energy is proportional to the square of velocity. The plot of the graph of kinetic energy vs. velocity would be

   (A) a straight horizontal line.
   (B) a straight diagonal line sloping upward.
   (C) a parabola.
   (D) a hyperbola.
   (E) a circle.

8. The cosine of an angle in a right triangle is equal to the

   (A) sine of the angle.
   (B) tangent of the angle.
   (C) hypotenuse of the triangle.
   (D) side adjacent to the angle.
   (E) ratio of the side adjacent to the angle and the hypotenuse of the triangle.

9. Which of the following quantities is NOT a vector quantity?

    (A) displacement
    (B) mass
    (C) resultant
    (D) equilibrant
    (E) 10 km at 30° north of east

10. The resultant of the two displacement vectors 3 m east and 4 m north is

    (A) 5 m northeast.
    (B) 7 m northeast.
    (C) 1 m southwest.
    (D) 1 m northeast.
    (E) 12 m northeast.

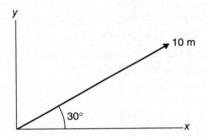

11. The x-component of the vector shown is most nearly (sin 30° = 0.5, cos 30° = 0.87, tan 30° = 0.58)

    (A) 10 m.
    (B) 5 m.
    (C) 8.7 m.
    (D) 5.8 m.
    (E) 100 m.

12. Two displacement vectors, each having a y-component of 10 km, are added together to form a resultant that forms an angle of 60° from the +x-axis. What is the magnitude of the resultant? (sin 60° = 0.87, cos 60° = 0.5)

    (A) 23 m
    (B) 40 m
    (C) 12 m
    (D) 20 m
    (E) 30 m

SOLUTIONS TO MEASUREMENT, SCALARS, AND VECTORS REVIEW QUESTIONS

1. C

A 3 followed by 8 zeros, or 3 multiplied by 10 eight times.

2. B

Mass is measured in kilograms, length in meters, and time in seconds.

3. D

The prefix *milli* means 10^{-3}.

4. D

$$1 \text{ km} \left(\frac{10^3 \text{m}}{\text{km}} \right) \left(\frac{10^9 \text{nm}}{\text{m}} \right) = 10^{12} \text{ nm}$$

5. A

Slope equals rise over run, which in this case would be $\frac{\Delta d}{\Delta t}$.

6. C

The total area can be calculated by adding the area bounded by $4(6 - 2) = 16$ and the area of the triangle bounded by $v = 4$ to $v = 8$ and $t = 6$ and $t = 2$: $\frac{1}{2}(8 - 4)(6 - 2) = 8$. Thus, the total area is $16 + 8 = 24$.

7. C

Since the kinetic energy is proportional to the square of the velocity, plotting *KE* vs. *v* would produce a parabola.

8. E

The cosine is defined as the ratio of the adjacent side to the hypotenuse.

9. B

Mass has no direction associated with it and therefore is a scalar, not a vector.

10. A

The two displacements represent the two legs of a right triangle. By the Pythagorean theorem, the hypotenuse is equal to

$$\sqrt{3^2 + 4^2} = 5 \text{ m northeast.}$$

11. C

The *x*-component of the vector is the side adjacent to the 30° angle and is found by $(10 \text{ m}) \cos 30° = 8.7 \text{ m}$.

12. A

The figure below shows that the two *y*-components add up to 20 m, which is the *y*-component of the resultant. The *y*-component of the resultant (20 m) is the opposite side to the 60° angle, and the magnitude of the resultant can be found by

$$\left(\frac{20 \text{ m}}{\sin 60°} \right) = 23 \text{ m.}$$

THINGS TO REMEMBER

- Exponents
  - Powers of ten
  - Scientific notation
  - The metric system and SI units
- Graphing
  - Linear graphs
  - Area under a curve
  - Parabolic graphs
- Trigonometry
- Scalars and vectors
  - Vector components
  - Adding vectors using components

Chapter 4: **Kinematics**

- Distance and Displacement
- Speed and Velocity
- Acceleration
- The Kinematic Equations for Uniformly Accelerated Motion
- Graphs of Motion

We begin our review of motion with the study of *kinematics*. Kinematics is the study of *how* things move; that is, how far things move (distance and displacement), how fast they move (speed and velocity), the rate of change of velocity (acceleration), and how much time passes during the changes. Kinematics is the study of the relationships between all of these things without regard to *why* something is moving, a question we will take up in the next chapter.

Kinematics is the study of how things move.

DISTANCE AND DISPLACEMENT

Distance can be defined as total length moved. If you run around a circular track, you have covered a distance equal to the circumference of the track. Distance is a scalar, which means it has no direction associated with it. *Displacement*, however, is a vector, representing a change in position. Displacement is defined as the straight-line distance between two points, and is a vector pointing from an object's initial position toward its final position. In our previous example, if you run around a circular track and end up at the same place you started, your displacement is zero, since there is no distance between your starting point and your ending point. For more discussion on displacement and other vectors, see chapter 3.

Distance is a scalar and *displacement* is a vector.

SPEED AND VELOCITY

Average speed is defined as the total distance a moving object covers divided by the total time it takes to cover that distance:

$$\text{average speed} = \frac{\text{total distance}}{\text{total time}}, \text{ or}$$

$$v = \frac{d}{t},$$

where *v* stands for speed, *d* for distance, and *t* for time.

Example: A sprinter can run 100 meters in 11 seconds. Find her average speed.

Solution: $v = \frac{d}{t} = \frac{100 \text{ m}}{11 \text{ s}} = 9.1 \text{ m/s}$

Average velocity is defined a little differently from *average speed*. While average speed is the total distance divided by the total time, average velocity is the change in position divided by the change in time. Since velocity is a vector, we must define it in terms of another vector, displacement **s**. Often, average speed and average velocity are interchangeable for the purposes of the SAT Subject Test: Physics. Speed is the magnitude of velocity; that is, speed is the scalar component of the velocity vector. For example, if you are driving west at 55 miles per hour, we say that your speed is 55 mph, and your velocity is 55 mph west. We will use the letter *v* for both speed and velocity in our calculations, and we will take the direction of velocity into account when necessary.

> *Speed* is a scalar and *velocity* is a vector.

ACCELERATION

Acceleration *a* is defined as the rate of change of velocity *v*, or the change in velocity *v* divided by the change in time *t*:

$$\text{acceleration} = \frac{\text{change in velocity}}{\text{change in time}}$$

$$a = \frac{\Delta v}{\Delta t}$$

> *Acceleration* is the rate at which velocity is changing.

The Greek letter Δ stands for "change in," or final quantity (in this case, velocity) minus initial quantity.

Acceleration tells us how fast velocity is changing. For example, if you start from rest on the goal line of a football field and begin walking up to a speed of 2 m/s for the first second, then up to 4 m/s for the second second, then up to 6 m/s for the third second, you are speeding up with an average acceleration of 2 m/s for each second you are walking. We write the following:

> *Velocity* is the rate of change of displacement, and *acceleration* is the rate of change of velocity.

$$a = \frac{\Delta v}{\Delta t} = \frac{2 \text{ m/s}}{1 \text{ s}} = 2 \text{ m/s/s} = 2 \text{ m/s}^2$$

In other words, you are changing your speed by 2 m/s for each second you walk. If you start with a high velocity and slow down, you are still accelerating, but your acceleration would be in the opposite direction of the initial motion. If you assume the initial direction to be positive, then your acceleration would be negative.

Example: A car moving initially at 10 m/s accelerates up to 30 m/s during the course of 4 seconds. Find the acceleration of the car.

Solution: The car's initial velocity v_i = 10 m/s, the final velocity v_f = 30 m/s, and the time interval Δt = 4 s. The acceleration can be found by the following equation:

$$a = \frac{\Delta v}{\Delta t} = \frac{v_f - v_i}{\Delta t} = \frac{30 \text{ m/s} - 10 \text{ m/s}}{4 \text{ s}} = 5 \text{ m/s}^2$$

Usually, the change in speed Δv is calculated by the final speed v_f minus the initial speed v_i. The initial and final speeds are called instantaneous speeds, since they each occur at a particular instant in time and are not average speeds.

THE KINEMATIC EQUATIONS FOR UNIFORMLY ACCELERATED MOTION

Kinematics is the study of the relationships between distance and displacement, speed and velocity, acceleration, and time. The kinematic equations are the equations of motion that relate these quantities to each other. These equations assume that the acceleration of an object is *uniform*, that is, constant for the time interval we are interested in. The kinematic equations listed below would not work for calculating velocities and displacements for an object that is accelerating erratically. Fortunately, the SAT Subject Test: Physics only deals with uniform acceleration, so the kinematic equations will be very helpful in solving problems on the test.

Kinematic Equations

Equation 1 $\bar{v} = \dfrac{\Delta s}{\Delta t}$

Equation 2 $s = \dfrac{1}{2}(v_f + v_i)t$

Equation 3 $\bar{a} = \dfrac{\Delta v}{\Delta t} = \dfrac{v_f - v_i}{\Delta t}$

Equation 4 $v_f = v_i + at$

Equation 5 $s = v_i t + \dfrac{1}{2}at^2$

Equation 6 $v_f^2 = v_i^2 + 2as$

where t = time, v_i = initial velocity, v_f = final velocity (or the velocity at the end of a time interval), a = acceleration, and s = displacement (or change in position, $\Delta x = x_f - x_i$).

> The *kinematic equations* relate distance, position, displacement, velocity, acceleration, and time to each other.

Notice that in some of the equations above we have chosen to replace the time interval Δt with a t, representing total time. Also, these equations are the scalar form of the kinematic equations rather than the vector form. Remember that if we have a moving object with a displacement, velocity, or acceleration in the opposite direction of another vector quantity, we must use a negative sign to distinguish opposite direction.

When solving problems using the kinematic equations, we need to write down which quantities are given in the statement of the problem and the quantity we want to find, and use the equation that includes all of them.

Example: A car traveling initially at a speed of +12 m/s accelerates at a rate of +4 m/s² for a time of 5 s. What is the car's speed at the end of 5 s?

Solution: Let's write down the quantities we are given in the problem:

$$v_i = +12 \text{ m/s}$$
$$a = +4 \text{ m/s}^2$$
$$t = 5 \text{ s}$$

We want to find the final velocity v_f, so we look at the list of equations and find the one that includes v_i, a, t, and v_f. Equation 4 contains all of these quantities, so:

$$v_f = v_i + at = 12 \text{ m/s} + (4 \text{ m/s}^2)(5 \text{ s}) = +32 \text{ m/s}.$$

Example: The car in the above example now slows down at the rate of −2 m/s² for a distance of 60 meters. What is the car's velocity after covering this distance?

Solution: Organizing the new given quantities, we have the following:

$$v_i = +32 \text{ m/s}$$
$$a = -2 \text{ m/s}^2$$
$$s = 60 \text{ m}$$

We are to find the final velocity v_f after the car travels 60 m. Notice that we are not given time in this example, so we need to match up the given quantities with an equation that does not include time, such as Equation 6:

$$v_f^2 = v_i^2 + 2as$$

$$v_f = \sqrt{v_i^2 + 2as} = \sqrt{(32 \text{ m/s})^2 + 2(-2 \text{ m/s}^2)(60 \text{ m})} = +28 \text{ m/s}$$

If you had difficulty working through that last one without a calculator, don't worry; the numbers chosen for the SAT Subject Test: Physics will be simple enough for you to do the calculations without a calculator. You can find more examples using these equations in the review questions and explanations at the end of this chapter.

Free Fall

An object is in *free fall* if it is falling freely under the influence of gravity. Any object, regardless of its mass, falls near the surface of the Earth with an acceleration of 9.8 m/s², which we will denote with the letter g. We will round the free fall acceleration g to 10 m/s² for the purpose of the SAT Subject Test: Physics. This free fall acceleration assumes that there is no air resistance to impede the motion of the falling object, and this is a safe assumption on the SAT Subject Test: Physics unless you are told differently for a particular question on the exam.

Since the free fall acceleration is constant, we may use the kinematic equations to solve problems involving free fall. We simply need to replace the acceleration a with the specific free fall acceleration g in each equation.

Example: A ball is dropped from rest from a high window of a tall building and falls for 3 seconds.

Neglecting air resistance:

  (A)   What is the speed of the ball?
  (B)   What is the distance the ball has fallen from where it was released?
  (C)   What is the ball's acceleration?

Solution: First, let's list the quantities given or implied in this problem.

  $v_i = 0$, since the ball is dropped from rest

  $t = 3$ s

  $a = g = 10$ m/s², since the ball is falling freely under the influence of gravity

(A)   We are looking for the speed v_f after 3 s, so we find an equation that includes v_f, v_i, a, and t. Equation 4 gives

$$v_f = v_i + gt = 0 + (10 \text{ m/s}^2)(3 \text{ s}) = 30 \text{ m/s}.$$

(B)   The distance fallen can be found by Equation 5, choosing the downward direction as positive, and this gives:

$$s = v_i t + \frac{1}{2} gt^2 = (0)(3 \text{ s}) + \frac{1}{2}(10 \text{ m/s}^2)(3 \text{ s})^2 = 45 \text{ m}.$$

(C)   After 3 s of free fall, the ball is still accelerating at 10 m/s². The ball's *speed* is increasing, but the *rate* at which its speed is increasing (its *acceleration*) is constant.

Example: Suppose another ball is thrown upward with an initial velocity of 5 m/s from the window in the previous example. What is the ball's velocity (magnitude and direction) after 8 seconds?

Solution: In this case, the ball is thrown upward, and since gravity acts downward, we must assign a negative sign to either the acceleration of the ball, which is still 10 m/s² while it's in the air, or the initial velocity. Let's call the initial velocity positive since it is directed upward, and the acceleration negative since it is directed downward. The given quantities can be listed as follows:

$$v_i = +5 \text{ m/s}$$
$$t = 8 \text{ s}$$
$$a = g = -10 \text{ m/s}^2$$

We are trying to find v_f.

> If velocity and acceleration are in opposite directions in the same problem, we must give a negative sign to one of them and a positive sign to the other.

Equation 4 has everything we need:

$$v_f = v_i + at = (+5 \text{ m/s}) + (-10 \text{ m/s}^2)(8 \text{ s}) = -75 \text{ m/s}.$$

Thus, after 8 seconds, the ball is moving downward with a speed of 75 m/s.

Projectile Motion

Projectile motion results when an object is thrown either horizontally through the air or at an angle relative to the ground. In both cases, the object moves through the air with a constant horizontal velocity (neglecting air friction) and at the same time is falling freely under the influence of gravity. In other words, the projected object is moving horizontally and vertically at the same time, and the resulting path of the projectile, called the *trajectory*, has a parabolic shape. For this reason, projectile motion is considered to be *two-dimensional* motion.

> The horizontal velocity of a projectile is constant, but the vertical velocity is changed by gravity.

The motion of a projectile can be broken down into constant velocity and zero acceleration in the horizontal direction, and a changing velocity in the vertical direction due to the acceleration of gravity. Let's label any quantity in the horizontal direction with the subscript *x*, and any quantity in the vertical direction with the subscript *y*. If we fire a cannonball from a cannon on the ground pointing up at an angle θ, the ball will follow a parabolic path and we can draw the vectors associated with the motion at each point along the path:

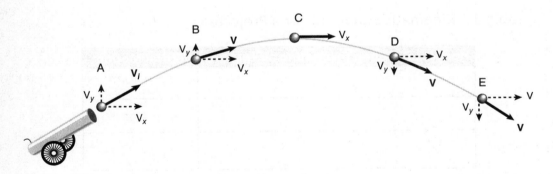

At each point, we can draw the horizontal velocity vector $\mathbf{v}_x$ and the vertical velocity vector $\mathbf{v}_y$. The vertical acceleration vector $\mathbf{g}$, which is simply the acceleration due to gravity, is directed downward at each point along the path. Notice that the length of the horizontal velocity vector and the acceleration due to gravity vector do not change, since they are constant. The absolute value vertical velocity decreases as the ball rises and increases as the ball falls. The motion of the ball is symmetric; that is, the velocity and acceleration of the ball on the way up is the same as on the way down, with the vertical velocity being zero at point C and reversing its direction at this point.

At any point along the trajectory, the velocity vector is the vector sum of the horizontal and vertical velocity vectors; that is, $\mathbf{v} = \mathbf{v}_x + \mathbf{v}_y$.

By the Pythagorean theorem

$$v = \sqrt{v_x^2 + v_y^2},$$

and

$$v_x = v\cos\theta$$
$$v_y = v\sin\theta$$
$$\theta = \tan^{-1}\left(\frac{v_y}{v_x}\right).$$

In both the horizontal and vertical cases, the acceleration is constant; that is, zero in the horizontal direction and 10 m/s² downward in the vertical direction. Therefore, we can use the kinematic equations to describe the motion of a projectile, as shown in Table 4.1.

Table 4.1:Kinematic Equations for a Projectile

Horizontal Motion (neglecting air friction)	Vertical Motion
$a_x = 0$	$a_y = g = 10$ m/s²
$v_x = \dfrac{s_x}{t}$	$v_y = v_{iy} + gt$
$s_x = v_x t$	$s_y = v_{iy}t + \dfrac{1}{2}gt^2$

If the acceleration **g** and the initial vertical velocity **v**$_{iy}$ are in opposite directions, we must give one of them a negative sign.

Example: A table tennis ball is launched from a level floor at an angle of 60° from the horizontal with an initial velocity of 6 m/s. (cos 60° = 0.5; sin 60° = 0.87; tan 60° = 1.73)

Neglecting air resistance:

    (A)   What is the maximum height reached by the ball?

    (B)   How much time does it take for the ball to land on the floor?

    (C)   How far horizontally does the ball travel before hitting the floor?

Solution: First, let's write down the quantities we are given:

$$\theta = 60°$$
$$v_i = 6 \text{ m/s}$$
$$g = 10 \text{ m/s}^2$$

(A)   At the ball's maximum height, $v_{fy} = 0$. We can use a vertical kinematic equation to find the time t_1 it takes to reach this maximum height, then find the maximum height.

$$v_{fy} = v_{iy} + gt_1$$
$$0 = (v \sin \theta) - gt_1$$

Note that g is negative, since the initial velocity is upward and positive.

$$t_1 = \frac{v \sin \theta}{g} = \frac{(6 \text{ m/s}) \sin 60°}{10 \text{ m/s}^2} = 0.5 \text{ s}$$

Then the height of the ball from the ground at this time is

$$s_y = v_{iy}t_1 - \frac{1}{2} gt_1^2 = (6 \text{ m/s}) \sin 60°(0.5 \text{ s}) - \frac{1}{2}(10 \text{ m/s}^2)(0.5 \text{ s})^2 = 1.35 \text{ m}.$$

Thus, the ball is located 1.35 m above the ground after 0.5 s.

(B)   By symmetry, the time t_2 it takes for the ball to land on the floor is twice the time it takes for the ball to reach maximum height. So,

$$t_2 = 2(0.5 \text{ s}) = 1 \text{ s}.$$

(C)   The horizontal distance traveled by the ball before hitting the ground is:

$$s_x = v_x t_2 = (v \cos \theta)t_2 = (6 \text{ m/s}) \cos 60°(1 \text{ s}) = 3 \text{ m}.$$

This maximum horizontal distance is also called the *range* of the projectile.

GRAPHS OF MOTION

Let's take some time to review how we interpret the motion of an object when we are given the information about it in graphical form. On the SAT Subject Test: Physics, you will need to be able to interpret three types of graphs: displacement vs. time, velocity vs. time, and acceleration vs. time.

Displacement vs. Time

Consider the displacement vs. time graph below:

> The slope of a displacement vs. time graph is velocity.

Since the graph is a straight, diagonal line, the slope is constant. As we discussed in chapter 3, the slope of a line is the rise divided by the run. The rise in this case is the displacement, or change in position, and the run is the change in time. Thus:

$$\text{slope of an } s \text{ vs. } t \text{ graph} = \frac{rise}{run} = \frac{\Delta x}{\Delta t} = velocity.$$

A constant slope in this case means a constant velocity. Remember, position and time are changing, but the velocity (slope) is constant.

Velocity vs. Time

Consider the velocity vs. time graph below:

In this case, the straight diagonal line means that the velocity is changing with time; that is, the object is accelerating. Thus:

$$\text{slope of a } v \text{ vs. } t \text{ graph} = \frac{rise}{run} = \frac{\Delta v}{\Delta t} = acceleration.$$

The constant slope in this case means constant acceleration. Remember, the velocity is changing with time, but the acceleration is constant.

As we discussed in chapter 3, the area under a velocity vs. time graph is the displacement.

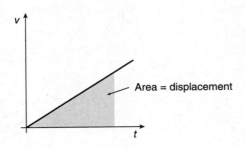

> The slope of a *velocity vs. time* graph is acceleration, and the area under a *velocity vs. time* graph is the displacement.

If the velocity is changing, then the slope of a displacement vs. time graph must also be changing. For constant acceleration, the displacement vs. time graph would be a parabola:

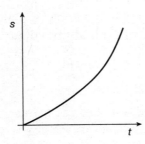

On this graph, the slope (velocity) is constantly increasing, indicating that the object is accelerating. The shape is parabolic because displacement is proportional to the square of time, as we've seen in the kinematic equations relating displacement and time for constant acceleration.

Acceleration vs. Time

Since the SAT Subject Test: Physics typically deals with only constant acceleration, any graph of acceleration vs. time on the exam would likely be a straight horizontal line:

This graph tells us that the acceleration of this object is +10 m/s². If the object were accelerating negatively, the horizontal line would be below the time axis.

Example: A football player catches a ball at his goal line ($x = 0$) at $t = 0$, and his motion is then graphed on the displacement vs. time graph below.

(A)   During which interval is the player accelerating away from his goal line?

(B)   What is his velocity between points B and C?

(C)   Describe his motion between points C and D.

(D)   What is his velocity (magnitude and direction) during the interval from 4 s to 6 s?

Solution:

(A)   The player is accelerating during the interval A to B, since the graph is parabolic. This tells us that his velocity is increasing as he runs away from the goal line.

(B)   The player's velocity between points B and C is the slope of the line between these two points.

$$\text{slope} = \frac{rise}{run} = \frac{\Delta x}{\Delta t} = \frac{20 \text{ m} - 10 \text{ m}}{3 \text{ s} - 2 \text{ s}} = 10 \text{ m/s}$$

(C)   During the interval from C to D, the time changes from 3 s to 4 s, but the player's position is not changing. He remains at rest at a distance of 20 m from the goal line, and thus his velocity is zero during this time interval. We could also say that since the slope of the line is zero, his velocity is zero, and he is at rest.

(D)   The player's velocity between 4 s and 6 s is found by the slope of the line in that interval:

$$\text{slope} = \frac{rise}{run} = \frac{\Delta x}{\Delta t} = \frac{0 \text{ m} - 20 \text{ m}}{6 \text{ s} - 4 \text{ s}} = -10 \text{ m/s}$$

Since the slope is negative, the velocity is negative, which does *not* mean the player is slowing down. A negative velocity means the player is running back toward his own goal line, that is, he is moving backward compared to his motion in intervals AB and BC.

Example: The graph below represents the velocity vs. time graph for a car.

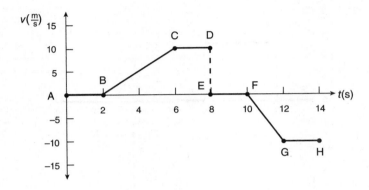

(A)   During which intervals is the car at rest?

(B)   During which intervals is the car moving at a constant nonzero velocity? State the velocity at each of these intervals.

(C)   There are two intervals during which the car is accelerating. Find the acceleration in each of these intervals.

(D)   Sketch the acceleration vs. time graph that corresponds to the motion of the car from 0 s to 14 s.

Solution:

(A)   The car is at rest when the velocity is zero: A to B and E to F.

(B)   The velocity of the car is constant from C to D, when its velocity is +10 m/s, and from G to H, when its velocity is −10 m/s. The car is traveling backward during the interval G to H compared to the interval C to D.

(C)   The car is accelerating during intervals B to C and F to G. During the interval B to C, the acceleration can be found by finding the slope of the *v* vs. *t* graph:

$$\text{slope of a } v \text{ vs. } t \text{ graph} = \frac{rise}{run} = \frac{\Delta v}{\Delta t} = \frac{10\,\text{m/s} - 0}{6\,\text{s} - 2\,\text{s}} = +2.5\ \text{m/s}^2.$$

During the interval F to G:

$$\text{slope} = \frac{rise}{run} = \frac{\Delta v}{\Delta t} = \frac{-10\,\text{m/s} - 0}{12\,\text{s} - 10\,\text{s}} = -5\ \text{m/s}^2.$$

In this last case, the car is still speeding up (from 0 to −10 m/s²); it's just speeding up in a negative direction.

(D)   The acceleration vs. time graph looks like this:

KINEMATICS REVIEW QUESTIONS

Unless otherwise noted, use $g = 10$ m/s^2 and neglect air resistance for all questions.

1. Which of the following statements is true?

   (A) Displacement is a scalar and distance is a vector.
   (B) Displacement is a vector and distance is a scalar.
   (C) Both displacement and distance are vectors.
   (D) Neither displacement nor distance are vectors.
   (E) Displacement and distance are always equal.

2. Which of the following is the best description of a velocity?

   (A) 60 miles per hour
   (B) 30 meters per second
   (C) 30 km at 45° north of east
   (D) 40 km/hr
   (E) 50 km/hr southwest

3. A jogger runs 3 km in 0.3 hr, then 7 km in 0.70 hr. What is the average speed of the jogger?

   (A) 10 km/hr
   (B) 3 km/hr
   (C) 1 km/hr
   (D) 0.1 km/hr
   (E) 100 km/hr

4. A motorcycle starts from rest and accelerates to a speed of 20 m/s in a time of 5 s. What is the motorcycle's average acceleration?

   (A) 100 m/s^2
   (B) 80 m/s^2
   (C) 40 m/s^2
   (D) 20 m/s^2
   (E) 4 m/s^2

5. A bus starting from a speed of +12 m/s slows to +6 m/s in a time of 3 s. The average acceleration of the bus is

   (A) 2 m/s^2.
   (B) 4 m/s^2.
   (C) 3 m/s^2.
   (D) –2 m/s^2.
   (E) –4 m/s^2.

6. A train accelerates from rest at a rate of 4 m/s^2 for a time of 10 s. What is the train's speed at the end of 10 s?

   (A) 14 m/s
   (B) 6 m/s
   (C) 2.5 m/s
   (D) 0.4 m/s
   (E) 40 m/s

7. A football player starts from rest 20 meters from the goal line and accelerates away from the goal line at 2 m/s^2. How far from the goal line is the player after 4 s?

   (A) 8 m
   (B) 28 m
   (C) 32 m
   (D) 36 m
   (E) 52 m

8. A stone is dropped from rest. What is the acceleration of the stone immediately after it is dropped?

   (A) zero
   (B) 5 m/s^2
   (C) 10 m/s^2
   (D) 20 m/s^2
   (E) 30 m/s^2

Questions 9–11 refer to the following.

A ball is thrown straight upward with an initial velocity of +15 m/s.

9. What is the ball's acceleration just after it is thrown?

    (A) zero
    (B) 10 m/s² upward
    (C) 10 m/s² downward
    (D) 15 m/s² upward
    (E) 15 m/s² downward

10. How much time does it take for the ball to rise to its maximum height?

    (A) 25 s
    (B) 15 s
    (C) 10 s
    (D) 5 s
    (E) 1.5 s

11. What is the approximate maximum height reached by the ball?

    (A) 23 m
    (B) 15 m
    (C) 11 m
    (D) 8 m
    (E) 5 m

12. Which of the following is NOT true of a projectile launched from the ground at an angle (neglecting air resistance)?

    (A) The horizontal velocity is constant.
    (B) The vertical acceleration is upward during the first half of the flight, and downward during the second half of the flight.
    (C) The horizontal acceleration is zero.
    (D) The vertical acceleration is 10 m/s².
    (E) The time of flight can be found by horizontal distance divided by horizontal velocity.

13. A projectile is launched horizontally from the edge of a cliff 20 m high with an initial speed of 10 m/s. What is the horizontal distance the projectile travels before striking the level ground below the cliff?

    (A) 5 m
    (B) 10 m
    (C) 20 m
    (D) 40 m
    (E) 60 m

14. A projectile is launched from level ground with a velocity of 40 m/s at an angle of 30° from the ground. What will be the vertical component of the projectile's velocity just before it strikes the ground? (sin 30° = 0.5, cos 30° = 0.87)

    (A) 10 m/s
    (B) 20 m/s
    (C) 30 m/s
    (D) 35 m/s
    (E) 40 m/s

15. Each of the choices below shows a pair of graphs. Which choice shows the pair of graphs that are equivalent to each other?

    (A)

    (B)

    (C)

    (D)

    (E)

Questions 16–17 refer to the graph below.

Consider the velocity vs. time graph.

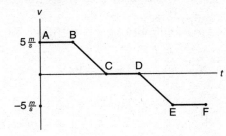

16. During which interval is the object at rest?

(A) AB

(B) BC

(C) CD

(D) DE

(E) EF

17. During which interval is the speed of the object increasing?

(A) AB

(B) BC

(C) CD

(D) DE

(E) EF

SOLUTIONS TO KINEMATICS REVIEW QUESTIONS

1. B

Displacement is the straight-line length from an origin to a final position and includes direction, whereas distance is simply length moved.

2. E

Velocity is a vector and, therefore, direction should be included.

3. A

Average speed is total distance divided by total time. The total distance covered by the jogger is 10 km and the total time is 1 hour, so the average speed is 10 km/hr.

4. E

$$a = \frac{\Delta v}{\Delta t} = \frac{20 \text{ m/s}}{5 \text{ s}} = 4 \text{ m/s}^2$$

5. D

$$a = \frac{v_f - v_i}{t} = \frac{6 \text{ m/s} - 12 \text{ m/s}}{3 \text{ s}} = -2 \text{ m/s}^2$$

6. E

$$v_f = v_i + at = 0 + (4 \text{ m/s}^2)(10 \text{ s}) = 40 \text{ m/s}$$

7. D

$$x_f = x_i + v_i t + \tfrac{1}{2}at^2 = (20 \text{ m}) + 0 + \frac{1}{2}(2 \text{ m/s}^2)(4 \text{ s})^2 = 36 \text{ m}$$

8. C

The acceleration due to gravity is 10 m/s² downward at all points during the stone's fall.

9. C

After the ball is thrown, the only acceleration it has is the acceleration due to gravity, 10 m/s² downward.

10. E

At the ball's maximum height, $v_f = 0$. Thus:

$$v_f = v_i + gt = 0$$

$$t = \frac{v_i}{g} = \frac{15 \text{ m/s}}{10 \text{ m/s}^2} = 1.5 \text{ s}$$

11. C

$$s = \frac{1}{2}gt^2 = \frac{1}{2}(10 \text{ m/s}^2)(1.5 \text{ s})^2 = 11.25 \text{ m}$$

12. B

Since the vertical acceleration is due to gravity, it is always downward.

13. C

First we find the time of flight, which can be calculated from the height.

$$d = \frac{1}{2}gt^2, \text{ so } t = \sqrt{\frac{2d}{g}} = \sqrt{\frac{2(20 \text{ m})}{10 \text{ m/s}^2}} = 2 \text{ s}$$

Then, $x = v_x t = (10 \text{ m/s})(2 \text{ s}) = 20 \text{ m}$.

14. B

Neglecting air resistance, the y-component of the velocity projectile just before it lands is equal to the y-component of the velocity when it is first fired:

$$v_y = (40 \text{ m/s})\sin 30° = 20 \text{ m/s}$$

15. B

Both graphs imply the object is accelerating.

16. C

The object is at rest during the interval in which the velocity is zero.

17. D

The speed is increasing from zero at point D to −5 m/s at point E, implying the object is going backward but speeding up from D to E.

THINGS TO REMEMBER

- Distance and displacement
- Speed and velocity
- Acceleration
- The kinematic equations for uniformly accelerated motion
  - Free fall
  - Projectile motion
- Graphs of motion
  - Displacement vs. time
  - Velocity vs. time
  - Acceleration vs. time

Chapter 5: **Dynamics**

- Newton's First Law of Motion
- Newton's Second Law of Motion
- Newton's Third Law of Motion

In the last chapter, we discussed *kinematics*, the study of *how* motion occurs. In this chapter, we review *dynamics*, the study of the *causes* of motion, namely, *forces*. A force is a push or a pull. As we discussed in chapter 3, a force is a vector quantity, and, therefore, has magnitude (size) and direction (angle). The SI unit for force is the *newton*, named for the originator of the study of dynamics, Isaac Newton. In 1687, Newton published his three laws of motion.

NEWTON'S FIRST LAW OF MOTION

The first law of motion states that an object in a state of constant velocity (including zero velocity) will continue in that state unless acted upon by an unbalanced, or net, force. Thus, a book at rest on your desk will remain at rest until you or something else applies a force to it. The property of the book that causes it to follow Newton's first law of motion is its *inertia*. Inertia is the resistance of an object to changing its state of motion or state of rest. It is difficult to push a car to get it moving from a state of rest because of its inertia, just as it is difficult to stop a moving car because of its inertia. We measure inertia by measuring the mass of an object, or the amount of material it contains. Thus, the SI unit for inertia would be the kilogram. We often refer to Newton's first law as the *law of inertia*. Remember, you don't need an unbalanced force to keep an object at rest or moving at a constant velocity; its own inertia takes care of that.

Newton's first law is the *law of inertia*.

NEWTON'S SECOND LAW OF MOTION

The law of inertia tells us what happens to an object when there are no unbalanced forces acting on it. Newton's second law tells us what happens to an object that *does* have an unbalanced force acting on it: It accelerates in the direction of the unbalanced force. Another name for an unbalanced force is a *net force*, meaning a force that is not canceled by any other force acting on the object. Sometimes, the net force acting on an object is called an *external force*.

> Newton's second law can be written as: force equals mass times acceleration.

Newton's second law can be stated like this: *A net force acting on a mass causes that mass to accelerate in the direction of the net force. The acceleration is proportional to the force* (if you double the force, you double the amount of acceleration), *and inversely proportional to the mass of the object being accelerated* (twice as big a mass will only be accelerated half as much by the same force). In equation form, we write Newton's second law as

$$F_{net} = ma,$$

where F_{net} and a are vectors pointing in the same direction. We see from this equation that the newton is defined as a $kg \cdot m/s^2$, which is the equivalent of a little less than a quarter of a pound.

Example: Two ropes pull on a 50 kg cart as shown below. What is the acceleration of the cart?

$F_2 = 200 \text{ N}$ ← [m = 50 kg] → $F_1 = 300 \text{ N}$

Solution: Before calculating the acceleration of the cart using Newton's second law, we must first find the net force. Since the rope on the right is pulling with a force that is greater than the force pulling to the left, the net force must be to the right and equal to the difference between the forces, since they are acting in opposite directions.

$$F_{net} = F_1 - F_2 = 300 \text{ N} - 200 \text{ N} = 100 \text{ N to the right.}$$

$$\text{Then, } a = \frac{F_{net}}{m} = \frac{100 \text{ N}}{50 \text{ kg}} = 2 \text{ m/s}^2 \text{ to the right.}$$

But what if the forces are acting at an angle other than 0° or 180°?

Example: Two forces act on a 40 kg sled resting on ice as shown from the top view below. What is the magnitude and direction of the acceleration of the sled?

Top View

$F_1 = 100$ N

$\sin 30° = \cos 60° = 0.5$

$\cos 30° = \sin 60° = 0.87$

60°

30°

$F_2 = 174$ N

Solution: Once again we need to find the net force before we can find the acceleration of the sled. Since the weight of the sled or the normal force exerted by the ground on the sled do not affect the acceleration of the sled in this case, we will not include them in our diagram. Let's break the forces down into their components:

$$F_{1y} \quad \mathbf{F_1}$$

60°

F_{1x}

F_{2x}

30°

$F_{2y} \qquad \mathbf{F_2}$

$F_{1x} = F_1 \cos 60° = (100 \text{ N})(0.5) = 50 \text{ N to the right}$

$F_{2x} = F_2 \cos 30° = (174 \text{ N})(0.87) = 150 \text{ N to the right}$

$F_{1y} = F_1 \sin 60° = (100 \text{ N})(0.87) = 87 \text{ N toward the top of the page}$

$F_{2y} = -F_2 \sin 30° = (174 \text{ N})(0.5) = -87 \text{ N toward the bottom of the page}$

Notice that the *y*-components of the forces cancel out, so we are left with a net force to the right:

$$F_{net} = F_{1x} + F_{2x} = 50 \text{ N} + 150 \text{ N} = 200 \text{ N to the right.}$$

So, the acceleration of the sled is

$$a = \frac{F_{net}}{m} = \frac{200 \text{ N}}{40 \text{ kg}} = 5 \text{ m/s}^2 \text{ to the right.}$$

Weight

As mentioned earlier, mass is a measure of the inertia of an object. If you take a 1 kg mass to the moon, it will still have a mass of 1 kg. Mass does not depend on gravity, but weight does. The *weight* of an object is defined as the amount of gravitational force acting on its mass. Since weight is a force, we can calculate it using Newton's second law:

$$\mathbf{F_{net}} = \mathbf{ma} \text{ becomes } \mathbf{Weight} = \mathbf{mg}$$

Mass is the measure of the amount of substance in an object, and is measured in kilograms. *Weight* is the gravitational force pulling down on an object, and is measured in newtons.

In the preceding equation, the specific acceleration associated with weight is, not surprisingly, the acceleration due to gravity. Like any force, the SI unit for weight is the newton.

Example: Find the weight in newtons of a girl having a mass of 40 kg.

Solution: $W = mg = (40 \text{ kg})(10 \text{ m/s}^2) = 400 \text{ N}$.

Since one newton is a little less than a quarter of a pound, this girl weighs about 100 lbs in U.S. Customary units.

Static Equilibrium

A system is said to be *static* if it has no velocity and no acceleration. In other words, it's at rest and it's going to stay that way. According to Newton's first law, *if an object is in static equilibrium, the net force on the object must be zero*. That doesn't mean there are no forces acting on it; it means there are no *unbalanced* forces acting on it.

> Always draw all of the forces acting on an object before answering a question about the forces or net force.

Example: Three ropes are attached as shown below. The tension forces in the ropes are T_1, T_2, and T_3, and the mass of the hanging ball is 50 kg. What is the magnitude of the tension in each of the three ropes? ($\sin 30° = \cos 60° = 0.5$; $\sin 60° = \cos 30° = 0.87$)

Solution: Since the system is in equilibrium, the net force on the system must be zero. We start by drawing a *free-body force diagram* of all the forces acting on point O. A free-body force diagram is a vector diagram of all of the forces acting on a mass.

Tension T_1 is simply equal to the weight of the hanging ball:

$$T_1 = W = mg = (50 \text{ kg})(10 \text{ m/s}^2) = 500 \text{ N}$$

To find T_2 and T_3, we can break them down into their vector components:

$$T_{2x} = T_2 \cos 30° \text{ and } T_{2y} = T_2 \sin 30°$$
$$T_{3x} = T_3 \cos 30° \text{ and } T_{3y} = T_3 \sin 30°$$

Since the forces are in equilibrium, the vector sum of the forces in the x-direction must equal zero. Therefore:

$$T_{2x} = T_{3x}$$
$$T_2 \cos 30° = T_3 \cos 30°$$
$$T_2 = T_3$$

The sum of the forces in the y-direction must also be zero:

$$T_{2y} + T_{3y} = W$$
$$T_2 \sin 30° + T_3 \sin 30° = W$$
$$T_2 (0.5) + T_3(0.5) = 500 \text{ N}$$

Since $T_2 = T_3$, it follows that each tension is also equal to 500 N.

Blocks and Pulley

A typical example used to illustrate weight and Newton's second law is a blocks and pulley system. Let's look at a couple of examples of the blocks and pulley system.

Example: Two blocks of mass m and $3m$ are connected by a string that passes over a pulley of negligible mass and friction, as shown below. The system is released from rest. In terms of the acceleration due to gravity g, what is the acceleration of the system?

Solution: First, we should draw a free-body force diagram for each block. There are two forces acting on each of the masses: weight downward and the tension in the string upward. Our free-body force diagrams should look like this:

Writing Newton's second law for each of the blocks:

$$F_{net} = ma \qquad\qquad F_{net} = 3ma$$
$$(T - mg) = ma \qquad\qquad (3mg - T) = 3ma$$
$$T = mg + ma \qquad\qquad T = 3mg - 3ma$$

Notice that the tension T acting on block m is greater than block m's weight, but block $3m$ has a greater weight than the tension T. This is, of course, the reason block $3m$ accelerates downward and block m accelerates upward. The magnitude of the tension acting on each block is the same, and the magnitudes of their accelerations are the same. Setting their tensions equal to each other, we get:

$$mg + ma = 3mg - 3ma.$$

Canceling the masses and solving for a, we get:

$$a = \frac{1}{2}g.$$

Of course, the block of mass m accelerates upward, while the block $3m$ accelerates downward.

Example: A block of mass m rests on a horizontal table of negligible friction. A string is tied to the block, passed over a pulley, and another block of mass $4m$ is hung on the other end of the string, as shown in the figure below. Find the acceleration of the system.

Solution: Once again, let's draw a free-body force diagram for each of the blocks, and then apply Newton's second law.

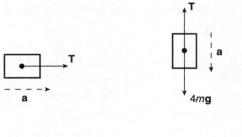

$$F_{net} = ma$$
$$T = ma$$

$$F_{net} = 4ma$$
$$(4mg - T) = 4ma$$
$$T = 4mg - 4ma$$

Setting the two equations for T equal to each other:

$$ma = 4mg - 4ma$$
$$a = \frac{4}{5}g$$

Could you have guessed at this solution before we worked it out? If the hanging mass $4m$ were not connected to the mass m on the table, it would fall freely at g. Since it is connected to the mass, the weight of mass $4m$ must accelerate $4m + m = 5m$ of mass, resulting in an acceleration only $\frac{4}{5}$ that of free-fall acceleration.

> See if you can make an educated guess at the answer to a question before working it out, and eliminate impossible or unreasonable answers.

NEWTON'S THIRD LAW OF MOTION

Newton's third law is sometimes called the *law of action and reaction*. It states that for every action force, there is an equal and opposite reaction force. For example, let's say your physics book weighs 6 N. If you set it on a level table, the book exerts 6 N of force on the table. By Newton's third law, the table must exert 6 N back up on the book. If the table could not return the 6 N of force on the book, the book would sink into the table. We call the force the table exerts on the book the *normal force*. *Normal* is another word for perpendicular, because the normal force always acts perpendicularly to the surface that is applying the force (in this case, the table). The force the book exerts on the table and the force the table exerts on the book are called an *action-reaction pair*.

> Newton's third law is the *law of action and reaction*.

> The normal force F_N is the reaction force that a surface exerts on an object and is perpendicular to the surface.

Friction

Friction is a resistive force between two surfaces that are in contact with each other. Friction always opposes the relative motion between the two surfaces. There are two types of friction: *static friction* and *kinetic friction*. Static friction is the resistive force between two surfaces that are not moving relative to each other, but that would be moving if there were no friction. A block at rest on an inclined board would be an example of static friction acting between the block and the board. If the block began to slide down the board, the friction between the surfaces would no longer be static, but would be kinetic, or sliding, friction. Sliding friction is typically less than static friction for the same two surfaces in contact.

We can define a ratio that quantifies the roughness between two surfaces in contact with each other. This ratio is the frictional force between the surfaces divided by the normal force acting on the surfaces, and is called the *coefficient of friction*. The coefficient of friction is represented by the Greek letter μ (mu). Equations for the coefficients of static and kinetic friction are

$$\mu_s = \frac{f_s}{F_N} \text{ and } \mu_k = \frac{f_k}{F_N}$$

where f_s is the static frictional force, f_k is the kinetic frictional force, and F_N is the normal force*. Sometimes the normal force is represented by N, but as this is easily confused with the newton (N), the unit for force, F_N will be used to represent the normal force throughout this book. (Note: There are times when these equations are not quite valid, but we don't have to worry about those cases for the SAT Subject Test: Physics.)

Example: A 2 kg block rests on a rough horizontal table as shown below. A rope is attached to the block and is pulled with a force of 8 N. As a result, the block accelerates at 2.5 m/s². What is the coefficient of kinetic friction μ_k between the block and the table?

> The frictional force between two surfaces is actually due to the interaction between the electrons in the atoms contained in the two surfaces.

$$a = 2.5 \text{ m/s}^2$$
$$- - - \rightarrow$$

| 2 kg | $\bullet \rightarrow$ $F_{rope} = 8$ N |

Solution: First, let's draw all of the forces acting on the block:

$$F_N \uparrow$$

$$f_K \leftarrow \qquad \bullet \qquad \rightarrow F_{rope} = 8 \text{ N}$$

$$mg \downarrow$$

---

* These equations are accurate for material covered in the SAT Subject Test. However, technically speaking, we should write $\mu_s = \frac{f_{s_{max}}}{F_N}$, where $f_{s_{max}}$ is the maximum possible static friction force that can exist under the specific conditions given.

In the vertical direction, the normal force F_N must be equal and opposite to the weight W down. Thus:

$$F_N = W = mg = (2 \text{ kg})(10 \text{ m/s}^2) = 20 \text{ N}.$$

In the horizontal direction, the net force is the difference between the force F_{rope} the rope exerts on the block and the force of friction f_k on the block:

$$F_{net} = (F_{rope} - f_k) = ma,$$
$$f_k = F_{rope} - ma = 8 \text{ N} - (2 \text{ kg})(2.5 \text{ m/s}^2) = 3 \text{ N}.$$

The coefficient of friction is

$$\mu_k = \frac{f_k}{F_N} = \frac{3 \text{ N}}{20 \text{ N}} = 0.15.$$

Notice that the coefficient of friction doesn't have any units, since it is the ratio of two forces. This is the coefficient of kinetic friction, since the block is moving.

Inclined Plane

If the surface on which the block rests is not horizontal but inclined at an angle, the normal force is not equal and opposite the weight of the block. Let's look at an example.

Example: A 3 kg block is placed on a rough inclined plane. The coefficient of static friction between the block and the plane is 0.2, and the angle of incline is 30°. Will the block slide down the plane, or remain at rest? (sin 30° = cos 60° = 0.5; cos 30° = sin 60° = 0.87)

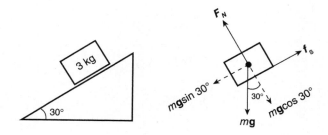

Solution: We see in the free-body force diagram that the frictional force points up the incline to oppose the motion (or impending motion) of the block. What we really want to know is whether or not the component of the weight directed down the incline (mgsin 30°) is greater than the magnitude of the frictional force f_s directed up the incline. Calculating each of those forces, we get:

$$mg \sin 30° = (3 \text{ kg})(10 \text{ m/s}^2)(0.5) = 15 \text{ N down the incline}.$$

The normal force F_N is equal and opposite to the component of the weight that is perpendicular to the ramp, expressed as $mg\cos 30°$. So:

$$f_s = \mu_s F_N = \mu_s(mg\cos 30°) = (0.2)(3 \text{ kg})(10 \text{ m/s}^2)(0.87)$$
$$= 5.2 \text{ N up the incline.}$$

Thus, the force down the incline is greater than the force up the incline, and the block will overcome friction to slide down the incline.

DYNAMICS REVIEW QUESTIONS

1. The amount of force needed to keep a 0.1 kg hockey puck moving at a constant speed of 5 m/s on frictionless ice is

   (A) zero.
   (B) 0.1 N.
   (C) 0.5 N.
   (D) 5 N.
   (E) 50 N.

2. A force of 20 N is needed to overcome a frictional force of 5 N and accelerate a 3 kg mass across a floor. What is the acceleration of the mass?

   (A) 4 m/s^2
   (B) 5 m/s^2
   (C) 7 m/s^2
   (D) 20 m/s^2
   (E) 60 m/s^2

3. A force of 50 N directed at an angle of 45° from the horizontal pulls a 70 kg sled across a frictionless pond. The acceleration of the sled is most nearly (sin 45° = cos 45° = 0.7)

   (A) 0.5 m/s^2.
   (B) 0.7 m/s^2.
   (C) 5 m/s^2.
   (D) 35 m/s^2.
   (E) 50 m/s^2.

4. Which of the following is true of the magnitudes of tensions T_1, T_2, and T_3 in the ropes in the diagram shown?

   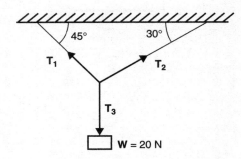

   (A) The magnitude of tension T_3 must be greater than 20 N.
   (B) The magnitude of the tension T_2 is greater than T_1.
   (C) The sum of the y-components of T_1 and T_2 is equal to 20 N.
   (D) The sum of the magnitudes of T_1 and T_2 is equal to T_3.
   (E) The sum of the magnitudes of T_2 and T_3 is equal to T_1.

5. Two blocks of mass m and $5m$ are connected by a light string that passes over a pulley of negligible mass and friction. What is the acceleration of the masses in terms of the acceleration due to gravity, g?

   (A) $4g$

   (B) $5g$

   (C) $6g$

   (D) $\dfrac{4}{5}g$

   (E) $\dfrac{2}{3}g$

6. A 1 kg block rests on a frictionless table and is connected by a light string to another block of mass 2 kg. The string is passed over a pulley of negligible mass and friction. What is the acceleration of the masses?

(A) 5 m/s²
(B) 6.7 m/s²
(C) 10 m/s²
(D) 20 m/s²
(E) 30 m/s²

7. A ball falls freely toward the Earth. If the action force is the Earth pulling down on the ball, the reaction force is

(A) the ball pulling up on the Earth.
(B) air resistance acting on the ball.
(C) the ball striking the Earth when it lands.
(D) the inertia of the ball.
(E) There is no reaction force in this case.

8. Friction

(A) can occur only between two surfaces that are moving relative to one another.
(B) is equal to the normal force divided by the coefficient of friction.
(C) opposes the relative motion between two surfaces in contact.
(D) only depends on one of the surfaces in contact.
(E) is always equal to the applied force.

9. A 2 kg wooden block rests on an inclined plane as shown.

The frictional force between the block and the plane is most nearly (sin 30° = 0.5, cos 30° = 0.87, tan 30° = 0.58)

(A) 2 N.
(B) 10 N.
(C) 12 N.
(D) 17 N.
(E) 20 N.

SOLUTIONS TO DYNAMICS REVIEW QUESTIONS

1. A

The law of inertia states that no force is needed to keep an object moving with a constant velocity.

2. B

The net force is 20 N − 5 N = 15 N, and the acceleration is

$$a = \frac{F_{net}}{m} = \frac{15 \text{ N}}{3 \text{ kg}} = 5 \text{ m/s}^2.$$

3. A

Only the x-component of the force accelerates the sled:
$F_x = (50 \text{ N}) \cos 45° = 35 \text{ N}$, and

$$a = \frac{F_x}{m} = \frac{35 \text{ N}}{70 \text{ kg}} = 0.5 \text{ m/s}^2.$$

4. C

$T_{1y} + T_{2y}$ must equal the weight, since the system is in static equilibrium.

5. E

The net force acting on the system is $5 mg - mg = 4 mg$. Thus, according to Newton's second law, $4 mg = 6 ma$, and $a = \frac{2}{3} g$.

6. B

The weight of the larger 2 kg block is the net force accelerating the entire system.

$$F_{system} = m_{larger} g = (2 \text{ kg})(10 \text{ m/s}^2) = 20 \text{ N}$$

$$a_{system} = \frac{F_{system}}{m_{system}} = \frac{(20 \text{ N})}{(1 \text{ kg} + 2 \text{ kg})} = \frac{20 \text{ N}}{3 \text{ kg}} = 6.7 \text{ m/s}^2$$

7. A

Newton's third law states that if the Earth is pulling on the ball, the ball is pulling on the Earth.

8. C

Friction acts on each of the surfaces in contact that are moving or have the potential for moving relative to each other.

9. B

Since the block is in static equilibrium, the frictional force must be equal and opposite to the component of the weight pointing down the incline:

$$f = mg \sin 30° = (2 \text{ kg})(10 \text{ m/s}^2) \sin 30° = 10 \text{ N}$$

THINGS TO REMEMBER

- Newton's first law of motion
- Newton's second law of motion
    - Weight
    - Static equilibrium
    - Blocks and pulley
- Newton's third law of motion
    - Friction
    - Inclined plane

Chapter 6: **Momentum and Impulse**

- Momentum
- Impulse
- Conservation of Momentum in One Dimension

MOMENTUM

The *momentum* of an object is defined as the product of its *mass* and the *velocity* at which it is moving. The usual symbol for momentum is *p*, and thus the equation for momentum is

$$p = mv.$$

Momentum is mass times velocity.

Since one of the components of momentum, velocity, is a vector, momentum is also a vector and is always in the same direction as the velocity. Momentum can be thought of as inertia in motion, and can be measured by how difficult it is to move a mass from rest or stop an object that is already moving. Since the momentum of an object includes both its mass and velocity, two different masses can have the same momentum depending on their respective velocities.

Example: How fast must a small car of mass 800 kg be moving in order to have the same momentum as a large truck of mass 2,000 kg moving at 20 m/s?

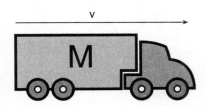

Solution: The momentum of the truck is

$$p = mv = (2{,}000 \text{ kg})(20 \text{ m/s}) = 40{,}000 \text{ kg(m/s)}.$$

Thus, the small car's speed can be found by

$$v = \frac{p}{m} = \frac{40{,}000 \text{ kg(m/s)}}{800 \text{ kg}} = 50 \text{ m/s}.$$

IMPULSE

Newton's second law states that an unbalanced (net) force acting on a mass will accelerate the mass in the direction of the force. Another way of saying this is that a net force acting on a mass will change its momentum. We can rearrange the equation for Newton's second law to emphasize the change in momentum:

$$F_{net} = ma = m\left(\frac{\Delta v}{\Delta t}\right)$$

or

$$F\Delta t = m\Delta v = mv_f - mv_i$$

Impulse is the product of the force acting and the time during which it acts.

The left side of the equation ($F\Delta t$) is called the *impulse*, and the right side ($m\Delta v$) is the *change in momentum*. This equation reflects the *impulse-momentum theorem*, and in words can be stated: *A force acting on a mass during a time causes the mass to change its momentum.* The unit for impulse is the newton-second (N·s).

Example: Consider the force vs. time graph below.

(A) What is the impulse acting on the object between 2 s and 4 s?

(B) What is the change in momentum between 2 s and 4 s?

(C) If the mass of the object is 10 kg and it has a velocity of 2 m/s at 2 s, what is its velocity at 4 s?

Solution:

(A) The impulse $F\Delta t$ is the area under the graph from 2 s to 4 s:

$$Area = F\Delta t = (20 \text{ N})(4 \text{ s} - 2 \text{ s}) = 40 \text{ N·s}$$

(B) The impulse-momentum theorem states that the change in momentum of an object is equal to the impulse applied:

$$change \text{ } in \text{ } momentum = F\Delta t = 40 \text{ N·s}$$

(C) The impulse-momentum theorem states that $F\Delta t = m(v_f - v_i)$. Thus, we get the following:

$$40 \text{ N s} = (10 \text{ kg})(v_f - 2 \text{ m/s})$$

where v_f is the velocity at a time of 4 s.

Solving for v_f, we get $v_f = 6$ m/s.

CONSERVATION OF MOMENTUM IN ONE DIMENSION

We've seen that if you want to change the momentum of an object or a system of objects, Newton's second law says that you have to apply an unbalanced force. This implies that if there are no unbalanced forces acting on a system, the total momentum of the system must remain constant. This is another way of stating Newton's first law, the law of inertia, discussed in chapter 5. If the total momentum of a system remains constant during a process, such as an explosion or collision, we say that the momentum is *conserved*. There are three typical examples of conservation of momentum questions on the SAT Subject Test: Physics: recoil, inelastic collision, and elastic collision.

> There are three types of conservation of momentum problems: recoil, inelastic collision, and elastic collision.

Recoil

Example: A 3 kg rifle that is initially at rest contains a bullet with a mass of 0.03 kg. The bullet is fired from the rifle at a speed of 300 m/s toward the east. What is the recoil velocity of the rifle?

Solution: Since the rifle and bullet were motionless before the rifle was fired, the total momentum of the system is zero both before and after the rifle was fired, since all forces in this case are internal and don't change the total momentum of the system. We write the momentum for each mass before and after the rifle is fired, and solve for the recoil velocity of the rifle. We will denote any velocity or momentum that occurs after a process with a *prime* (').

Momentum before firing = Momentum after firing

$$p_o = p_b' + p_R'$$

$$0 = m_b v_b' + m_R v_R'$$

$$0 = (0.03 \text{ kg})(300 \text{ m/s}) + (3 \text{ kg})v_R'$$

$$v_R' = -3 \text{ m/s}$$

Note that the recoil velocity of the rifle is negative, indicating that it moves in the opposite direction of the bullet (west), as we would expect. Also note that the velocity of the rifle is one-hundredth of the velocity of the bullet, since the rifle is one hundred times more massive than the bullet. In other words, *the momentum of the bullet must be equal and opposite to the momentum of the rifle.*

We can generalize this result to an object that explodes and sends its fragments in several directions, as shown below. Again, the total vector momentum of the system before the explosion must equal the total vector momentum after the explosion.

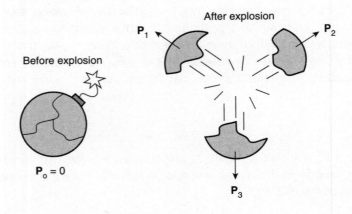

Inelastic Collision

An inelastic collision occurs when two colliding objects stick together after impact. Momentum is conserved in an inelastic collision, but kinetic energy is not.

Example: A car of mass 700 kg and moving at a speed of 30 m/s collides with a stationary truck of mass 1,400 kg, and the two vehicles lock together on impact. What is the combined velocity of the car and truck after the collision?

Solution: Once again, momentum is conserved in the collision.

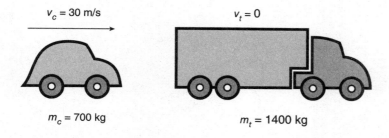

Before the inelastic collision

$v_c = 30$ m/s $v_t = 0$

$m_c = 700$ kg $m_t = 1400$ kg

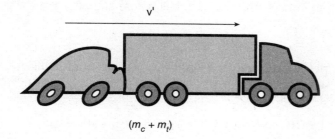

After the inelastic collision

v'

$(m_c + m_t)$

Momentum before collision = Momentum after collision

$$p_c = p_{c+t}'$$

$$m_c v_c = (m_c + m_t)v'$$

$$(700 \text{ kg})(30 \text{ m/s}) = (700 \text{ kg} + 1{,}400 \text{ kg})v'$$

$$v' = 10 \text{ m/s}$$

Elastic Collision

In an elastic collision, the colliding objects bounce off each other, and momentum is conserved. As we shall see in the next chapter, kinetic energy is also conserved in an elastic collision.

Example: A white pool ball of mass 0.5 kg moving at 10 m/s collides with a 0.4 kg red pool ball initially at rest. After the collision, the white pool ball continues in the same direction with a velocity of 1.1 m/s. Neglecting friction, what is the velocity of the red ball after the collision?

Before the elastic collision

$v_W = 10$ m/s $v_R = 0$

$m_W = 0.5$ kg $m_R = 0.4$ kg

After the elastic collision

$v_W' = 1.1$ m/s v_R'

Solution: Writing the momentum for each ball before and after the collision, we have the following:

Momentum before collision = Momentum after collision

$$m_w v_w + m_r v_r = m_w v_w' + m_r v_r'$$

$$(0.5 \text{ kg})(10 \text{ m/s}) + (0) = (0.5 \text{ kg})(1.1 \text{ m/s}) + (0.4 \text{ kg})v_r'$$

$$v_r' = 11.1 \text{ m/s to the right}$$

MOMENTUM AND IMPULSE REVIEW QUESTIONS

1. A hockey puck is sliding on the ice with a momentum of 5 kg·m/s when it is struck by a hockey stick giving it an impulse of 100 N • s in the direction of motion of the puck. Afterward, the momentum of the puck is

    (A) 500 kg·m/s.
    (B) 105 kg·m/s.
    (C) 100 kg·m/s.
    (D) 50 kg·m/s.
    (E) 20 kg·m/s.

2. A force acts on a mass as shown in the force vs. time graph.

    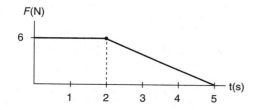

    The change in momentum of the mass between 2 s and 5 s is

    (A) 9 kg·m/s.
    (B) 18 kg·m/s.
    (C) 21 kg·m/s.
    (D) 30 kg·m/s.
    (E) 42 kg·m/s.

3. A cannonball is fired from a cannon so that the cannon recoils backward as the ball is fired forward. Which of the following statements is true?

    (A) The velocity of the cannonball is equal and opposite to the velocity of the cannon.
    (B) The mass of the cannonball and the cannon must be equal.
    (C) The momentum of the cannonball must be greater than the magnitude of the momentum of the cannon.
    (D) The momentum of the cannon must be equal to the magnitude of the momentum of the cannonball.
    (E) The momentum of the cannon must be greater than the magnitude of the momentum of the cannonball.

4. A 5,000 kg railroad car collides and sticks to a stationary railroad car of mass 7,000 kg and they move off together at a speed of 5 m/s. What was the speed of the 5,000 kg car before the collision?

    (A) 5 m/s
    (B) 12 m/s
    (C) 14 m/s
    (D) 35 m/s
    (E) 60 m/s

5. Which of the following quantities are conserved in an elastic collision?

    (A) momentum only
    (B) momentum and potential energy
    (C) kinetic energy only
    (D) momentum and kinetic energy
    (E) momentum and velocity

6. A 1 kg pool ball moving at +10 m/s strikes a 2 kg pool ball that is initially at rest. Which of the following statements is true immediately after the elastic collision?

    (A) The 1 kg pool ball is at rest.
    (B) The 2 kg ball must have a negative velocity.
    (C) The 2 kg ball's speed must be less than 10 m/s.
    (D) The two pool balls stick together.
    (E) The total kinetic energy of the two pool balls must be equal to 100 J.

SOLUTIONS TO MOMENTUM AND IMPULSE REVIEW QUESTIONS

1. B

The amount of impulse added is equal to the change in momentum. Thus:

$$5 \text{ kg·m/s} + 100 \text{ "N • s"} = 105 \text{ kg·m/s}$$

2. A

The area under the graph from 2 s to 5 s is equal to the impulse and therefore the change in momentum. The area under the triangle is

$$\frac{1}{2}(6 \text{ N})(3 \text{ s}) = 9 \text{ kg·m/s}$$

3. D

Conservation of momentum tells us that the momentum of the cannonball must be equal and opposite to the momentum of the cannon.

4. B

For the inelastic collision, momentum before the collision equals the momentum after the collision:

$$m_1 v_1 = (m_1 + m_2)v'$$

$(5{,}000 \text{ kg})v_1 = (12{,}000 \text{ kg})(5 \text{ m/s})$ yields $v_1 = 12 \text{ m/s}$

5. D

By definition, both momentum and kinetic energy are conserved in an elastic collision.

6. C

Since the 1 kg ball retains some of its momentum after the collision and transfers some of its momentum to the 2 kg ball, the speed of the 2 kg ball must be less than the original speed of the 1 kg ball.

THINGS TO REMEMBER

- Momentum
- Impulse
- Conservation of momentum in one dimension
    - Recoil
    - Inelastic collision
    - Elastic collision

Chapter 7: **Work and Energy**

- Work
- Energy
- Conservation of Energy
- Power

WORK

As you know by now, there are many words in physics that may be used quite differently outside the context of a physics course. The concept of *work* is certainly one of these words. In physics, work is defined as the scalar product of force **F** and displacement **s**, that is

$$W = \mathbf{F} \cdot \mathbf{s}.$$

Here, the force and displacement vectors are multiplied together in such a way that the product yields a scalar. Thus, work is not a vector, and has no direction associated with it. Since work is the product of force and displacement, it has units of newton-meters, or *joules* (J). A joule is the work done by applying a force of one newton through a displacement of one meter. One joule is about the amount of work you do in lifting your calculator to a height of one meter.

In the equation for work above, the scalar product of force and displacement can also be written as

$$W = Fs \cos\theta,$$

where θ is the angle between the applied force and the displacement. Let's look at a couple of examples.

> *Work* is the scalar product of force and displacement.

Example: A box is pulled across a horizontal floor of negligible friction with a horizontal force of 40 N through a displacement of 10 m. How much work is done on the box?

Solution: Since the force and the displacement are in the same direction, we can write:

$$W = Fs = (40 \text{ N})(10 \text{ m}) = 400 \text{ J}$$

Example: Suppose the force applied to the box in the previous example were directed at 60° above the horizontal as shown in the figure below. If the box is pulled by this force through a displacement of 10 m, how much work is done on the box? (sin 60° = cos 30° = 0.87; sin 30° = cos 60° = 0.5)

QUICK QUIZ

A boy pushes on a stationary brick wall with a force of 50 N for a time of 15 seconds. How much work did he do on the wall?

(A) 750 J
(B) 50 J
(C) 15 J
(D) none

Answer: (D) none. If the wall is not displaced, there is no work done on it.

Solution: To determine the amout of work done, we must only consider the component of the force that lies in the direction of the displacement, namely $F\cos\theta$. Then the work done is

$$W = Fs \cos 60° = (40 \text{ N})(10 \text{ m})(0.5) = 200 \text{ J}.$$

Thus, the person pulling the box across the floor only accomplishes half as much work by pulling up at an angle of 60°. This does not, however, mean that the person is only half as tired when he finishes the job; work is not a measure of how much effort is expended while performing the work. It is a measure of the product of the force that was applied in the direction of the displacement. Work is also a measure of the energy that was transferred while the force was being applied.

ENERGY

Energy is the ability to do work.

Energy is the ability to do work, and when work is done, there is always a transfer of energy. Energy can take on many forms, such as potential energy, kinetic energy, and heat energy. The unit for energy is the same as the unit for work, the joule. This is because *the amount of work done on a system is exactly equal to the change in energy of the system*. This is called the *work-energy theorem*. Let's look at two examples of the work-energy theorem.

Potential Energy

Potential energy is the energy a system has because of its position or configuration. When you stretch a rubber band, you store energy in the rubber band as elastic potential energy. When you lift a mass upward against gravity, you do work on the mass and therefore change its energy. The work you do on the mass gives the mass potential energy relative to the ground. To lift it, you must apply a force equal to the weight *mg* of the mass through a displacement height *h*.

> *Potential energy* is the potential for doing work.

The work done in lifting the mass is

$$W = Fs = (mg)h,$$

which must also equal its potential energy,

$$PE = mgh.$$

Example: A 5 kg bowling ball is lifted straight up to a shelf 2 meters above the floor. What is the work done on the bowling ball, and how much potential energy does the ball have when it is on this shelf?

Solution: The work done in lifting the bowling ball to a height of 2 m is

$$W = mgh = (5 \text{ kg})(10 \text{ m/s}^2)(2 \text{ m}) = 100 \text{ J}.$$

The potential energy of the ball must also be 100 J relative to the floor, since all of the work done on the ball went into increasing its potential energy.

Kinetic Energy

Kinetic energy is the energy an object has because it is moving. The kinetic energy of a moving object depends on its mass and the square of its velocity:

> *Kinetic energy* is energy of motion.

$$KE = \frac{1}{2}mv^2$$

But in order for a mass to gain kinetic energy, work must be done on the mass to push it up to a certain speed or to slow it down. The work-energy theorem states that the change in kinetic energy of an object is exactly equal to the work done on it, assuming there is no change in the object's potential energy.

Example: A 500 kg car is accelerated from rest by a force of 2,000 N for a displacement of 400 m. What is the speed of the car at the end of 400 m?

Solution: The work done on the car is equal to its change in kinetic energy. The work done is

$$W = Fs = (2{,}000 \text{ N})(400 \text{ m}) = 800{,}000 \text{ J}.$$

Thus, the 800,000 J is also equal to the change in kinetic energy of the car:

$$800{,}000 \text{ J} = \Delta KE = \frac{1}{2} m v_f^2 - \frac{1}{2} m v_i^2$$

$$800{,}000 \text{ J} = \frac{1}{2}(500 \text{ kg}) \, v_f^2 - \frac{1}{2}(500 \text{ kg})(0)^2$$

Solving for v_f, we get 56.6 m/s.

CONSERVATION OF ENERGY

If work is done on a system of objects by an outside agent, then the energy of the system changes. Energy can be lost from a system if the objects in the system do work on objects outside of the system. In summary, energy is conserved in isolated, or insulated, systems— systems in which the particles do not interact with objects outside the defined system. We say that total energy for these systems is *conserved*; that is, it remains constant during any process. This is also called the *law of conservation of energy*.

As an example, let's consider a 10 kg stone that sits just on the edge of a cliff 10 meters above the ground.

$m = 10$ kg

$h = 10$ m

The potential energy of the stone relative to the ground is

$$PE = mgh = (10 \text{ kg})(10 \text{ m/s}^2)(10 \text{ m}) = 1{,}000 \text{ J}.$$

If the stone slips off the edge of the cliff and falls, the potential energy of the stone begins changing into kinetic energy as the stone gains speed while losing height above the ground. Both the stone's potential and kinetic energies change, but the total amount of energy is conserved. In other words, the sum of the potential energy and kinetic energy at any time is equal to the total energy, which remains constant throughout the fall. The chart below summarizes the changes in potential and kinetic energies as the stone falls.

> *Conservation of energy* means that the total energy of a system remains constant.

	PE	KE	Total E
10 m	1,000 J	0	1,000 J
7.5 m	750 J	250 J	1,000 J
5 m	500 J	500 J	1,000 J
2.5 m	250 J	750 J	1,000 J
0	0	1,000 J	1,000 J

We can use the fact that the sum of the potential and kinetic energies remains constant during free fall to solve for quantities such as speed.

Example: What is the speed of the stone in the example above just before it strikes the ground?

Solution: Conservation of energy states that the total energy at the top of the cliff equals the total energy at the bottom of the cliff. Thus:

$$PE_{top} + KE_{top} = PE_{bottom} + KE_{bottom}$$

But the KE at the top and the PE at the bottom are zero, so we are left with:

$$PE_{top} = KE_{bottom}$$

$$mgh = \frac{1}{2}mv_{bottom}^2$$

$$v = \sqrt{2gh} = \sqrt{2(10 \text{ m/s}^2)(10 \text{ m})} = 14.1 \text{ m/s}$$

These same principles can be applied to a block sliding down a frictionless ramp, a pendulum swinging from a height, and many other situations. We could use Newton's laws and kinematics to solve these types of problems, but usually conservation of energy is easier to apply:

$$PE_{top} = KE_{bottom}$$

POWER

Work can be done slowly or quickly, but the time taken to perform the work doesn't affect the amount of work done, since there is no element of time in the definition for work. However, if you do the work quickly, you are operating at a higher power level than if you do the work slowly. *Power is defined as the rate at which work is done.* Often we think of electricity when we think of power, but it can be applied to mechanical work and energy as easily as it is applied to electrical energy. The equation for power is

$$P = \frac{work}{time},$$

and it has SI units of joules/second or watts (W). A machine is producing 1 watt of power if it is doing 1 joule of work every second. A 100 watt light bulb uses 100 joules of energy each second.

Example: A motor lifts a 100 kg crate onto a deck that is 5 meters high in a time of 10 seconds. How much power does the machine produce?

> *Power* is the rate at which work is done.

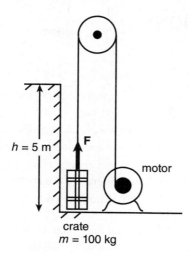

Solution: Power is work divided by time:

$$P = \frac{W}{t} = \frac{mgh}{t} = \frac{(100 \text{ kg})(10 \text{ m/s}^2)(5 \text{ m})}{10 \text{ s}} = 500 \text{ watts}$$

Any motor could do this same amount of work, but not necessarily as quickly, and therefore not at this 500 watt power level. For example, a small motor could lift the 100 kg crate if it were first broken into 1 kg pieces. Then the small motor could lift one piece at a time to the height of 5 meters and accomplish the same amount of work at a lower power level.

The letter W can stand for weight, work, or watt. Read the test questions carefully to be sure you know which one is being asked about in the question.

WORK AND ENERGY REVIEW QUESTIONS

1. Which of the following is NOT true of work?

   (A) It is the scalar product of force and displacement.

   (B) It is a vector that is always in the same direction as the force.

   (C) It is measured in joules.

   (D) It has the same units as energy.

   (E) It takes energy to perform work.

2. A 5 kg box is pushed across a level floor with a force of 50 N for a displacement of 10 m, then lifted to a height of 3 m. What is the total work done on the box?

   (A) 250 J

   (B) 500 J

   (C) 650 J

   (D) 2,500 J

   (E) 7,500 J

3. A 30 kg cart is pushed up the inclined plane shown by a force **F** to a height of 5 m.

   What is the potential energy of the cart when it reaches the top of the inclined plane?

   (A) 1,500 J

   (B) 630 J

   (C) 600 J

   (D) 300 J

   (E) 150 J

4. The work done on a system

   (A) always changes the potential energy of the system.

   (B) always changes the kinetic energy of the system.

   (C) always changes the momentum of a system.

   (D) can change either the potential energy or kinetic energy of the system.

   (E) is not related to the energy of the system.

5. A ball falls from a height h from a tower. Which of the following statements is true?

   (A) The potential energy of the ball is conserved as it falls.

   (B) The kinetic energy of the ball is conserved as it falls.

   (C) The difference between the potential energy and the kinetic energy is a constant as the ball falls.

   (D) The sum of the kinetic and potential energies of the ball is a constant.

   (E) The momentum of the ball is constant as the ball falls.

6. A 0.5 kg ball is dropped from a third-story window that is 10 m above the sidewalk. What is the speed of the ball just before it strikes the sidewalk?

   (A) 5 m/s

   (B) 10 m/s

   (C) 14 m/s

   (D) 28 m/s

   (E) 200 m/s

7. Drew lifts a 50 kg crate onto a truck bed 1 meter high in 2 seconds. Perry lifts fifty 1 kg boxes onto the same truck in a time of 2 minutes. Which of the following statements is true?

(A) Drew does more work than Perry does.

(B) Perry does more work than Drew does.

(C) They do the same amount of work, but Drew operates at a higher power level.

(D) They do the same amount of work, but Perry operates at a higher power level.

(E) Drew and Perry do the same amount of work and operate at the same power level.

8. A crane can lift a 600 kg mass to a height of 20 m in 2 minutes. The power at which the crane is operating is

(A) 1,000 watts.

(B) 6,000 watts.

(C) 60,000 watts.

(D) 240,000 watts.

(E) 1,440,000 watts.

SOLUTIONS TO WORK AND ENERGY REVIEW QUESTIONS

1. B

Work is a scalar, not a vector.

2. C

$$\text{Total work} = Fs + mgh = (50\,\text{N})(10\text{ m}) +$$
$$(5\text{ kg})(10\text{ m/s}^2)(3\text{ m}) = 650\text{ J}$$

3. A

The potential energy is only equal to the work done against gravity:

$$PE = mgh = (30\text{ kg})(10\text{ m/s}^2)(5\text{ m}) = 1{,}500\text{ J}$$

4. D

Work done equals either a change in potential energy or kinetic energy, or sometimes both.

5. D

The total energy is the sum of the potential and kinetic energies, and must remain constant.

6. C

Potential energy at the top equals the kinetic energy at the bottom:

$$mgh = \frac{1}{2}mv^2$$
$$(0.5\text{ kg})(10\text{ m/s}^2)(10\text{ m}) = \frac{1}{2}(0.5\text{ kg})v^2$$
$$v = 14\text{ m/s}$$

7. C

Drew and Perry do the same amount of work, but Drew does it faster and therefore operates at a higher power level.

8. A

$$P = \frac{work}{time} = \frac{mgh}{t} = \frac{(600\text{ kg})(10\text{ m/s}^2)(20\text{ m})}{120\text{ s}}$$
$$= 1{,}000\text{ watts}$$

THINGS TO REMEMBER

- Work
- Energy
  - Potential energy
  - Kinetic energy
- Conservation of energy
- Power

Chapter 8: **Circular Motion and Rotation**

- Uniform Circular Motion
- Torque
- Angular Momentum

UNIFORM CIRCULAR MOTION

Up until this chapter, we've been reviewing motion in a straight line. The law of inertia states that if an object is moving, it will continue moving in a straight line at a constant velocity until a net force causes it to speed up, slow down, or change direction. Imagine a ball moving in a straight line in space, but tied to a string as shown in the figure below.

The ball will continue to move in a straight line until it reaches the end of the string, at which time it will be pulled to a central point *O* and begin moving in a circle. As long as the string is pulled toward this central point, the ball will continue moving in a circle at a constant speed. *An object moving in a circle at a constant speed is said to be in uniform circular motion (UCM).* Notice that even though the speed is constant, the velocity vector is not constant, since it is always changing direction due to the central force that the string applies to the ball, which we will call the *centripetal force* $\mathbf{F}_c$. *Centripetal* means "center-seeking."

> *Centripetal force* is the center-seeking force that causes an object to follow a circular path.

> The three vectors associated with UCM are velocity, centripetal force, and centripetal acceleration.

There are three vectors associated with uniform circular motion: *velocity* (**v**), *centripetal force* (**F**$_c$), and *centripetal acceleration* (**a**$_c$). These vectors are drawn in the diagram below.

Notice that the velocity vector is tangent to the path of the ball and points in the direction the ball would move if the string were to break at that instant. The centripetal force and acceleration are both pointing toward the center. Although the centripetal force does not change the speed of the ball, it is always pulling the ball away from its inertial straight-line path and toward the center of the circle. Thus, the centripetal force accelerates the ball toward the center of the circle, constantly changing its direction.

> *Period* is the time for one revolution, and *frequency* is the number of revolutions per unit time.

The time it takes for the ball to complete one revolution is called the *period* (*T*). Since period is a time, we will measure it in seconds, minutes, hours, or even years. On the other hand, *frequency* (*f*) is the number of revolutions the ball makes per unit time. Units for frequency would include:

$$\frac{revolutions}{second}, \frac{revolutions}{hour}$$

Units for frequency can be any time unit divided into revolutions or cycles. Another name for rev/s is *hertz*. We can relate all of these quantities in the equations that follow.

The constant speed of any object can be found by

$$v = \frac{d}{t}.$$

For an object moving in a circle and completing one revolution, the speed of the object can be found by

$$v = \frac{circumference}{period} = \frac{2\pi r}{T}, \text{ where } r \text{ is the radius of the circle,}$$

and the centripetal acceleration is

$$a_c = \frac{v^2}{r}.$$

Newton's second law states that the net force and acceleration must be in the same direction and are related by the following equation:

$$\mathbf{F}_{net} = m\mathbf{a} = \frac{mv^2}{r}$$

Some other examples of centripetal force are the gravitational force keeping a satellite in orbit, and friction between a car's tires and the road that causes the car to turn in a circle.

Example:

A 100 kg racecar moves around a flat circular track of radius 50 m with a constant speed. The car makes one revolution around the track every 10 seconds. Find

(A)   the speed of the car.

(B)   the acceleration of the car.

(C)   the force between the tires and the road that keeps the car moving in a circle.

Top View

Solution:

(A)   The speed of the car is

$$v = \frac{circumference}{period} = \frac{2\pi r}{T} = \frac{2(3.14)(50 \text{ m})}{10 \text{ s}} = 31.4 \text{ m/s}.$$

(B)   The acceleration of the car is

$$a_c = \frac{v^2}{r} = \frac{(31.4 \text{ m/s})^2}{50 \text{ m}} = 19.7 \text{ m/s}^2.$$

(C)   The frictional force between the tires and the road provides the centripetal force and is

$$F_c = ma_c = (100 \text{ kg})(19.7 \text{ m/s}^2) = 1{,}970 \text{ N}.$$

TORQUE

Torque is the result of a force acting at a distance from a rotational axis, and it may cause a rotation about the axis only if there is a component of the force perpendicular to the radius. Torque is the product of the perpendicular component of the force ($F_\perp$) and the distance (*r*) (as in radius) from the rotational axis:

$$\text{Torque} = F_\perp r$$

The unit for torque is the *newton-meter*. To open a hinged door, you apply a force perpendicular to the door at the doorknob, which is mounted a certain distance from the hinges, and create a torque that causes the door to rotate around the hinges. When you use a wrench to tighten a bolt, you apply a force at the end of the wrench and perpendicular to it to get the most torque to turn the bolt. The distance from the rotational axis (r) is sometimes called the lever arm length; a lever is a rigid object used to apply a force around a rotational axis.

For a system in static equilibrium, the sum of the forces must equal zero, and the sum of the torques must also equal zero. This is illustrated in the next example.

Example: Two children sit on a seesaw that is 9 m long and pivots on an axis at its center. The first child has a mass m_1 of 20 kg and sits at the left end of the seesaw, while the second child has a mass m_2 of 40 kg and sits somewhere on the seesaw to the right of the axis. At what distance r_2 from the axis should the second child sit to keep the seesaw horizontal?

Solution: For the seesaw to remain horizontal, the torque on the left must equal and act in the opposite direction as the torque on the right. The forces acting on the seesaw on either side are just the weight (mg) of each child. So

torque on the left = torque on the right, or

$$F_1 r_1 = F_2 r_2,$$

where each force is applied perpendicular to the seesaw board,

$$(m_1 g)r_1 = (m_2 g)r_2.$$

Canceling the g's and solving for r_2 we get

$$r_2 = \frac{m_1 r_1}{m_2} = \frac{(20 \text{ kg})(4.5 \text{ m})}{40 \text{ kg}} = 2.25 \text{ m to the right of the axis.}$$

Could you have guessed this answer before we worked it out? Since the child on the right is twice as heavy as the child on the left, he should sit half as far from the axis on the right side to balance the torque the lighter child is producing on the left side.

ANGULAR MOMENTUM

In an earlier chapter, we studied linear momentum (p), which is the product of the mass of an object and its velocity. For an object moving in a curved path such as a circle, we can also define its *angular momentum*. Consider a ball on the end of a string that is being swung in a circular path. Its angular momentum (L) is defined as the product of its mass, velocity, and radius of orbit:

$$L = mvr.$$

We are interested in angular momentum because, as long as there are no net external torques, the quantity *mvr* is conserved. For example, consider a ball on the end of a string that is passed through a vertical glass tube and swung in a horizontal circle at a large radius R. If we pull the string through the tube to shorten the radius to r, the speed must increase to make up for the loss in radius to conserve angular momentum:

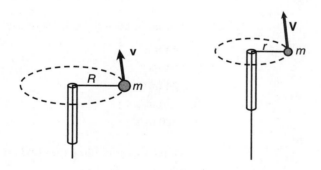

angular momentum before = angular momentum after, or

$$mvR = mVr.$$

We will revisit the law of conservation of angular momentum when we review gravitation and satellite orbits in chapter 10.

CIRCULAR MOTION AND ROTATION REVIEW QUESTIONS

Questions 1–2 refer to the following diagram.

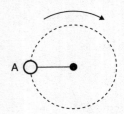

1. A ball on the end of a string is swung in a horizontal circle, rotating clockwise as shown. When the ball is at point A, the direction of the velocity, centripetal force, and centripetal acceleration vectors, respectively, are

    (A) →   ←   ←
    (B) ↓   →   →
    (C) ↓   →   ←
    (D) ↑   →   →
    (E) ↓   →   →

2. If the string were suddenly cut when the ball is at point A in the figure above, the subsequent motion of the ball would be

    (A) to move to the right.
    (B) to move to the left.
    (C) to move to the top of the page.
    (D) to move to the bottom of the page.
    (E) to move up and to the left.

Questions 3–5 refer to the following diagram.

A 30 kg child sits on the edge of a carnival ride at a radius of 2 m. The ride makes 2 revolutions in 4 s.

3. The period of revolution for this ride is

    (A) $\frac{1}{2}$ rev/s.

    (B) $\frac{1}{2}$ s.

    (C) 2 rev/s.

    (D) 2 s.

    (E) 4 s.

4. The speed of the child is most nearly

    (A) 4 m/s.
    (B) 6 m/s.
    (C) 24 m/s.
    (D) 120 m/s.
    (E) 360 m/s.

5. The force that is holding the child on the ride is most nearly

    (A) 30 N.
    (B) 180 N.
    (C) 300 N.
    (D) 540 N.
    (E) 4,320 N.

6. Torque

   (A) is the vector product of force and lever arm length.

   (B) is a scalar and has no direction associated with it.

   (C) is always equal to force.

   (D) is always greater for shorter lever arms.

   (E) must always equal zero.

7. Two blocks of mass 3 kg and 4 kg hang from the ends of a rod of negligible mass marked in seven equal parts.

   At which of the points indicated should a string be attached if the rod is to remain horizontal when suspended from the string?

   (A) A

   (B) B

   (C) C

   (D) D

   (E) E

8. A ball is tied to a string that passes through a glass tube and is attached to a hanging mass.

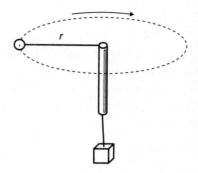

   The tube is held vertically as the ball is swung in a horizontal circle at a radius r and speed v. If the string is pulled through the tube by hanging a larger mass on the string so that the radius becomes $\frac{1}{2}r$, the speed of the ball will become

   (A) $\frac{1}{2}v$.

   (B) $2v$.

   (C) $3v$.

   (D) $4v$.

   (E) v (unchanged).

SOLUTIONS TO CIRCULAR MOTION AND ROTATION REVIEW QUESTIONS

1. D

The velocity vector points tangent to the circle in the direction that the ball is moving at the instant when it is at point A, which is toward the top of the page. The centripetal force and acceleration both point toward the center of the circle.

2. C

Since the ball is moving toward the top of the page at the instant when it is at point A, it would move in that direction if the string were to be cut there.

3. D

The period is $\dfrac{4 \text{ s}}{2 \text{ rev}} = 2 \text{ s}$.

4. B

$$v = \frac{2\pi r}{T} = \frac{2\pi(2 \text{ m})}{2 \text{ s}} = 6 \text{ m/s}$$

5. D

The force holding the child on is the centripetal force:

$$F = \frac{mv^2}{r} = \frac{(30 \text{ kg}) (6 \text{ m/s})^2}{2 \text{ m}} = 540 \text{ N}.$$

6. A

Torque is a vector and it is the product of force and lever arm length.

7. B

The string must be hung a little closer to the 4 kg mass than the 3 kg mass so that the torque to the left of the string will equal the torque to the right of the string. We can write (3 kg)(4 length units) = (4 kg)(3 length units).

8. B

According to conservation of angular momentum, if the radius is halved, the speed will double.

THINGS TO REMEMBER

- Uniform circular motion
- Torque
- Angular momentum

Chapter 9: **Vibrations**

- The Dynamics of Harmonic Motion
- Energy Considerations in Harmonic Motion

Another type of motion commonly found in nature is *vibrational motion*, which we sometimes call *harmonic motion*. An object is in harmonic motion if it follows a repeated path at regular time intervals. Two common examples of harmonic motion often studied in physics are a mass on a spring and a pendulum.

> An object is moving with *harmonic motion* if it follows a repeated path at constant time intervals.

Mass on a spring

Pendulum

THE DYNAMICS OF HARMONIC MOTION

As an object vibrates, it has both a *period* and a *frequency*. Recall that the period of vibration is the time it takes for one complete cycle of motion (i.e., the time it takes for the object to return to its original position). For a pendulum, this would be the time for one complete swing, forward and back. The frequency is the number of cycles per unit time, such as cycles per second, or hertz. The period and frequency of a pendulum depend only on the length of the pendulum and the acceleration due to gravity. The lowest point in the swing of a pendulum is called the *equilibrium position*, and the maximum displacement from equilibrium is called the *amplitude*. The amplitude can be measured by the maximum angle or by the linear horizontal distance from equilibrium, as shown below.

Since the pendulum vibrates about the equilibrium position, there must be a force that is trying to restore it back toward the center of the swing. This force is called the *restoring force*, and it is greatest at the amplitude and zero as the pendulum passes through the equilibrium position. Newton's second law tells us that if there is a net force, there must be an acceleration, and if the force is maximum at the amplitude, the acceleration must be maximum at the amplitude as well. The velocity, however, is zero at the amplitude and maximum as it passes through the equilibrium position. It might be helpful to think of the swing of a pendulum in terms of energy. At maximum amplitude, the pendulum mass has maximum potential energy and no kinetic energy. As it passes through the equilibrium position, all of the potential energy has been converted to kinetic energy.

We can apply these same concepts to a mass vibrating at the end of a spring. On the following figure, we've labeled the equilibrium position, the amplitude, maximum force and acceleration, and maximum velocity.

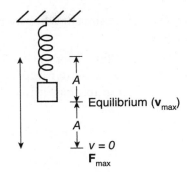

The period and frequency of a mass vibrating on a spring depend on the stiffness of the spring. For a stiffer spring, it takes more force to stretch the spring to a particular length. The amount of force needed per unit length is called the *spring constant* (k), measured in newtons per meter. The relationship between force, stretched length, and k for an ideal (or linear) spring is called *Hooke's law*:

$$F_{spring} = kx,$$

where x is the stretched length of the spring. For an ideal spring, the stretch is proportional to the force. If we pull with twice the force, the spring will stretch twice as far.

> A linear spring follows *Hooke's law*: The force is proportional to the distance the spring is stretched.

Example: The graph below represents the force F vs. stretched length x for two springs.

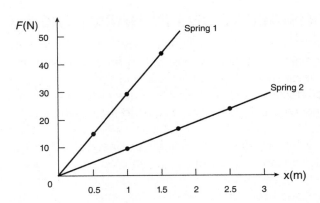

(A)   Which is the stiffer spring? Explain.

(B)   What is the spring constant for Spring 2?

> **QUICK QUIZ**
>
> Which of the following occur at the same time for a swinging pendulum?
>
> maximum force, maximum velocity, maximum acceleration, amplitude, equilibrium position
>
> Answer: The maximum force and acceleration occur when the pendulum is at its amplitude, and the maximum velocity occurs at the equilibrium position.

Solution:

(A)   Spring 1 is the stiffer spring, since it takes more force to stretch it the same length as Spring 2.

(B)   We can find the spring constant k for Spring 2 by taking the ratio of the force to the stretch for a particular interval. In other words, we can find the slope of the F vs. x graph for Spring 2.

$$k = \frac{25 \text{ N} - 10 \text{ N}}{2.5 \text{ m} - 1 \text{ m}} = 10 \frac{\text{N}}{\text{m}}$$

ENERGY CONSIDERATIONS IN HARMONIC MOTION

As an object vibrates in harmonic motion, energy is transferred between potential energy and kinetic energy. Consider a mass sitting on a surface of negligible friction and attached to a linear spring. If we stretch a spring from its equilibrium (unstretched) position to a certain displacement, we do work on the mass against the spring force. By the work-energy theorem, the work done is equal to the stored potential energy in the spring. If we release the mass and allow it to begin moving back toward the equilibrium position, the potential energy begins changing into kinetic energy. As the mass passes through the equilibrium position, all of the potential energy has been converted into kinetic energy, and the speed of the mass is maximum. The kinetic energy in turn begins changing into potential energy, until all of the kinetic energy is converted into potential energy at maximum compression.

The compressed spring then accelerates the mass back through the equilibrium to the original starting position, and the entire process repeats itself. If we neglect friction on the surface and in the spring, the total energy of the system remains constant; that is,

total energy = potential energy + kinetic energy = a constant.

Thus, whatever potential energy is lost must be gained as kinetic energy, and vice versa.

Example: Consider the mass suspended on a spring. The mass vibrates between levels A and C, and level B is halfway between A and C. Assume there is no loss of energy due to friction as the mass oscillates, and the potential energy at point B is zero.

> The *total energy* of a mass on a spring or a pendulum is the sum of the potential and kinetic energies.

(A)   At which point(s) is the speed of the mass the greatest?

(B)   At which point(s) is the potential energy the greatest?

(C)   If the potential energy at point A is 20 joules, what is the kinetic energy at point B?

Solution:

(A)   The speed of the mass is the greatest at point B as it passes through the equilibrium position.

(B)   The potential energy is the greatest when it is equal to the total energy (i.e., when the kinetic energy is zero). Thus, the potential energy is greatest at points A and C, at the greatest displacement from the equilibrium position.

(C)   If the potential energy is zero at point B, then all of the potential energy at point A is converted into kinetic energy as the mass passes through B. Thus, the kinetic energy at B must be 20 joules.

Example: A pendulum swings back and forth between points A and C as shown below. B is the midpoint between points A and C.

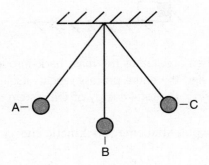

Which of the following statements are true?

(A)   The potential energy at A is equal to the kinetic energy at C.
(B)   The kinetic energy at B is equal to the total energy of the pendulum.
(C)   The pendulum has both kinetic energy and potential energy at point A.
(D)   The potential energy is maximum at points A and C.
(E)   The kinetic energy is maximum at point B.

Solution:

(A)   False. Since the mass is at rest at points A and C, there is no kinetic energy at A and C.

(B)   True. Since there is no potential energy at point B, all of the energy of the pendulum must be kinetic at that point.

(C)   False. The pendulum has no kinetic energy at point A, since it is momentarily at rest at that point.

(D)   True. Since points A and C are at the amplitude of the swing of the pendulum, the potential energy of the pendulum is maximum at these points.

(E)   True. The pendulum accelerates as it falls from point A to point B, and it reaches its maximum speed at point B, and therefore its maximum kinetic energy.

VIBRATIONS REVIEW QUESTIONS

1. According to Hooke's law for a mass vibrating on an ideal spring, doubling the stretch distance will

   (A) double the velocity of the mass.
   (B) double the force that the spring exerts on the mass.
   (C) quadruple the force the spring exerts on the mass.
   (D) double the period.
   (E) double the frequency.

2. For an ideal spring, the slope of a force vs. displacement graph is equal to

   (A) the work done by the spring.
   (B) the amplitude.
   (C) the period.
   (D) the frequency.
   (E) the spring constant.

3. Consider the force vs. displacement graph shown for an ideal spring.

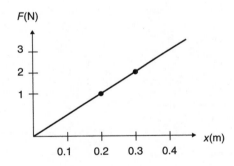

   The work done in stretching the spring from 0.2 m to 0.3 m is

   (A) 1 J.
   (B) 10 J.
   (C) 0.10 J.
   (D) 0.15 J.
   (E) 1.5 J.

4. A pendulum swings with an amplitude θ as shown.

   If the amplitude is increased and the pendulum is released from a greater angle,

   (A) the period will decrease.
   (B) the period will increase.
   (C) the period will not change.
   (D) the frequency will increase.
   (E) the frequency will decrease.

5. A mass on an ideal spring vibrates between points A and E as shown.

At which point is the acceleration of the mass the greatest?

(A) A
(B) B
(C) C
(D) D
(E) The acceleration is the same at all points.

6. A mass vibrates on an ideal spring as shown.

The total energy of the spring is 100 J. What is the kinetic energy of the mass at point B?

(A) 25 J
(B) 50 J
(C) 75 J
(D) 100 J
(E) 200 J

SOLUTIONS TO VIBRATIONS REVIEW QUESTIONS

1. B

Hooke's law states that the force is proportional to the stretch (displacement).

2. E

$$slope = \frac{\Delta F}{\Delta x} = k$$

3. D

The work done by the spring is equal to the area under the F vs. x graph from 0.2 m to 0.3 m, which is

$$(1)(0.1) + \frac{1}{2}(1)(0.1) = 0.15 \text{ J.}$$

4. C

The period (and thus the frequency) is not affected by a change in amplitude, only a change in length or gravity.

5. A

The acceleration is the greatest at the same point where the restoring force is the greatest: at the amplitude.

6. D

At point B, the equilibrium position, all of the energy is kinetic (100 J).

THINGS TO REMEMBER

- The dynamics of harmonic motion
- Energy considerations in harmonic motion

Chapter 10: **Gravity**

- Newton's Law of Universal Gravitation
- Orbiting Satellites

NEWTON'S LAW OF UNIVERSAL GRAVITATION

Gravitational Force

Newton's law of universal gravitation states that every mass in the universe attracts every other mass in the universe. The gravitational force between two masses is proportional to the product of the masses and inversely proportional to the square of the distance between their centers. The equation describing the gravitational force is

$$F_G = \frac{Gm_1m_2}{r^2},$$

where F_G is the gravitational force, m_1 and m_2 are the masses in kilograms, and r is the distance between their centers. The constant G simply links the units for gravitational force to the other quantities, and in the metric system happens to be equal to 6.67×10^{-11} Nm^2/kg^2. Because gravitational force is inversely proportional to the square of the distance from its sources, it is called an *inverse square law*. The questions on the SAT Subject Test: Physics will typically not use this constant, but will instead ask you about the proportionalities involved in the relationship between force, mass, and separation distance.

Example: Two planets each of mass m and separated by a distance r are attracted to each other by a gravitational force F_1. If the mass of one of the planets is doubled, and the distance between the planets is also doubled, what will be the new force between the masses in terms of F_1?

> Gravitational force is proportional to the product of the masses and inversely proportional to the square of the distance between their centers.

Solution: According to the equation for Newton's law of gravitation,

$$F_1 = \frac{Gmm}{r^2}.$$

Thus, the new force between the masses is

$$F_2 = \frac{G(2m)(m)}{(2r)^2} = \frac{2Gmm}{4r^2} = \frac{Gmm}{2r^2}.$$

So the new force F_2 is only half as much as the original force F_1. Note that regardless of the masses of the two objects, they always exert equal and opposite forces on each other.

Gravitational Acceleration

We've been treating the acceleration due to gravity as if it were a constant as long as we stay near the surface of the Earth. But if we travel an appreciable distance from the center of the Earth, such as twice the Earth's radius, the acceleration due to gravity is changed significantly. Like the gravitational force, the *gravitational acceleration* is inversely proportional to the square of the distance between the centers of the two masses. Thus, gravitational acceleration is also an inverse square law.

> Gravitational acceleration is proportional to gravitational force (Newton's second law).

Example: A ball is dropped near the surface of the Earth and accelerates toward the Earth with an acceleration of 10 m/s². With what initial acceleration will the ball fall if it is dropped from a height of three Earth radii from the center of the Earth?

Solution: Since the acceleration due to gravity is inversely proportional to the square of the distance from the center of the Earth, we can write

$$g \propto \frac{1}{r^2},$$

where the ∝ sign means "proportional to." If the ball is dropped at a height of three Earth radii, we have

$$g \propto \frac{1}{(3r)^2} = \frac{1}{9r^2}.$$

Thus, the acceleration due to gravity at three Earth radii is $\frac{1}{9}$ as much as it is near the Earth's surface (one Earth radius). At this height, the value for g is then

$$\frac{1}{9} \, (10 \text{ m/s}^2) = 1.1 \text{ m/s}^2.$$

ORBITING SATELLITES

As a satellite such as the Moon orbits the Earth, it is pulled toward the Earth with a gravitational force that is acting as a centripetal force. As described in chapter 8, the inertia of the satellite would cause it to tend to follow a straight-line path, but the centripetal gravitational force pulls it toward the center of the orbit. Although we often approximate the orbits of satellites around the Earth (or Sun, in the case of the orbits of the planets) as circular, they are actually elliptical, with the Earth (or Sun) located at one focus of the ellipse.

Comets follow highly elliptical orbits around the Sun. Halley's comet takes only a few months to get around the Sun on its closest approach, but it takes more than seven decades to reach its farthest point from the Sun and then return.

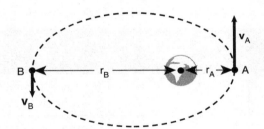

This means that there are times when the satellite is closer to the Earth than other times. If the satellite is at point A in the figure above, the gravitational force acting on the satellite is greater than at point B, and the speed at A is greater than at B. This is consistent with the law of conservation of angular momentum discussed in chapter 8:

angular momentum at A = angular momentum at B, or

$$mv_A r_A = mv_B r_B.$$

This equation shows that the closer the satellite gets to the planet (smaller r), the faster it goes (larger v). As the satellite orbits, potential energy and kinetic energy each change, but total energy (potential plus kinetic) remains constant.

Both the total energy and angular momentum of a satellite remain constant.

Example: A satellite orbiting the Earth moves from point A to point B in an elliptical orbit as shown below.

Fill in the table below with *increases*, *decreases*, or *constant* to describe the quantities related to the orbit as the satellite moves from point A to point B.

Quantity	Increases, Decreases, Constant
Speed	
Angular momentum	
Kinetic energy	
Total energy	
Gravitational force	

Solution:

Quantity	Increases, Decreases, Constant	Explanation
Speed	Decreases	The satellite is moving farther away from the planet and slowing down.
Angular momentum	Constant	Conservation of angular momentum
Kinetic energy	Decreases	Since the speed is decreasing, the kinetic energy must also be decreasing.
Total energy	Constant	Conservation of total energy
Gravitational force	Decreases	The satellite is getting farther away, thus the force is getting weaker due to the inverse square law.

GRAVITY REVIEW QUESTIONS

1. Which of the following diagrams of two planets would represent the largest gravitational force between the masses?

    (A)

    (B)

    (C)

    (D)

    (E)

2. A satellite is in orbit around the Earth. Consider the following quantities:

    I. distance from the center of the Earth

    II. mass of the Earth

    III. mass of the satellite

    The gravitational acceleration *g* depends on which of the above?

    (A) I only
    (B) I and II only
    (C) III only
    (D) I and III only
    (E) I, II, and III

3. As a satellite orbits the Earth, it passes points A and B. The satellite is traveling faster at point B than at point A. Consider the following statements:

    I. The gravitational force is greater at B than at A.

    II. The speed is greater at B than at A.

    III. The kinetic energy is greater at B than at A.

    IV. The angular momentum is greater at B than at A.

    Which of the above statements are true?

    (A) I only
    (B) I and II only
    (C) II only
    (D) I, II, and III only
    (E) I, II, III, IV

4. As a planet orbits the Sun, which of the following must remain constant?

    (A) velocity
    (B) gravitational force
    (C) radius of orbit
    (D) angular momentum
    (E) the product of mass and velocity

SOLUTIONS TO GRAVITY REVIEW QUESTIONS

1. B

Gravitational force is proportional to the product of the masses and inversely proportional to the square of the distance between the masses. Answers A and C are equivalent, while B is larger than either. Answers D and E are smaller than C.

2. B

The acceleration due to gravity does not depend on the mass of the orbiting (falling) object, but only on the mass of the Earth and the distance between the masses.

3. D

If the satellite is moving faster at B, then it is closer to the Earth at B; however, angular momentum is conserved as the satellite orbits, and is therefore constant at points A and B.

4. D

Angular momentum is conserved and must remain constant throughout the orbit.

THINGS TO REMEMBER

- Newton's law of universal gravitation
    - Gravitational force
    - Gravitational acceleration
- Orbiting satellites

Chapter 11: **Electric Fields, Forces, and Potentials**

- Charge
- Coulomb's Law
- Separation and Transfer of Charge in an Electroscope
- Electric Field

CHARGE

Charge is the fundamental quantity that underlies all electrical phenomena. The symbol for charge is q, and the SI unit for charge is the *Coulomb* (C). The fundamental carrier of negative charge is the electron, with a charge of -1.6×10^{-19} C. The proton, found in the nucleus of any atom, carries exactly the same charge as the electron, but is positive. The neutron, also found in the nucleus of the atom, has no charge. When charge is transferred, only electrons move from one atom to another. Thus, the transfer of charge is really just the transfer of electrons. We say that an object with a surplus of electrons is negatively charged, and an object having a deficiency of electrons is positively charged. Charge is conserved during any process, and so any charge lost by one object must be gained by another object.

The electron is the fundamental carrier of negative charge.

Charge is conserved during any process.

The Law of Charges

The law of charges states that like charges repel each other and unlike charges attract each other. This law is fundamental to understanding all electrical phenomena.

The law of charges: Like charges repel, unlike charges attract.

Example: Four charges, A, B, C, and D, exist in a region of space. Charge A attracts B, but B repels C. Charge C repels D, and D is positively charged. What is the sign of charge A?

Solution: If D is positive and it repels C, C must also be positive. Since C repels B, B must also be positive. A attracts B, so A must be negatively charged.

Example: Two charged spheres of equal size carry a charge of +6 C and −4 C, respectively. The spheres are brought in contact with one another for a time sufficient to allow them to reach an equilibrium charge. They are then separated. What is the final charge on each sphere?

Solution: The total charge on the two spheres is +6 C + −4 C = +2 C, and this is the magnitude of the equilibrium charge. When they are separated, they divide the charge evenly, each keeping a charge of +1 C.

COULOMB'S LAW

We know that two charges exert either an attractive or repulsive force on each other, but what is the nature of this force? It turns out that the force between any two charges follows the same basic form as Newton's law of universal gravitation; that is, the electric force is proportional to the magnitude of the charges and inversely proportional to the square of the distance between the charges. The equation for Coulomb's law is

$$F_E = \frac{Kq_1q_2}{r^2},$$

where F_E is the electric force, q_1 and q_2 are the charges, r is the distance between their centers, and K is a constant that happens to equal 9×10^9 Nm²/C². Usually, you will be asked questions about the proportionality between the quantities in Coulomb's law, rather than the equation.

Example: Two point charges q_1 and q_2 are separated by a distance r.

The following choices refer to the electric force on these two charges.

    (a)   It is quadrupled.

    (b)   It is doubled.

(c) It remains the same.

(d) It is halved.

(e) It is quartered.

(A) What happens to the force on q_2 if the charge on q_1 is doubled?

(B) What happens to the force on q_2 if the charge on q_1 is doubled and the distance between the charges is also doubled?

Solution:

(A) If q_1 is doubled, then

$$F = \frac{K(2q_1)(q_2)}{r^2} = 2F_E.$$

Thus, the new force between the charges is doubled, answer (b).

(B) If q_1 is doubled and r is doubled, then

$$F = \frac{K(2q_1)(q_2)}{(2r)^2} = \frac{2}{4}F_E = \frac{1}{2}F_E.$$

Thus, the new force is half as much as the original force, answer (d).

SEPARATION AND TRANSFER OF CHARGE IN AN ELECTROSCOPE

An electroscope is a device that consists of a metal ball or plate connected to a metal rod with two thin metal leaves attached at the bottom. The rod and leaves are insulated so as not to pick up any extra charges from the air. Remember, even neutral objects have charges in them; they just have an equal number of positive and negative charges. We can use other charged objects to redistribute the charges in a neutral object without actually changing the amount of charge.

Induction

We can use an electroscope to study how charges in the ball, rod, and leaves separate from one another when we bring another charged object near the electroscope or touch the ball of the electroscope with the charged object. For example, your physics teacher may have charged a hard rubber rod negatively by rubbing it on a piece of fur. The rod becomes negatively charged because it strips electrons off of the fur. If we bring

An electroscope can be used to study how charges distribute themselves.

the negatively charged rubber rod near the ball of the electroscope, the charges on the electroscope separate from each other. Use the diagram of the rod and electroscope below to draw how the positive and negative charges are distributed on the electroscope, then check your answer below.

Did you draw the ball as positive and the leaves as negative and repelling each other? The free electrons in the ball are repelled by the nearby negatively charged rod and therefore move down to the leaves of the electroscope. Since both leaves are then negative, they repel each other. We say that the ball of the electroscope is positively charged since it now has a lack of electrons. Your drawing should look like this:

But what if we touch the ball of the electroscope with the negatively charged rod? Draw the distribution of charges below.

The negative charges (electrons) flow into the electroscope, and we say that the electroscope is now negatively charged. This time, we didn't just separate charges in the metal, we actually transferred charge from one object to another by *conduction*, bringing the two objects in contact with each other. Your drawing should look like this:

The excess charge on an electroscope can be removed by touching it with a *ground*, which absorbs or transfers electrons from the electroscope and neutralizes the electroscope.

Conduction is the transfer of charge by actual contact.

Conductors, like metals, have electrons that are loosely bound to the outskirts of their atoms and can therefore easily move from one atom to another. An *insulator*, like wood or glass, does not have many loosely bound electrons, and therefore cannot pass charge easily.

ELECTRIC FIELD

An *electric field* is the condition of space around a charge (or distribution of charges) in which another charge will feel a force. Electric field lines always point in the direction in which a positive charge would feel a force. For example, if we take a charge Q to be the source of an electric field E, and we bring a very small positive "test" charge q nearby to test the strength and direction of the electric field, then q will feel a force that is directed radially away from Q as shown below.

> *Electric field* is the force per unit charge in a region of space.

The magnitude of the electric field is given by the equation

$$E = \frac{F}{q},$$

where electric field E is measured in newtons per coulomb, and F is the force acting on the charge q, which is feeling the force in the electric field. The test charge q would feel a force radially outward anywhere around the source charge Q, so we would draw the electric field lines around the positive charge Q like this:

> Electric field lines are always drawn in the direction in which a *positive* charge will feel a force.

Remember, electric field lines in a region are always drawn in the direction in which a positive charge would feel a force in that region. They can also represent the path a positive charge would follow in that region. The diagrams below show how we would draw the electric field lines around a negative charge, two positives, two negatives, and a positive and a negative charge.

> Electrons (*negative* charges) are moved when charge is transferred, but electric field lines are drawn in the direction a *positive* charge would move.

PE

V

Example: A charge of $+6 \times 10^{-6}$ C is brought near a negative charge in a region where the electric field strength due to the negative charge is 20 N/C. What are the magnitude and direction of the force acting on the positive charge?

$$(-Q) \quad \bullet{+q}$$

Solution: Electric field, force, and charge are related by the following equation, which can be solved for force:

$$F = qE = (6 \times 10^{-6} \text{ C})(20 \text{ N/C}) = 1.2 \times 10^{-4} \text{ N}$$

The force is directed radially inward toward the negative charge, since the positive charge is attracted to the negative charge.

Electric Potential

The *electric potential V* is defined in terms of the work we would have to do on a charge to move it against an electric field. For example, if we wanted to move a positive charge from point A to point B in the electric field shown below, we would have to do work on the charge, since the electric field would push against us.

> Electric *field* is the force per unit charge, and electric *potential* is the work per unit charge.

$$(+Q) \; \text{---} \bullet \longleftarrow \text{Work} \; \bullet{+q}$$
$$\quad \text{B} \qquad \text{A}$$
$$\Delta V = \frac{W}{q}$$

$$PE = \frac{kq_1 q_2}{r}$$

$$F_q = \frac{k q_1 q_2}{r^2}$$

Electrical Potential
$$\quad \hookrightarrow \quad V = \frac{kq}{r}$$

$$\Delta V = \frac{W}{q_o}$$

$$E = \frac{V}{r}$$
$$\llcorner \text{field}$$
$$\text{and}$$
$$\text{potential}$$

We say that there is a potential difference ΔV between points A and B, and the equation for potential difference between two points is

$$\Delta V = \frac{Work}{q},$$

and it is measured in joules/coulomb, or volts. When we apply potential difference to circuits in the next chapter, we will often call it *voltage*. If we place the charge q at point B and let it go, it would "fall" toward point A. We say that positive charges naturally want to move from a point of high potential (B) to low potential (A), and we refer to the movement of the positive charges as *current*. We will return to voltage and current in chapter 12.

Uniform Electric Field

We can create a uniform electric field in a region of space by taking two metal plates, setting them parallel to each other and separating them by a distance d, and placing a voltage V (as from a battery) across the plates so that one of the plates will be positive and the other negative.

The positive charges on the top plate will line up uniformly with the negative charges on the bottom plate so that each positive charge lines up with a negative charge directly across from it. This arrangement of charges creates electric field lines that run from the positive charges to the negative charges and are uniformly spaced to produce a uniform (constant) electric field everywhere between the plates. Conducting plates that are connected this way are called *capacitors*. Capacitors are used to store charge and electric field in a circuit that can be used at a later time. We will discuss capacitors further in chapter 12.

The electric field, voltage, and distance between the plates are related by the equation

$$E = \frac{V}{d}.$$

It follows from this equation that the unit for electric field is volts/meter, which is equivalent to newtons/coulomb.

Example: Two charged parallel conducting plates are separated by a distance d of 0.005 m and are connected across a battery such that the electric field between the plates is 300 V/m.

(A) What is the potential difference (voltage) of the battery that is connected across the plates?

(B) An electron is placed halfway between the plates. Describe the subsequent motion of the electron.

(C) A neutron is placed between the plates and near the top plate. Describe the force acting on the neutron at this location.

Solution:

(A) We are given the equation $E = \dfrac{V}{d}$, so it follows that

$$V = Ed = (300 \text{ V/m})(0.005 \text{ m}) = 1.5 \text{ volts.}$$

This voltage is typical for most batteries you use each day, such as size AA, C, or D.

(B) A negatively charged electron would experience a force upward toward the positive plate, and therefore would accelerate upward. We could also say that the electron will move in a direction opposite to the direction of the electric field, since electric field lines are always drawn in the direction a positive charge would move.

(C) Since a neutron has no charge, it will not experience a force from either the top or bottom plate, and consequently will not move.

ELECTRIC FIELDS, FORCES, AND POTENTIALS REVIEW QUESTIONS

1. When charge is transferred from one object to another, which of the following are actually transferred?

   (A) electrons
   (B) protons
   (C) neutrons
   (D) quarks
   (E) photons

2. Two conducting spheres of equal size have a charge of –3 C and +1 C, respectively. A conducting wire is connected from the first sphere to the second. What is the new charge on each sphere?

   (A) –4 C
   (B) +4 C
   (C) –1 C
   (D) +1 C
   (E) zero

3. If the electric force between two charges is attractive, which of the following must be true?

   (A) One charge is positive and the other charge is negative.
   (B) Both charges are positive.
   (C) Both charges are negative.
   (D) The two charges must be equal in magnitude.
   (E) The force must be directed toward the larger charge.

4. Two charges q_1 and q_2 are separated by a distance r and apply a force F to each other. If both charges are doubled, and the distance between them is halved, the new force between them is

   (A) $\frac{1}{2}F.$
   (B) $\frac{1}{2}F.$
   (C) $4F.$
   (D) $8F.$
   (E) $16F.$

   $F = \dfrac{\cancel{k}q_1 q_2}{r^2}$

   $= \dfrac{\cancel{k}q_1 q_2}{\frac{1}{4}} =$

5. Two uncharged spheres A and B are near each other. A negatively charged rod is brought near one of the spheres.

   The far right side of sphere B is

   (A) uncharged.
   (B) neutral.
   (C) positive.
   (D) negative.
   (E) equally positive and negative.

6. Two charges A and B are near each other, producing the electric field lines shown.

   What are the two charges A and B, respectively?

   (A) positive, positive
   (B) negative, negative
   (C) positive, negative
   (D) negative, positive
   (E) neutral, neutral

7. A force of 40 N acts on a charge of 0.25 C in a region of space. The electric field at the point of the charge is

   (A) 10 N/C.
   (B) 100 N/C.
   (C) 160 N/C.
   (D) 40 N/C.
   (E) 0.00625 N/C.

   $[F = Eq$

   $40 = E \cdot 0.25$

   $40 \circ 4 = E$

8. Electric potential

   (A) is a vector quantity.
   (B) is proportional to the work done in an electric field.
   (C) is always equal to the electric field.
   (D) is zero when a charge is in an electric field.
   (E) is measured in N/C.

9. Two conducting plates are separated by a distance of 0.001 m. A 9 V battery is connected across the plates. The electric field between the plates is

   (A) 9,000 V/m.
   (B) 900 V/m.
   (C) 9 V/m.
   (D) 0.009 V/m.
   (E) 0.00011 V/m.

$r = 0.001$

$V = 9$

$E = \dfrac{V}{r}$

$E = \dfrac{9}{0.001} = \dfrac{9}{\frac{1}{1000}} = 9 \cdot 1000$

Questions 10–11 refer to the following.

Two charged parallel plates are oriented as shown.

The following particles are placed between the plates, one at a time:

   I. electron
   II. proton
   III. neutron

10. Which of the particles would move to the right between the plates?

   (A) I and II only
   (B) I and III only
   (C) II and III only
   (D) II only
   (E) I only

11. Which of the particles would not experience a force while between the plates?

   (A) I and II only
   (B) II and III only
   (C) I only
   (D) III only
   (E) I, II, and III

SOLUTIONS TO ELECTRIC FIELDS, FORCES, AND POTENTIAL REVIEW QUESTIONS

1. A

Electrons are often free to move from one atom to another.

2. C

The total charge is –2 C, so when a wire connects the spheres, each sphere gets half of the –2 C, or –1 C each.

3. A

According to the law of charges, like charges repel each other and unlike charges attract each other.

4. E

$$F = \frac{Kq_1q_2}{r^2}$$

$$F_{new} = \frac{K(2q_1)(2q_2)}{\left(\frac{1}{2}r\right)^2} = \frac{4Kq_1q_2}{\frac{1}{4}r^2} = 16\,F$$

5. D

The far right side of sphere B is negative, since the negative charges in the sphere are pushed as far away as possible by the negative charges on the rod.

6. D

Electric field lines begin on positive charges and end on negative charges; thus A is negative and B is positive.

7. C

$$E = \frac{F}{q} = \frac{40\text{ N}}{0.25\text{ C}} = 160\,\frac{\text{N}}{\text{C}}$$

8. B

Electric potential is defined as the work per unit charge in moving the charge to a particular place in an electric field.

9. A

$$E = \frac{V}{d}. = \frac{9\text{ V}}{0.001\text{ m}} = 9{,}000\,\frac{\text{V}}{\text{m}}$$

10. D

Only the positively charged proton would move to the right, toward the negatively charged plate.

11. D

Since the neutron has no charge, it would not experience a force in an electric field.

THINGS TO REMEMBER

- Charge
  - The law of charges
- Coulomb's law
- Separation and transfer of charge in an electroscope
- Electric field
  - Electric potential
  - Uniform electric field

Chapter 12: **Circuits**

- Current, Voltage, and Resistance
- Power and Joule's Law of Heating
- Circuits with More Than One Resistor
- Capacitance and Resistance-Capacitance Circuits

CURRENT, VOLTAGE, AND RESISTANCE

When we connect a battery, wires, and a light bulb in the circuit shown below, the bulb lights up. But what is actually happening in the circuit?

Recall from the previous chapter that the battery has a potential difference, or voltage, across its ends. One end of the battery is positive, and the other end is negative. When we connect the wires and light bulb to the battery in a complete circuit, charge begins to flow from one end of the battery, through the wires and the bulb, to the other end of the battery, causing the bulb to light. We say that the movement of positive charge from the positive end of the battery through the circuit to the negative end of the battery is called *conventional current*, or simply *current*. Current is the amount of charge moving through a conductor per second, and the unit for current is the coulomb/second, or *ampere*. We use the symbol *I* for current.

> Current (*I*) is defined as the flow of positive charge through a conductor, and is measured in *amperes*, or *amps*.

Technically speaking, it is (generally) negative charges and not positive charges that move through a circuit (although it is conventional to speak of positive charge flowing rather than negative charge flowing). When the battery is connected to the circuit, an electric field is set up such that the negative charges experience a force that push them in one direction through the wire. At the same time, positive charges experience a force in the opposite direction, but since the electrons that comprise the negative charge in matter are much more mobile than those particles (protons) that comprise the positive charge, it is actually the electrons (and not the positive charge) that are moving through the circuit. As the electrons move through the light bulb filament, they generate heat and light that causes the light bulb filament to glow. The SAT Subject Test: Physics generally uses the conventional current model of positive charge current flow in the direction of the motion of positive charges.

As charge moves through the circuit, it encounters *resistance*, or opposition to the flow of current. Resistance is the electrical equivalent of friction. In our previous circuit diagram, the wires and the light bulb would be considered resistances, although usually the resistance of the wires is neglected. When a larger voltage is used, more charge moves through the wire, and thus more current flows through the circuit. In other words, the current is directly proportional to the voltage. This implies that the ratio of voltage to current is a constant. This constant is defined as the *resistance*, and is measured in *ohms* (Ω). An ohm is a volt/amp. The relationship between voltage, current, and resistance is called *Ohm's law*:

$$V = IR$$

$$R = \frac{V}{I}$$

This relationship typically holds true for the purposes of the SAT Subject Test: Physics.

> *Resistance* is the opposition to the flow of current, and is measured in *ohms* (Ω).

> *Ohm's law* relates voltage, current, and resistance in the equation $R = \frac{V}{I}$.

Schematic Diagram Symbols for Circuits

Table 12.1 below summarizes the quantities discussed so far.

Table 12.1: Circuit Components

Quantity	Symbol	Unit	Schematic Symbol
Battery voltage	V	Volts (V)	
Current	I	Amps (A)	
Resistance	R	Ohms (Ω)	

Usually, when we draw circuit diagrams, we use the symbols in the table above. For example, the simple light bulb circuit would look like the following diagram.

If we wanted to actually measure the current through the resistor and the voltage across the resistor, we would connect an *ammeter* (to measure current) in series with the resistor, and a *voltmeter* (to measure voltage) in parallel with the resistor, as shown below.

We place the ammeter in *series* with the resistor so that the same current will pass through the ammeter and the resistor, and we place the voltmeter in *parallel* with the resistor so that the voltage will be the same across the voltmeter and the resistor. Ammeters have a low resistance so as not to add to the total resistance of the circuit (and thus decrease the current in the circuit), and voltmeters have a high resistance so that current will not want to flow through them and bypass the resistor.

POWER AND JOULE'S LAW OF HEATING

In chapter 7 we defined *power* as the rate at which work is done, or the rate at which energy is transferred. When current flows through a resistor, heat is produced, and the amount of heat produced in joules per second is equal to the power in the resistor. The heating in the resistor is called *joule heating*, and the power dissipated in the resistor follows *Joule's law of heating*. The equation that relates power to the current, voltage, and resistance in a circuit is

Power in a circuit is the energy used per unit time, measured in *watts*.

$$P = IV = I^2R = \frac{V^2}{R}.$$

The unit for power is the joule/second, or *watt*.

Example: A simple circuit consists of a 12 volt battery and a 6 Ω resistor.

(A) Draw a schematic diagram of the circuit, and include an ammeter, which measures the current through the resistor, and a voltmeter, which measures the voltage across the resistor.

(B) What will the ammeter and voltmeter read?

(C) What is the power dissipated in the resistor?

Solution:

(A) The schematic diagram would look like this:

Note that the ammeter is placed in series with the resistor, and the voltmeter is placed in parallel with the resistor.

(B) The ammeter reads the current, which we can calculate using Ohm's law:

$$I = \frac{V}{R} = \frac{12 \text{ V}}{6 \text{ Ω}} = 2 \text{ A}$$

The voltmeter will read 12 V, since the potential difference across the resistor must be equal to the potential difference across the battery. As we will see later, if there were more than one resistor in the circuit, they would not necessarily get 12 volts each.

(C) The power can be found by the following equation:

$$P = IV = (2 \text{ A})(12 \text{ V}) = 24 \text{ watts}$$

CIRCUITS WITH MORE THAN ONE RESISTOR

When two or more resistors are placed in a circuit, there are basically three ways to connect them: in series, in parallel, or a combination of series and parallel.

Series Circuits

Two or more resistors of any value placed in a circuit in such a way that the same current passes through each of them is called a *series circuit*. Consider the following series circuit, which includes a voltage source ε (which stands for *emf*, an older term for voltage) and three resistors R_1, R_2, and R_3.

The rules for dealing with series circuits are as follows:

1. The total resistance in a series circuit is the sum of the individual resistances:

$$R_{total} = R_1 + R_2 + R_3$$

2. The total current in the circuit is

$$I_{total} = \frac{V_{total}}{R_{total}}.$$

This current must pass through each of the resistors, so each resistor also gets I_{total} that is, $I_{total} = I_1 = I_2 = I_3$.

3. The voltage divides proportionally among the resistances according to Ohm's law:

$$V_1 = I_1R_1;\ V_2 = I_2R_2;\ V_3 = I_3R_3$$

Example: Three resistors of 2 Ω, 6 Ω, and 10 Ω are connected in series with a 9 volt battery.

(A) Draw a schematic diagram of the circuit that includes an ammeter to measure the current through the 2 Ω resistor, and a voltmeter to measure the voltage across the 10 Ω resistor.

(B) What will the ammeter read?

(C) What will the voltmeter read?

Solution:

(A) The schematic diagram for the circuit looks like this:

(B) The current through each resistor is equal to the total current in the circuit, so the ammeter will read the total current regardless of where it is placed, as long as it is placed in series with the resistances:

$$I_{total} = \frac{V_{total}}{R_{total}} = \frac{9\ V}{2\ \Omega + 6\ \Omega + 10\ \Omega} = 0.5\ A$$

(C) The voltmeter will read the voltage across the 10 Ω resistor, which is NOT 9 volts. The 9 volts provided by the battery is divided proportionally among the resistances. The voltage across the 10 Ω resistor is

$$V_{10} = I_{10}R_{10} = (0.5\ A)(10\ \Omega) = 5\ V.$$

Parallel Circuits

> In a *series* circuit, the resistors get the same current. In a *parallel* circuit, the resistors get the same voltage.

Two or more resistors of any value placed in a circuit in such a way that each resistor has the same potential difference across it is called a *parallel circuit*. Consider the parallel circuit below, which includes a voltage source ε and three resistors R_1, R_2, and R_3.

The rules for dealing with parallel circuits are as follows:

1. The total resistance in a parallel circuit is given by the following equation:
$$\frac{1}{R_{total}} = \frac{1}{R_1} + \frac{1}{R_2} + \frac{1}{R_3}$$

2. The voltage across each resistance is the same: $V_{total} = V_1 = V_2 = V_3$

3. The current divides in an inverse proportion to the resistance:
$$I_1 = \frac{V_1}{R_1};\ I_2 = \frac{V_2}{R_2};\ I_3 = \frac{V_3}{R_3},$$

where R_1, R_2, and R_3 are equal to each other.

Example: The resistors of resistance 2 Ω, 3 Ω, and 12 Ω are connected in parallel to a battery of voltage 24 V.

(A) Draw a schematic diagram of the circuit that includes an ammeter to measure only the current through the 2 Ω resistor, and a voltmeter to measure the voltage across the 12 Ω resistor.

(B) What is the total resistance in the circuit?

(C) What will the ammeter read?

(D) What will the voltmeter read?

Solution:

(A) The schematic diagram for the circuit looks like this:

(B) The total resistance in the circuit is found by the following:

$$\frac{1}{R_{total}} = \frac{1}{R_1} + \frac{1}{R_2} + \frac{1}{R_3} = \frac{1}{2\,\Omega} + \frac{1}{3\,\Omega} + \frac{1}{12\,\Omega} = \frac{6}{12\,\Omega} + \frac{4}{12\,\Omega} + \frac{1}{12\,\Omega} = \frac{11}{12\,\Omega}$$

Notice that this fraction is not the total resistance, but $\frac{1}{R_{total}}$. Thus, the total resistance in this circuit must be

$$\frac{12}{11}\,\Omega.$$

> The equation for the total resistance in parallel comes from the fact that the total current is the sum of the individual currents in the circuit, and each resistor gets the same voltage:
> $$\frac{V_{total}}{R_{total}} = \frac{V_1}{R_1} + \frac{V_2}{R_2} + \cdots,$$
> where all the V's are equal.

(C) Since the ammeter is placed in series only with the 2 Ω resistance, it will measure the current passing only through the 2 Ω resistance. Recognizing that the voltage is the same (24 V) across each resistance, we calculate that

$$I_2 = \frac{V_2}{R_2} = \frac{24\ V}{2\ \Omega} = 12\ A.$$

(D) Each resistance is connected across the 24 V battery, so the voltage across the 12 Ω resistance is 24 V.

Combination Series and Parallel Circuits

Consider the combination circuit below.

We see that R_1 is in parallel with R_2, and R_3 is in series with the parallel combination of R_1 and R_2. Let's find (A) the total resistance, (B) the total current in the circuit, (C) the voltage across each resistor, and (D) the current through each resistor.

(A)   Before we can find the total resistance of the circuit, we need to find the equivalent resistance of the parallel combination of R_1 and R_2:

$$\frac{1}{R_{12}} = \frac{1}{R_1} + \frac{1}{R_2} = \frac{1}{20\ \Omega} + \frac{1}{30\ \Omega} = \frac{3}{60\ \Omega} + \frac{2}{60\ \Omega} = \frac{5}{60\ \Omega},$$

which implies that the combination of R_1 and R_2 has an equivalent resistance of $60/5\ \Omega = 12\ \Omega$. Then the total resistance of the circuit is $R_{total} = R_{12} + R_3 = 12\ \Omega + 40\ \Omega = 52\ \Omega$.

(B)   The total current in the circuit is

$$I_{total} = \frac{V_{total}}{R_{total}} = \frac{13\text{ V}}{52\ \Omega} = 0.25\text{ A}.$$

(C)   The voltage provided by the battery is divided proportionally among the parallel combination of R_1 and R_2 (with R_1 and R_2 having the same voltage across them), and R_3. Since R_3 has the total current passing through it, we can calculate the voltage across R_3 as

$$V_3 = I_3 R_3 = (0.25\text{ A})(40\ \Omega) = 10\text{ V}.$$

This implies that the voltage across R_1 and R_2 is the remainder of the 13 V provided by the battery. Thus, the voltage across R_1 and R_2 is

$$13\text{ V} - 10\text{ V} = 3\text{ V}.$$

(D)   The current through R_3 is the total current in the circuit, 0.25 A. Since we know the voltage and resistance of the other resistors, we can use Ohm's law to find the current through each:

$$I_1 = \frac{V_1}{R_1} = \frac{3\text{ V}}{20\ \Omega} = 0.15\text{ A} \quad \text{and} \quad I_2 = \frac{V_2}{R_2} = \frac{3\text{ V}}{30\ \Omega} = 0.10\text{ A}$$

Notice that I_1 and I_2 add up to the total current in the circuit, 0.25 A.

CAPACITANCE AND RESISTANCE-CAPACITANCE CIRCUITS

Capacitance

Let's revisit the conducting parallel plates we discussed in chapter 11. Recall that if we connect a battery to the plates, charge flows from the battery onto the plates, with one plate becoming positively charged with a charge +q, and the other plate negatively charged with a charge −q.

The capacitance of the plates is defined as

$$C = \frac{q}{V},$$

where q is the charge on one of the plates, and V is the voltage across the plates. The unit for capacitance is the coulomb/volt, or *farad*. The capacitance of a capacitor is proportional to the area of each plate and inversely proportional to the distance between the plates. In symbols, it is

$$C \propto \frac{A}{d}.$$

The purpose of a *capacitor* is to store charge and electric field in a circuit that can be used at a later time.

> *Capacitance* is charge per unit voltage, and depends only on the geometry of the plates.

Example: A capacitor has a capacitance C_0. What is the effect on the capacitance if (A) the area of each plate is doubled? and (B) the distance between the plates is halved?

Solution:

(A) If the area of each plate is doubled (assuming the plates have equal area), we can find the new capacitance by the following equation:

$$C \propto \frac{(2)A}{d} = 2C_0$$

Twice the area gives twice the capacitance.

(B) If the distance between the plates is halved (i.e., the plates are brought closer together), the new capacitance is

$$C \propto \frac{A}{\frac{1}{2}d} = 2C_0.$$

Bringing the plates closer together increases the capacitance, in this case by a factor of two.

Resistance-Capacitance Circuits

A resistance-capacitance (RC) circuit is simply a circuit containing a battery, a resistor, and a capacitor in series with one another.

When the switch is moved to position *a*, current begins to flow, and the capacitor begins to fill up with charge. Initially, the current is ε/R by Ohm's law, but then it decreases as time goes on until the capacitor is full of charge and will not allow any more charge to flow out of the battery.

> An RC circuit can store charge and release it later.

This leads us to two rules we can follow when dealing with capacitors in an RC circuit:

1. An empty capacitor does not resist the flow of current, and thus acts like a wire.

2. A capacitor that is full of charge will not allow current to flow, and thus acts like a broken wire.

If we move the switch to position *b*, the battery is taken out of the circuit, and the capacitor begins to drain its charge through the resistor, creating a current in the opposite direction to the current flowing when the battery was connected.

Eventually, the current will die out because of the heat energy lost through the resistor.

Example: A 12 V battery is connected in series to a 3 Ω resistor and an initially uncharged capacitor. Determine the current in the circuit (A) immediately after the battery is connected to the resistor and capacitor, and (B) a long time later.

Solution:

(A) Immediately after the circuit is connected, the capacitor is still empty and thus acts like a wire. We can redraw the circuit like this:

The current, then, is $I = \dfrac{V}{R} = \dfrac{12\text{ V}}{3\text{ }\Omega} = 4$ A.

(B) The current begins to decrease as the capacitor fills up with charge, and after a long time, the capacitor is full of charge, and the current stops flowing completely. Thus, $I = 0$ a long time later.

CIRCUITS REVIEW QUESTIONS

Questions 1–3 refer to the following.

Two resistors of 2 Ω and 4 Ω are placed in series with a 12 V battery.

(handwritten) V = IR

12 = (1)(0)

↳ I = 2

1. Which of the following statements is true?

   (A) The 2 Ω will get more current than the 4 Ω resistor since it has less resistance.

   (B) The 4 Ω will get more current than the 2 Ω resistor since it has more resistance.

   (C) The voltage drop across the 2 Ω and 4 Ω resistors will be the same.

   (D) The voltage drop across the 2 Ω resistor will be more than that across the 4 Ω resistor.

   (E) The voltage drop across the 4 Ω resistor will be more than that across the 2 Ω resistor.

2. The current in the 2 Ω resistor is

   (A) 6 A.
   (B) 4 A.
   (C) 3 A.
   (D) 2 A.
   (E) 1 A.

   (handwritten) V = IR
   V = (2)(2) = 4

   V = IR
   V = (1)(B)

3. The voltage across the 4 Ω resistor is

   (A) 3 V.
   (B) 4 V.
   (C) 6 V.
   (D) 8 V.
   (E) 12 V.

   (handwritten) V = 6

   V = IR

Questions 4–6 refer to the following.

Two resistors of 3 Ω and 6 Ω are placed in parallel with a 6 V battery. Three ammeters and two voltmeters are placed in the circuit as shown.

(handwritten) I = 3

no voltage

4. Which of the following statements is true of the voltmeters?

   (A) Voltmeter 1 and voltmeter 2 will read the same voltage.

   (B) Voltmeter 1 will read 6 V.

   (C) Voltmeter 2 will read 6 V.

   (D) Voltmeter 2 will read the correct voltage across the 3 Ω resistor.

   (E) Both voltmeters will read the correct voltage across the 6 Ω resistor.

5. Which ammeter will read the highest amount of current?

   (A) Ammeter 1
   (B) Ammeter 2
   (C) Ammeter 3
   (D) All three will read the same current.
   (E) All three will read zero current.

6. What is the correct reading on ammeter 2?

   (A) 0
   (B) 1 A
   (C) 2 A
   (D) 3 A
   (E) 6 A

   (handwritten) V = IR
   6 = I(2)
   I = 3

(handwritten bottom left)
$\dfrac{1}{R_{total}} = \dfrac{1}{8} + \dfrac{1}{6}$

2 = R_{total}

7. What is the total current flowing in the circuit
    shown?

(A) 4 A

(B) 3 A

(C) 2 A

(D) $\dfrac{4}{3}$ A

(E) $\dfrac{3}{4}$ A

$v = IR \quad IR$

$4 = (1)\left(\dfrac{1}{2} + \dfrac{1}{4}\right)$

4

$4 = I\left(\dfrac{4}{3}\right)$

$4 \cdot \dfrac{3}{4} = I$

8. A resistance-capacitance circuit is connected as
    shown.

After a long time, the current in the
2 Ω resistor is

(A) 0

(B) 10 A

(C) 8 A

(D) 2 A

(E) 1 A

$V = IR$

$2V = (1)(2)$

$V = IR$

$V = I(10)$

$10 = I(10)$

$I = 1$

SOLUTIONS TO CIRCUITS REVIEW QUESTIONS

1. E

Since both resistors get the same current, the 4 Ω resistor experiences a greater voltage drop than the 2 Ω resistor, since the 4 Ω has more resistance.

2. D

The total resistance in the series circuit is the sum of the resistors, or 6 Ω. The current in the 2 Ω resistor is the same as the total current in the circuit, which is

$$I = \frac{V}{R} = \frac{12\text{ V}}{6\text{ Ω}} = 2\text{ A}.$$

3. D

Since the 4 Ω resistor represents $\frac{2}{3}$ of the total resistance, it will get $\frac{2}{3}$ of the total voltage, or 8 V.

4. B

The voltage across the 6 Ω resistor is 6 V since it is in parallel with the battery. Voltmeter 2 is incorrectly placed in the circuit and will read zero volts.

5. A

Ammeter 1 is in a position to measure the total current in the circuit before it splits up to go through the 3 Ω and 6 Ω resistors.

6. B

Ammeter 2 measures only the current through the 6 Ω resistor: $I = \dfrac{6\text{ V}}{6\text{ Ω}} = 1\text{ A}$.

7. B

The total resistance can be found by

$$\frac{1}{R_t} = \frac{1}{2\text{ Ω}} + \frac{1}{4\text{ Ω}} = \frac{3}{4\text{ Ω}},$$

which means that $R_t = {}^4\!/_3$ Ω. So the total current in the circuit is

$$I = \frac{V}{R} = \frac{4\text{ V}}{\frac{4}{3}\text{ Ω}} = 3\text{ A}.$$

8. E

After a long time, the capacitor is full of charge and does not allow any more current to flow through it. Thus, the current from the battery will only flow through the resistors and the current will be

$$I = \frac{10\text{ V}}{10\text{ Ω}} = 1\text{ A}.$$

THINGS TO REMEMBER

- Current, voltage, and resistance
  - Schematic diagram symbols for circuits
- Power and Joule's law of heating
- Circuits with more than one resistor
  - Series circuits
  - Parallel circuits
  - Combination series and parallel circuits
- Capacitance and resistance-capacitance circuits

Chapter 13: **Magnetic Fields and Forces**

- Magnetism
- Electromagnetic Induction

MAGNETISM

More than 2,000 years ago in the Greek province of Magnesia were found pieces of iron ore called *lodestones* that would attract or repel each other. When one of these magnetic stones was suspended from a string, one side of the stone would align itself to point in a northerly direction. Eventually, this end of the magnet was labeled *north* and the other end *south*. Later, it was suggested that the Earth itself is a magnet, and the stones were simply aligning themselves with the Earth's magnetic field. A *magnetic field B* is defined as the space around a magnet in which another magnet will feel a force; the magnetic field is measured in *teslas* (T). Magnetic field lines have no beginning and no end, but generally are drawn from the north pole of a magnet to its south pole. The magnetic fields most often appearing on the SAT Subject Test: Physics are those of a bar magnet, the Earth, and a horseshoe magnet, each shown below.

> Magnetic field lines generally point from north to south.

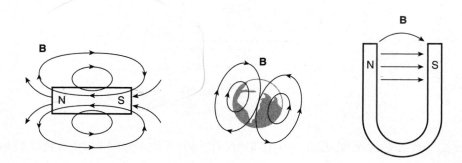

A material becomes magnetic when it is placed in a strong external magnetic field, and the clusters of atoms with similar magnetic orientations, called *domains*, become aligned

> A *domain* is a cluster of magnetically aligned atoms.

with the external magnetic field. Obviously, some materials are more easily magnetized than others, but the reasons for this are typically not covered on the SAT Subject Test: Physics.

Magnetic Field Produced by a Current-Carrying Wire

Fundamentally, magnetic fields are produced by moving charges. This is why all atoms are tiny magnets, since the electrons around the nucleus of the atom are moving charges and are therefore magnetic. Prior to 1820, it was generally believed that there was no physical connection between electricity and magnetism. But in that year, Oersted discovered that a current-carrying wire is magnetic, or as we would say in today's language, creates a magnetic field around itself. The magnetic field produced by a current-carrying wire circulates around the wire in a direction given by what we will refer to as the *first right-hand rule*.

First Right-Hand Rule: Place your right thumb in the direction of the current *I*, and your fingers will curl around in the direction of the magnetic field produced by that current.

In determining the direction of a magnetic field due to the flow of *electrons* in a wire, we would use the left hand instead of the right hand. (Remember: Current is positive, but electrons are negative.)

Another way of denoting any vector that points into the page or out of the page (in this case, the magnetic field vector) is to use an X to represent a vector pointing into the page, and a dot (●) to represent a vector pointing out of the page. Thus, the magnetic field around the current-carrying wire above can be drawn as:

Force on a Current-Carrying Wire in an External Magnetic Field

Since a current-carrying wire creates a magnetic field around itself according to the first right-hand rule, every current-carrying wire is a magnet. Thus, if we place a current-carrying wire in an external magnetic field, it will experience a force. The

out of
north
into the south

magnetism 2 Tesla
└ denoted
by B

direction of the force acting on the wire is given by what we will call the *second right-hand rule*.

Second Right-Hand Rule: Place your fingers in the direction of the magnetic field (north to south) with your thumb in the direction of the current in the wire, and the magnetic force on the wire will come out of your palm.

(1) I

(2) B

(3) F

> Use your right hand for conventional current flow or moving positive charges, and your left hand for electron flow or moving negative charges.

Again, you would use your left hand to find the direction of the magnetic force if you were given electron flow instead of conventional current.

The equation for finding the force on a current-carrying wire in a magnetic field is

$$F = ILB \sin \theta,$$

where *I* is the current in the wire, *L* is the length of wire in the magnetic field, *B* is the magnetic field, and θ is the angle between the length of wire and the magnetic field. If the angle is 90°, the equation becomes simply *F = ILB*.

Example: A wire carrying a 20 A current has a length L = 0.10 m between the poles of a magnet at an angle of 45°, as shown. The magnetic field is uniform and has a value of 0.5 T. What is the magnitude and direction of the magnetic force acting on the wire? (sin 45° = cos 45° = 0.7)

Top View

Solution: The magnitude of the force on the wire is found by the following:

$$F = ILB \sin \theta = (20 \text{ A})(0.10 \text{ m})(0.5 \text{ T}) \sin 45°$$

$$F = 0.7 \text{ N}$$

The direction of the force can be found by the second right-hand rule. Place your fingers in the direction of the magnetic field, and your thumb in the direction of the length (and current), which is perpendicular to the magnetic field, and we see that the force is out of the page.

Note that the length must have a component that is perpendicular to the magnetic field, or there will be no magnetic force on the wire. In other words, if the wire is placed parallel to the magnetic field, sin 0° = 0, and the force will also be zero.

Force on a Charged Particle in a Magnetic Field

Since a moving charge creates a magnetic field around itself, it will also feel a force when it moves through a magnetic field. The direction of the force acting on such a charge is given by the second right-hand rule, with the thumb pointing in the direction of the velocity of the charge. We use our right hand for moving positive charges, and our left hand for moving negative charges. The equation for finding the force on a charge moving through a magnetic field is

$$F = qvB \sin \theta,$$

where q is the charge in Coulombs, v is the velocity in m/s, B is the magnetic field in teslas, and θ is the angle between the velocity and the magnetic field. If the angle is 90°, then the equation becomes $F = qvB$.

Example: A proton enters a magnetic field **B** that is directed into the page. The proton has a charge $+q$ and a velocity v, which is directed to the right, and enters the magnetic field perpendicularly. Describe the resulting path of the proton.

```
  X        X        X   B into page

  X        X        X

q+ ●────→ v

  X        X        X
```

Solution: As the proton enters the magnetic field, it will initially feel a force that is directed upward, as we see from using the second right-hand rule. The path of the proton will curve upward in a circular path, with the magnetic force becoming a centripetal force, changing the direction of the velocity to form the circular path. The radius of this circle can be found by setting the magnetic force equal to the centripetal force as shown in the following diagram.

> A charge must be moving across magnetic field lines to feel a force.

> Use the second right-hand rule to find the direction of the force on a charge in a magnetic field.

$$\text{magnetic force} = \text{centripetal force}$$

$$qvB = \frac{mv^2}{r}$$

$$r = \frac{mv}{qB}$$

ELECTROMAGNETIC INDUCTION

For several years after Oersted discovered that a current flowing through a wire produced a magnetic field, several scientists, including Faraday in England and Henry in New York, tried to verify whether or not the opposite were true: Can a magnetic field produce a current? Faraday and Henry independently discovered that an electric current could be produced by moving a magnet through a coil of wire, or, equivalently, by moving a wire through a magnetic field. Generating a current this way is called *electromagnetic induction*.

> Moving a magnet through a coil of wire and generating a current is called *electromagnetic induction*.

Moving a wire into a magnetic field

The amount of voltage and current produced in a coil of wire depends on how quickly the magnetic field lines are crossed by the wire. For example, if the magnet is moved through the coil slowly, hardly any current is produced in the coil. If the magnet is moved through the coil quickly, a larger amount of current is produced in the coil. Also, a greater number of coils will produce a greater induced voltage and current. The direction of the current induced is dependent on the direction in which the magnet or wire is moving.

The principle of electromagnetic induction is the basis for a *generator*. A generator converts mechanical energy into electrical energy. To create your own generator, place a loop of wire on an axle in a magnetic field, as shown below. As the loop is rotated, the wire crosses magnetic field lines and generates a current in the loop. That current can be used to light a light bulb or power a city. All of our electrical power is generated in a similar way.

> A *generator* converts mechanical energy into electrical energy.

QUICK QUIZ

Which of the following can increase the amount of voltage induced in a coil of wire (there may be more than one correct answer)?

(A) move the magnet faster through the coil

(B) move a stronger magnet through the coils of wire

(C) move the magnet through more coils of wire

(D) move more coils of wire around a magnet

(E) move more magnets simultaneously through a coil of wire

Answer: All of the above can increase the amount of voltage generated in a coil of wire.

more coils = more electricity

anti-parallel cut

MAGNETIC FIELDS AND FORCES REVIEW QUESTIONS

1. A wire carries a current, creating a magnetic field around itself as shown.

    The current in the wire is

    (A) directed to the right.
    (B) directed to the left.
    (C) equal to the magnetic field.
    (D) in the same direction as the magnetic field.
    (E) zero.

    Questions 2–3 refer to the following.

    A wire carrying a current of 2 A is placed in a magnetic field of 0.1 T as shown.

    The length of wire in the magnetic field is 0.3 m.

2. The force on the wire is directed

    (A) into the page.
    (B) out of the page.
    (C) toward the top of the page.
    (D) toward the bottom of the page.
    (E) to the left.

3. The magnitude of the force on the wire is

    (A) 0.06 N.
    (B) 2.0 N.
    (C) 6.7 N.
    (D) 0.15 N.
    (E) 0.015 N.

    Questions 4–5 refer to the following.

    An electron enters a magnetic field as shown.

4. The electron will experience a force that is initially

    (A) into the page.
    (B) out of the page.
    (C) toward the top of the page.
    (D) toward the bottom of the page.
    (E) to the left.

5. The subsequent path of the electron is a

    (A) parabola.
    (B) straight line.
    (C) spiral or helix.
    (D) hyperbola.
    (E) circle.

6. For electromagnetic induction to occur,

    (A) a magnet must be at rest within a coil of wire.
    (B) a coil of wire must be at rest relative to the magnet.
    (C) a magnet must move through a coil of wire.
    (D) a magnet and a coil must have the same velocity.
    (E) a magnet must be pointing north.

7. A magnet moves into a coil of wire, inducing a current in the wire. If the magnet is pulled back out of the coil in the opposite direction as it went into the coil, which of the following will occur?

    (A) There will be a current produced in the coil in the same direction as before.

    (B) There will be a current produced in the coil in the opposite direction as before.

    (C) There will be no current produced in the coil.

    (D) The current produced must be stronger than before.

    (E) The current produced must be weaker than before.

8. A generator   *induction*

    (A) converts mechanical energy into electrical energy.

    (B) converts electrical energy into mechanical energy.

    (C) converts heat energy into mechanical energy.

    (D) converts electrical energy into heat energy.

    (E) converts nuclear energy into heat energy.

SOLUTIONS TO MAGNETIC FIELDS AND FORCES REVIEW QUESTIONS

1. A

By the first right-hand rule, if the fingers curl up and over the wire toward you, the current must be to the right.

2. B

According to the second right-hand rule, the fingers point to the right in the direction of the magnetic field, the thumb points toward the bottom of the page in the direction of the current, and the force comes out of the palm and out of the page.

3. A

$$F = ILB = (2 \text{ A})(0.1 \text{ T})(0.3 \text{ m}) = 0.06 \text{ N}$$

4. B

We use the second left-hand rule, since the electron is a negative charge, placing our fingers toward the bottom of the page, and the thumb to the right, in the direction of the component of the velocity that crosses the magnetic field lines. The force, then, comes out of the palm and out of the page.

5. C

The electron will orbit a magnetic field line but will also continue to move toward the bottom of the page, spiraling downward.

6. C

The magnet and coil must be moving relative to each other.

7. B

Pushing the north end of a magnet into a coil will produce a current in the opposite direction than if the north end were pulled out of the coil. Opposite magnet velocities will create opposite currents.

8. A

In a generator, mechanical energy is used to move magnets and wires in such a way that they produce electrical energy in the form of a current.

THINGS TO REMEMBER

- Magnetism
  - Magnetic field produced by a current-carrying wire
  - Force on a current-carrying wire in an external magnetic field
  - Force on a charged particle in a magnetic field
- Electromagnetic induction

Chapter 14: **General Wave Properties**

- Basic Properties of Mechanical Waves
- Sound Waves and the Doppler Effect
- Reflection, Refraction, Diffraction, and Interference of Mechanical Waves
- Standing Waves

A *mechanical wave* is a traveling disturbance in a medium that transfers energy from one place to another. A *medium* is the substance through which a wave moves, such as water for a water wave, or air for a sound wave. An *electromagnetic wave* is a vibration of an electric and magnetic field that travels through space at an extremely high speed and does not need a medium through which to travel. Visible light, radio waves, and microwaves are all examples of electromagnetic waves. We will return to electromagnetic waves later.

> Waves transfer energy from one place to another.

BASIC PROPERTIES OF MECHANICAL WAVES

There are two types of mechanical waves. *Transverse waves* vibrate in a direction that is perpendicular to the direction of motion of the wave. For example, if you hold the end of a horizontal spring and vibrate your hand up and down, you create a transverse wave in the spring that travels from one end to the other.

> The two types of waves are *transverse* and *longitudinal*.

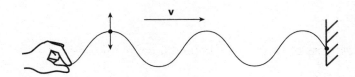

If you gather the spring up into a bunch and let it go, you create a *longitudinal wave*, in which the spring vibrates in a direction that is parallel to the direction of motion of the wave.

sound – ~~from~~ longitd'

light tran

Sound is a common example of a longitudinal wave, since the air through which a sound wave moves is repeatedly compressed and expanded.

> Harmonic motion and wave motion are very closely related.

Since an object vibrating with simple harmonic motion can create a wave in a medium, it is not surprising that many of the terms we discussed in chapter 9 can also be applied to waves. A wave has a *period*, the time it takes for a wave to vibrate once; a *frequency*, the number of waves that pass a given point per second; and an *amplitude*, the maximum displacement of a wave, or its height. But a wave also has length. The length of one complete vibration of a wave is called the *wavelength*, and is denoted by the Greek letter *lambda*, λ. The figure below illustrates these quantities.

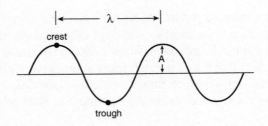

The *crest* is the highest point on the wave and the *trough* is the lowest point on the wave. The wavelength can be measured from one crest to the next crest, or from one trough to the next trough.

The speed of a wave can be found by the equation $v = f\lambda$, where v is the speed, f is the frequency, and λ is the wavelength. Since frequency is the reciprocal of period, we can also write this equation as

$$v = \frac{\lambda}{T}.$$

The speed of all types of waves can be found using this equation.

Example: Consider the following diagram of a wave.

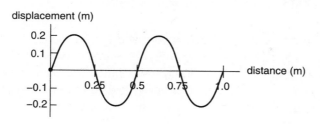

(A)   What is the wavelength of the wave?

(B)   What is the amplitude of the wave?

(C)   If the speed of the wave is 12 m/s, what is the frequency of the wave?

(D)   What is the period of the wave?

> The wave equation is $v = f\lambda$.

Solution:

(A)   The wavelength is the length of one full cycle of the wave, 0.5 m.

(B)   The amplitude of the wave is the vertical height from the zero line, which is 0.2 m.

(C) $f = \dfrac{v}{\lambda} = \dfrac{12 \text{ m/s}}{0.5 \text{ m}} = 24 \dfrac{\text{cycles}}{\text{s}} = 24 \text{ Hertz}$

(D)   Period $T = \dfrac{1}{f} = \dfrac{1}{24 \text{ Hz}} = 0.04 \text{ s}$

> The *period* is the time for one vibration of the wave; the *wavelength* is the length of one wave.

Thus, it takes 0.04 seconds for one full vibration of this wave.

SOUND WAVES AND THE DOPPLER EFFECT

Sound is a mechanical longitudinal wave, and therefore must have a medium to travel through. Sound generally travels at about 340 m/s in air, but travels at considerably higher speeds in more dense media such as water or steel. The characteristics of sound and how we detect and perceive these characteristics are summarized in the table below.

Sound Characteristic	Detected As
Frequency	Pitch
Amplitude	Loudness or volume
Harmonics	Quality or tone

> Sound is a mechanical longitudinal wave.

The third characteristic, *harmonics*, is the combination of several simultaneous frequencies that give a sound its special tone. For example, we can tell the difference between a trumpet and a clarinet because our ear detects each instrument's unique harmonics, even if they are playing the same pitch at the same loudness. For the same reason, we can tell the difference between two voices.

The *Doppler effect* is the apparent change in pitch due to relative motion between a sound source and a listener.

When a sound source is moving toward you, you hear a slightly higher pitch than if the sound source is at rest relative to you. By the same token, when a sound source is moving away from you, you hear a slightly lower pitch. This phenomenon is called the *Doppler effect*. For example, if a train is traveling toward you while blowing its horn at a certain pitch, the waves will appear to be arriving at your ear more frequently, increasing the pitch you perceive.

If the train blows its horn while traveling away from you, the waves will appear to be arriving at your ear less frequently, decreasing the pitch you perceive.

Weather forecasters use radio waves and the Doppler effect to detect the movement of clouds in our atmosphere.

Of course, the frequency of the horn produced by the train is not actually changing, but you perceive a change due to the relative motion between you and the train. The Doppler effect also occurs when a light source is moving toward or away from us. The light spectrum of a star, for example, is shifted toward the red (low frequency) end if the star is moving away from us, and would be shifted toward the blue (high frequency) end of the spectrum if it were to move toward us.

REFLECTION, REFRACTION, DIFFRACTION, AND INTERFERENCE OF MECHANICAL WAVES

Four ways you can affect a wave: reflection, refraction, diffraction, interference.

Let's discuss four ways you can affect a wave. *Reflection* is the bouncing of a wave off of a barrier. The *law of reflection* states that the angle of incidence of a wave is equal to the angle of reflection of the wave as measured from a line normal (perpendicular) to the barrier. This simply means that the wave will bounce off at the same angle at which it came in.

Refraction is the bending of a wave due to a change in medium. A water wave moving from deep water to shallow water will bend its path, slow down, and shorten its wavelength.

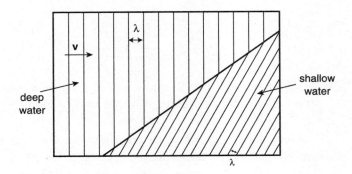

The speed of the wave and its wavelength always change when a wave undergoes refraction, but its frequency does not change. According to the equation $v = f\lambda$, a slower speed means having a shorter wavelength, and a higher speed means having a longer wavelength.

Diffraction is the bending of a wave around a barrier, such as water waves bending around a rock in a stream, or sound waves bending around the corner of a building. When water waves pass through a narrow opening, the sides of the waves drag on the walls of the opening, causing these parts of the wave to lag behind the center of the wave and creating a semicircular wave pattern, as shown in the figure below.

> *Refraction* is the bending of a wave due to a change in medium; *diffraction* is the bending of a wave around a barrier.

When two waves are traveling in the same medium at the same time, they *interfere* with each other. For example, consider two waves moving toward each other in the same rope. If the waves are moving on the same side of the rope, they build on each other and create a larger amplitude wave when they occupy the same space at the same time. This is called *constructive interference,* and the large wave produced at that instant is called an *antinode*.

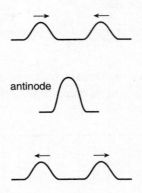

We say that the waves are *in phase* when they interfere constructively. After the waves pass through each other, they continue moving as if they never interfered.

If two waves of equal amplitude approach each other on opposite sides of the rope, they interfere *destructively*: that is, the waves destroy each other for the instant they are occupying the same point on the rope and a *node* is created at that point. A node is a point of no displacement, in this case resulting in a flat rope.

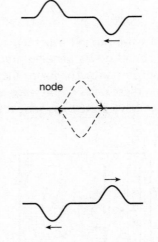

We say that the waves are *out of phase* when they interfere destructively. Once again, after the waves pass through each other, they continue moving as if they never interfered.

STANDING WAVES

The term *standing wave* is an oxymoron, since waves must move and never actually stand still. But waves can appear to stand still when two identical waves traveling in opposite directions in the same medium at the same time create a series of nodes and antinodes. Consider a rope tied to a wall. If we send a wave down the rope toward the wall, the wave reflects off the wall on the opposite side from which it was sent, according to the law of reflection.

> A *standing wave* is a series of nodes and antinodes.

If we continue to send regular waves down the rope and they continue to reflect off the wall, the incident and reflected waves will reinforce each other in some places and cancel each other in other places. The result is a series of antinodes (loops) where constructive interference is occurring, and nodes (points of no displacement between the loops) where destructive interference is occurring. We call this pattern a standing wave.

Another type of standing wave is produced when water waves are passed through two openings, called a double-slit, and an interference pattern results. The semicircular wave patterns that emerge from the slits interfere with each other, creating nodes and antinodes, and we see a pattern like the one in the figure below.

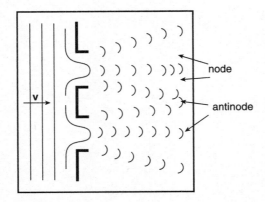

Since light is a wave, we will apply all of the characteristics of waves that we have discussed to the characteristics of light in the next few chapters.

GENERAL WAVE PROPERTIES REVIEW QUESTIONS

Questions 1–3 refer to the following graph.

0.2 s

1. The wavelength of the wave shown above is

    (A) 0.5 m.
    (B) 1.0 m.
    (C) 2.0 m.
    (D) 4.0 m.
    (E) 6.0 m.

2. The amplitude of the wave shown above is

    (A) 0.5 m.
    (B) 1.0 m.
    (C) 2.0 m.
    (D) 4.0 m.
    (E) 6.0 m.

3. The frequency of the wave shown above is

    (A) 2 Hz.
    (B) 4 Hz.
    (C) 5 Hz.
    (D) 0.4 Hz.
    (E) 0.2 Hz.

    $f = \dfrac{1}{P}$

4. A girl on the beach watching water waves sees 4
    waves pass by in 2 seconds, each with a wavelength
    of 0.5 m. The speed of the waves is

    (A) 0.25 m/s.
    (B) 0.5 m/s.
    (C) 1.0 m/s.
    (D) 2.0 m/s.
    (E) 4.0 m/s.

5. The Doppler effect produces apparent changes in

    (A) loudness.
    (B) pitch.
    (C) amplitude.
    (D) velocity.
    (E) acceleration.

6. As a wave passes from a spring to another spring
    with a greater tension,

    (A) the speed of the wave decreases.
    (B) the frequency of the wave increases.
    (C) the frequency of the wave decreases.
    (D) the amplitude of the wave increases.
    (E) the speed of the wave increases.

    longer
    λ

    └ spread
    pattern
    wider

7. The diffraction of a wave through a single opening
    produces

    (A) refraction.
    (B) an angle of incidence.
    (C) a semicircular wave pattern.
    (D) an increase in speed of the wave.
    (E) a decrease in speed of the wave.

$P = \dfrac{0.5}{r}$

$P = 2$

$v = \lambda \cdot f$
$= 2 \cdot 0.5$

8. Two waves approach each other in the same rope at the same time, as shown.

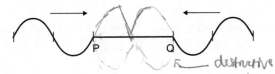

destructive interaction

When the two waves are exactly between points P and Q, the shape of the rope will be

(A) P Q

(B) P Q

(C) P Q

(D) P Q

(E) P Q

9. A standing wave is produced in a vibrating string as shown.

If the length of the string is 1.5 m and the frequency of the vibrating motor is 60 Hz, the speed of the wave is

(A) 15 m/s.
(B) 20 m/s.
(C) 40 m/s.
(D) 60 m/s.
(E) 90 m/s.

$f = 60 \, Hz \longrightarrow$

$c = \lambda \cdot f$

$c =$

SOLUTIONS TO GENERAL WAVE PROPERTIES REVIEW QUESTIONS

1. C

The wavelength is the length of one full cycle.

2. A

The amplitude is half the distance from trough to crest, or $\frac{1}{2}$ (1.0 m) = 0.5 m.

3. C

The wave vibrates two times per 0.4 s, so the frequency is $\frac{2\,\text{cycles}}{0.4\,\text{s}}$ = 5 Hz.

4. C

The frequency is $\frac{4\,\text{waves}}{2\,\text{s}}$ = 2 Hz, and the speed $v = f\lambda$ = (2 Hz)(0.5 m) = 1.0 m/s.

5. B

The pitch of a moving sound source sounds higher if it is moving toward you, and lower if it is moving away from you.

6. E

A wave will travel faster in a tight spring than a loose spring.

7. C

The center of the wave passes through the opening while the edges of the wave drag on the sides of the opening.

8. B

When both waves are exactly between P and Q, one wave's trough is superposed on the other wave's crest, causing the waves to interfere destructively, canceling each other out.

9. D

The wavelength is the length of two loops and is 1 m. The speed of the wave is $v = f\lambda$ = (60 Hz)(1 m) = 60 m/s.

THINGS TO REMEMBER

- Basic properties of mechanical waves
- Sound waves and the Doppler effect
- Reflection, refraction, diffraction, and interference of mechanical waves
- Standing waves

Chapter 15: **Reflection and Refraction of Light**

- Electromagnetic Waves
- Reflection of Light
- Refraction of Light
- Total Internal Reflection

ELECTROMAGNETIC WAVES

As we briefly discussed in the last chapter, an electromagnetic wave is a vibration of an electric and magnetic field that moves through space at an extremely high speed. The electromagnetic wave spectrum, listed from lowest frequency to highest frequency, includes radio waves, microwaves, infrared, visible light, ultraviolet, X-rays, and gamma rays. They are all a result of the same phenomena, and although they have different wavelengths and frequencies, they all travel through a vacuum at exactly the same speed: 3×10^8 m/s, or about 670 million miles per hour. This speed is often referred to as the speed of light, although light is just one example of an electromagnetic wave. More accurately, this speed is the speed of any electromagnetic wave in a vacuum. In any case, the speed of an electromagnetic wave is given the symbol c, from the Latin word *celeritas*, meaning "swift."

> All electromagnetic waves travel at the same speed in a vacuum, 3×10^8 m/s.

Example: Red light has a wavelength of 7×10^{-7} m. What is the frequency of red light?

Solution: We are given the wavelength of the red light, and we know the speed of the light as well, $c = 3 \times 10^8$ m/s. The frequency can be found using the following wave equation:

$$f = \frac{c}{\lambda} = \frac{3 \times 10^8 \text{ m/s}}{7 \times 10^{-7} \text{ m}} = 4.3 \times 10^{14} \text{ Hz}$$

If the visible colors of light are listed from long wavelength (low frequency) to short wavelength (high frequency), they would follow this order: red, orange, yellow, green, blue, and violet (ROYGBV).

REFLECTION OF LIGHT

Any wave that bounces off of a barrier follows the *law of reflection*: The angle of incidence is equal to the angle of reflection as measured from a line normal (perpendicular) to the barrier. In the case of light, the barrier is often a mirror.

> *Law of reflection:* The angle of incidence equals the angle of reflection as measured from the normal line.

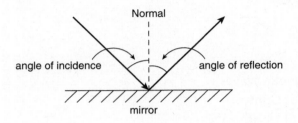

This is why if someone can see you in a mirror, you can see them in the mirror as well.

REFRACTION OF LIGHT

If you put a pencil in a clear glass of water, the image of the pencil in the water appears to be bent and distorted. The light passing from the air into the water is *refracted*, bending due to the fact that it's passing from one medium to another. If we consider a single beam of laser light, we can observe it as it passes from air into a piece of glass.

> *Refraction* is the bending of a light ray due to a change in medium.

The angle θ_i from the normal line at which the beam approaches the glass from the air is called the *angle of incidence*. The angle θ_r from the normal line in the glass is the *angle of refraction*. As the light passes from the air (a less dense medium) into the glass (a more dense medium), the beam bends toward the normal. When the beam of light exits the glass and passes back into the air, it bends away from the normal at the same angle it entered the glass from the air.

> The *angle of reflection* is the angle at which light bounces off a barrier, and the *angle of refraction* is the angle at which light bends through a substance. Both are measured from a line normal to the surface, but they are not equal.

The light bends toward the normal in the glass because the beam slows down as it enters the glass. In most cases, light travels more slowly in a more dense medium. Recall that, in most cases, sound travels faster in a more dense medium; however, sound is a mechanical wave, while light is an electromagnetic wave. The ratio of the speed of light in air (approximately a vacuum) to the speed of light in the glass (or any other medium) is called the *index of refraction n*:

> The *index of refraction* tells us how much light slows down in a more dense medium.

$$n = \frac{c}{v_{glass}}$$

Example: The index of refraction for water is 1.3. What is the speed of light in water?

Solution: Since $n = \dfrac{c}{v_{water}}$, then

$$v_{water} = \frac{c}{n} = \frac{3 \times 10^8 \text{ m/s}}{1.3} = 2.3 \times 10^8 \text{ m/s}.$$

Prism Dispersion

Each color in the spectrum refracts just a little differently from every other color. This is why we can separate white light into its component colors by passing it through a prism. The shorter wavelengths slow down and bend more than the longer wavelengths, so violet bends the most, and red the least:

hi f → more bend

White light
R
O
Y
G
B
V
Prism

Snell's Law of Refraction

We can relate the index of refraction to the angles of incidence and refraction by using *Snell's law of refraction*:

> *Snell's law of refraction* relates the angles of incidence and refraction to the index of refraction.

$$n_1 \sin \theta_1 = n_2 \sin \theta_2,$$

where n_1 and n_2 are the indices of refraction of the first and second media, and θ_1 and θ_2 are the angles of incidence and refraction, respectively.

Example: A beam of light enters the flat surface of a diamond from the air at an angle of 30° from the normal. The angle of refraction in the diamond is measured to be 12° from the normal. What is the index of refraction of this diamond? Interpret your answer physically. (sin 30° = 0.5, sin 12° = 0.2)

Solution: Let medium 1 be air and medium 2 be diamond. Using Snell's law, we can find n_2, the index of refraction of the diamond:

$$n_1 \sin \theta_1 = n_2 \sin \theta_2,$$

where $n_1 = 1$ for air, $\theta_1 = 30°$, and $\theta_2 = 12°$. Then we have

$$n_2 = \frac{n_1 \sin \theta_1}{\sin \theta_2} = \frac{(1) \sin 30°}{\sin 12°} = 2.5.$$

This means that the light travels 2.5 times slower in the diamond than it does in air.

TOTAL INTERNAL REFLECTION

Consider a waterproof laser that you can put under the water to shine a beam of light up out of the water into the air. If you shine the light at a small angle relative to the normal, the light will emerge from the water and bend away from the normal as it enters the air.

As you increase the angle at which the laser is pointed at the surface of the water, the refracted angle also increases, eventually causing the refracted ray to bend parallel to the surface of the water.

The angle of incidence in this case is called the *critical angle*, θ_c. If the laser is pointed at an angle greater than the critical angle, the beam will not emerge from the water, but will reflect back into the water.

This phenomenon is called *total internal reflection*. The inside surfaces of a glass prism in a pair of binoculars can become like mirrors, reflecting light inside the prism if the light is pointed at the surface at an angle greater than the critical angle. Total internal reflection is the also the principle behind the transmitting of light waves through transparent fiber optic cable for communication purposes.

REFLECTION AND REFRACTION OF LIGHT REVIEW QUESTIONS

1. Which of the following lists the electromagnetic waves from longest wavelength to shortest wavelength?

    (A) X-ray, ultraviolet, visible light
    (B) visible light, ultraviolet, X-ray
    (C) ultraviolet, X-ray, visible light
    (D) ultraviolet, visible light, X-ray
    (E) X-ray, visible light, ultraviolet

2. In a vacuum, all electromagnetic waves have the same

    (A) amplitude.
    (B) frequency.
    (C) wavelength.
    (D) intensity.
    (E) speed.

3. Violet light has a frequency of 7.5×10^{14} Hz. The wavelength of violet light is most nearly

    (A) 2.25×10^{23} m.
    (B) 2.5×10^{6} m.
    (C) 4×10^{-7} m.
    (D) 7.5×10^{-7} m.
    (E) 2.25×10^{7} m.

4. In the figure shown, the angle of incidence is θ.

    Which angle is the angle of reflection?

    (A) 1
    (B) 2
    (C) 3
    (D) 4
    (E) 5

5. A beam of light passes from the air through a thick piece of glass as shown.

    Which of the following angles is the angle of refraction?

    (A) 1
    (B) 2
    (C) 3
    (D) 4
    (E) 5

6. The speed of light in a piece of crown glass is 2×10^{8} m/s. What is the index of refraction of crown glass?

    (A) 2
    (B) 1.5
    (C) 0.67
    (D) 0.33
    (E) 0.2

7. A beam of light passes from air into glass. Which of the following statements is true?

   (A) The angle of incidence is greater than the angle of refraction in the glass.

   (B) The angle of incidence is less than the angle of refraction in the glass.

   (C) The angle of incidence is equal to the angle of refraction in the glass.

   (D) The frequency of the light decreases.

   (E) The frequency of the light increases.

8. Total internal reflection occurs when

   (A) light passes from air into water.

   (B) light refracts as it exits glass into air.

   (C) light reflects off of a mirror.

   (D) light passing through glass is reflected inside the glass.

   (E) the angle of incidence is less than the critical angle.

SOLUTIONS TO REFLECTION AND REFRACTION OF LIGHT REVIEW QUESTIONS

1. B

Visible light has the longest wavelength and lowest frequency of the three, and X-rays have the shortest wavelength and the highest frequency of the three.

2. E

All electromagnetic waves travel at 3×10^8 m/s in a vacuum.

3. C

$$\lambda = \frac{c}{f} = \frac{3 \times 10^8 \text{ m/s}}{7.5 \times 10^{14} \text{ Hz}} = 4 \times 10^{-7} \text{ m}$$

4. C

The angles of incidence and reflection are measured from the normal and are equal.

5. D

The angles of incidence and refraction are measured from the normal, and angle 2 is the angle of incidence and angle 4 is the angle of refraction in the glass.

6. B

$$n = \frac{c}{v} = \frac{3 \times 10^8 \text{ m/s}}{2 \times 10^8 \text{ m/s}} = 1.5$$

7. A

When the light enters the glass, the beam bends toward the normal line, causing the angle of refraction to be less than the angle of incidence. The frequency remains constant.

8. D

Total internal reflection implies that no light exits the glass since it is reflected inside the glass.

THINGS TO REMEMBER

- Electromagnetic waves
- Reflection of light
- Refraction of light
  - Prism dispersion
  - Snell's law of refraction
- Total internal reflection

Chapter 16: **Polarization, Diffraction, and Interference of Light**

- Polarization
- Diffraction and Interference

POLARIZATION

Light is a vibration of an electric and a magnetic field. If you could watch light waves coming toward you, you would see that they actually vibrate in many directions. We say the light is *polarized* when it is forced to vibrate in only one plane.

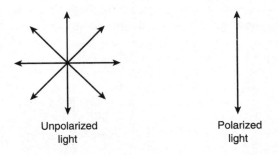

Unpolarized
light

Polarized
light

Polarizing sunglasses block out all but one of the vibrations of light so that considerably less light reaches your eyes after passing through the lenses. This is kind of like passing a rope through a picket fence and shaking the rope in many directions. The only wave that passes through the fence is vertical.

DIFFRACTION AND INTERFERENCE

Diffraction is the bending of a wave around a barrier or through an opening. If we pass a light wave through a narrow single slit, it will behave very similarly to the water waves discussed earlier, with the edges of the light waves lagging behind the center of the waves. If we place a screen opposite to the single-slit opening, we would see a bright light near the center of the screen with narrow lines becoming dimmer toward the edges of the screen. These lines form because of interference from light waves arriving from different locations within the slit.

If we replace the single-slit opening with a double-slit opening, the pattern on the screen changes. As the light passes through the two openings, it becomes two sources of light waves instead of one. These two light waves behave like the semicircular water waves we observed in chapter 14, interfering constructively in some places and destructively in others.

The pattern on the screen would consist of a central bright band of light, with alternating light and dark bands toward the edges of the screen, as depicted in the following diagram.

The bright bands on the screen are the places where constructive interference is occurring (antinodes), and the dark bands are a result of destructive interference (nodes). In 1801, Thomas Young was able to measure the wavelength of light waves using this double-slit diffraction pattern. He found that for a given distance between the slits and length from the slits to the screen, the width of the bright central antinode on the screen is proportional to the wavelength of the light. Thus, red light would produce a wider bright central band than violet light.

> The width of the central antinode produced in an interference pattern is proportional to the wavelength of the light.

POLARIZATION, DIFFRACTION, AND INTERFERENCE OF LIGHT REVIEW QUESTIONS

1. Making a light wave vibrate in only one plane is called

    (A) refraction.
    (B) reflection.
    (C) interference.
    (D) diffraction.
    (E) polarization.

2. If light is passed through a narrow, single-slit opening onto a screen, the pattern of light produced on the screen is

    (A) alternating bright and dark lines of equal width.
    (B) a bright central band of light with much smaller, dimmer bands toward the edges.
    (C) concentric circles of light.
    (D) one circle of light.
    (E) one band of light.

3. If light is passed through a double-slit opening onto a screen, the pattern produced on the screen is

    (A) a bright central band of light with slightly diminished, alternating bright and dark bands called antinodes and nodes.
    (B) a bright central band of light with tiny lines toward the edges of the screen.
    (C) a large circle of light with tiny circles around it.
    (D) equally sized concentric circles of light.
    (E) one antinode and no nodes.

4. Which of the following colors, when passed through a double-slit opening, will produce the widest central band of light?

    (A) red
    (B) orange
    (C) yellow
    (D) green
    (E) blue

$$y = \frac{\lambda \cdot L}{d \cdot m}$$

Solutions on following page.

SOLUTIONS TO POLARIZATION, DIFFRACTION, AND INTERFERENCE OF LIGHT REVIEW QUESTIONS

1.   E

All planes of vibration of the light except one are blocked when a light wave is polarized.

2.   B

The pattern would look like this:

3.   A

The pattern would look like this:

4.   A

The width of the central band is proportional to the wavelength of the light, and red has the longest wavelength of the colors listed.

THINGS TO REMEMBER

- Polarization
- Diffraction and Interference

Chapter 17: **Ray Optics**

- Mirrors
- Lenses

We can apply the principles of reflection and refraction to the images formed by mirrors and lenses.

MIRRORS

We will discuss three types of mirrors in this chapter: *plane, diverging*, and *converging*. A *plane mirror* is simply a flat mirror. From your everyday experience, you know that a plane mirror always produces an image that is the same size as the object (such as yourself in the morning), left-right reversed, and the same distance behind the surface of the mirror as the object is in front of the mirror. We say that the image formed by a plane mirror is *virtual*, since we cannot place a screen behind the mirror and see the image projected on the screen. A virtual image is one that cannot be projected onto a screen.

A *diverging mirror* is sometimes referred to as a *convex mirror*. You may have seen this type of mirror in the corner of a convenience store. The mirror diverges the rays of light that strike it, allowing the clerk at the store to see practically the entire store in one mirror. Light rays coming into the mirror parallel to its principal axis will diverge, or spread apart.

mirrors opposite lenses } *which you want*

light rays

principal axis

mirror

$2f = R$
of curvature

> The *focal length* is the distance from the center of the mirror or lens to the focal point of the rays.

Notice that the rays appear to originate from a point behind the mirror. This point is called the *virtual focus*, and the distance between the surface of the mirror at its center and the focal point is called the *focal length f*.

A *converging mirror* is sometimes referred to as a *concave mirror*. Light rays coming in parallel to the principal axis of the mirror will converge to a focal point.

light rays

mirror

> A diverging mirror is also called a convex mirror; a converging mirror is also called a concave mirror.

If you look into a converging mirror, you will at first see an image of yourself that is inverted (upside down), but then as you move closer to the mirror, you will see your image turn upright as you pass the focal point of the mirror. Satellite dishes act as converging mirrors for radio and TV waves, gathering them at a detector located at the focal point of the dish. Most research telescopes also use converging mirrors rather than lenses to focus light and study images.

LENSES

Lenses operate on the principle of refraction. A *diverging lens* is a lens that is thicker on the edges than it is in the middle, and it diverges the light rays that pass through it.

light rays

A diverging lens is sometimes referred to as a *concave lens.* The focal point of a diverging lens can be found by extending the diverging rays back behind the lens until they seem to meet.

A *converging lens* is a lens that is thicker in the middle than on the edges, and it converges parallel rays that pass through it.

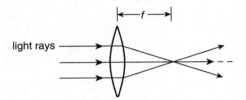

> A diverging lens is also called a concave lens; a converging lens is also called a convex lens.

Images Formed by a Converging (Convex) Lens

Let's take a closer look at the images formed by a converging lens. We said earlier that a *virtual image* is one that cannot be projected onto a screen. On the other hand, a *real image* is one that can be projected onto a screen. If your teacher uses an overhead projector in your classroom, the image projected on the screen is a real image. The image projected on a screen at a movie theater is also real. Under certain circumstances, a converging lens can create an image that can be real or virtual, upright or inverted, enlarged or reduced in size, or the same size as the object. It all depends on where the object is placed relative to the focal length of the lens.

> When you read the words *diverging* and *converging*, or *convex* and *concave*, be sure you identify whether the question is asking you about lenses or mirrors. The answers associated with lenses might be quite different from those associated with mirrors!

For our example, let's choose a burning candle as our object, since it produces light from the flame at the top of the candle. We'll first draw a side view of a converging lens, include a horizontal principal axis through the center of the lens, and mark the focal length of the lens on either side of it. We'll place the candle at a distance greater than twice the focal length from the center of the lens.

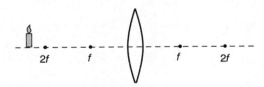

To find out what kind of image will be formed by the lens, we will draw two rays: one ray from the flame entering the lens parallel to the principal axis and bending through the focal point, and another ray from the flame that passes straight through the center of the lens without bending. The image is formed at the location of the intersection of these two rays.

> It takes at least two drawn rays to locate an image formed by a lens.

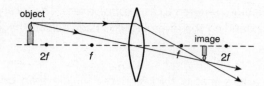

We see that in the case where the object (candle) distance from the lens is greater than twice the focal length, the image is inverted and reduced in size. The image is also real, so if we placed a screen at the location of the image, we would see the projection of a small inverted candle. The image formed by a converging lens is real if the object distance is greater than the focal length.

If we placed the candle at a distance from the lens equal to the focal length, our two rays would emerge parallel to each other, and no image would be formed.

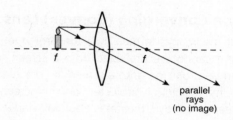

If we placed the candle inside the focal length, our two rays would diverge as they emerged from the lens. No image would be formed on the side opposite to the candle, but if we extended the rays backward, we would find that they seem to originate on the same side as the candle. The point from which they seem to originate is where a virtual image of the candle is formed.

A summary of the images formed by a converging lens is listed in Table 17.1 below, where d_o is the distance from the candle to the object and f is the focal length of the lens. A positive (+) image distance d_i implies that the image is formed on the opposite side of the lens as the object, and a negative (–) image distance implies that the image is formed on the same side as the object.

Table 17.1: Images Formed by a Converging Lens

Object Placement	Image Distance d_i	Real or Virtual	Upright or Inverted	Enlarged or Reduced
$d_o > 2f$	+	real	inverted	reduced
$d_o = 2f$	+	real	inverted	same size
$f < d_o < 2f$	+	real	inverted	enlarged
$d_o = f$	no image	no image	no image	no image
$d_o < f$	–	virtual	upright	enlarged

Note that all real images are inverted.

Magnification Using a Converging Lens

The amount by which an image is magnified by a converging lens is simply equal to the ratio of the image distance to the object distance, each measured from the lens.

$$M = \left| \frac{d_i}{d_o} \right|$$

> Magnification tells us how many times larger or smaller an image is than the object.

Example: A candle is placed a distance of 30 cm from a lens of focal length 20 cm, forming an image 60 cm from the lens. Describe the image formed by the lens and calculate the magnification of the image.

Solution: In this case, the candle is placed at $1.5f$, which is between f and $2f$. Consulting the table above, we see that the image formed is real, inverted, and larger than the object.

The magnification is

$$M = \left| \frac{d_i}{d_o} \right| = \frac{60 \text{ cm}}{30 \text{ cm}} = 2.$$

Thus, the image is twice as large as the object.

RAY OPTICS REVIEW QUESTIONS

1. A plane mirror will produce a virtual image

   (A) when the object distance is greater than the image distance.
   (B) when the object distance is less than the image distance.
   (C) when the object is on the principal axis of the mirror.
   (D) when the rays converge at the focal point of the mirror.
   (E) at all distances from the mirror.

2. Which of the following mirrors converge parallel light rays to a focal point?

   (A) plane
   (B) convex
   (C) concave
   (D) inverted
   (E) upright

3. Which of the following is true of a diverging lens?

   (A) Incoming parallel rays passing through the lens converge to a focal point.
   (B) The lens is thinner in the center than on the edges.
   (C) The lens is thicker in the center than on the edges.
   (D) Light must enter it parallel to the principal axis.
   (E) The lens must be flat on one side.

4. A candle is placed on the principal axis of a convex lens at a distance of 30 cm from the lens. The focal length of the lens is 10 cm. The image formed will be

   (A) real, upright, and enlarged.
   (B) real, inverted, and enlarged.
   (C) real, inverted, and smaller.
   (D) virtual, upright, and enlarged.
   (E) virtual, upright, and smaller.

5. A candle is placed on the principal axis of a convex lens at a distance of 10 cm from the lens. The focal length of the lens is 20 cm. The image formed will be

   (A) real, upright, and enlarged.
   (B) real, inverted, and enlarged.
   (C) real, inverted, and smaller.
   (D) virtual, upright, and enlarged.
   (E) virtual, upright, and smaller.

6. A candle is placed on the principal axis of a convex lens at a distance of 20 cm from the lens. The image formed is magnified 3 times. The image distance is

   (A) 7 cm.
   (B) 20 cm.
   (C) 60 cm.
   (D) 90 cm.
   (E) 120 cm.

SOLUTIONS TO RAY OPTICS REVIEW QUESTIONS

1. E

A plane (flat) mirror will reflect light and produce an image at any distance from the object.

2. C

A concave mirror is also called a converging mirror.

3. B

A diverging lens is also called a concave lens, and is thinner in the center than on the edges.

4. C

The candle is placed at a distance greater than twice the focal length, and so the image formed will be real, inverted, and smaller than the candle.

5. D

The candle is placed at a distance less than the focal length, and so the image formed will be virtual, upright, and enlarged. This is the case for a magnifying glass.

6. C

Since $Magnification = \dfrac{d_i}{d_o}$, then

$$d_i = (M)(d_o) = (3)(20 \text{ cm}) = 60 \text{ cm.}$$

THINGS TO REMEMBER

- Mirrors
- Lenses
  - Images formed by a converging (convex) lens
  - Magnification using a converging lens

Chapter 18: **Heat, Temperature, and Thermodynamics**

- Heat and Temperature
- Specific Heat and Heat Capacity
- Phase Changes
- The First and Second Laws of Thermodynamics

HEAT AND TEMPERATURE

There are three states of matter we will be discussing in these next few chapters: solid, liquid, and gas. The molecules of a solid are fixed in a rigid structure. The molecules of a liquid are loosely bound and may mix with one another freely, but the liquid still has a definite volume, although it takes the shape of its container. The molecules of a gas interact with each other only slightly, and generally move at high speeds compared to the molecules of a liquid or solid. But in all three states of matter, the molecules are moving and therefore have energy. They have potential energy because of the bonds between them and kinetic energy because the molecules have mass and speed. Relatively speaking, the potential energy between gas molecules can be ignored, so we will focus only on their kinetic energy. The sum of the potential and kinetic energies of the molecules in a substance is called the *internal energy* of the substance. When a warmer substance is brought into contact with a cooler substance, some of the kinetic energy of the molecules in the warmer substance is transferred to the cooler substance. The kinetic energy of molecules that is transferred spontaneously from a warmer substance to a cooler substance is called *heat energy*.

Temperature is the measure of how hot or cold a substance is, relative to some standard. It is the measure of the *average kinetic energy* of the molecules in a substance.

The two temperature scales used most widely in scientific applications are the Celsius scale and the Kelvin scale. The only difference between them is where each starts. On the Celsius scale, the freezing point of water is 0°C, and the boiling point of water

> *Heat* is the kinetic energy of molecules transferred from a warmer substance to a cooler one.

> *Temperature* is a measure of the average kinetic energy of the molecules in a substance.

(at standard pressure) is 100°C. The Kelvin scale has temperature units that are equal in size to the Celsius degrees, but the temperature of 0 Kelvin is *absolute zero*, defined as the temperature at which all molecular motion in a substance ceases. Zero Kelvin is equal to –273.15°C, so we can convert between the Kelvin scale and the Celsius scale by this equation:

$$K = °C + 273$$

(Note that we have rounded 273.15 to 273.)

QUICK QUIZ

What is the boiling point of water in Kelvins?

Answer: K = 100°C + 273 = 373 K

Mechanical Equivalent of Heat

The unit most often used for mechanical energy is the *joule*. Historically, the unit for heat has been the *calorie*. One calorie is defined as the heat needed to raise the temperature of one gram of water by one degree Celsius. In the mid-19th century, the British engineer James Joule showed there is a relationship between energy in the form of work in joules and energy in the form of heat in calories. Joule performed experiments that revealed that doing mechanical work on a substance can make its temperature rise. For example, rubbing your hands together causes them to heat up, and stirring a drink adds heat to it. The conversion between joules and calories is

$$1 \text{ calorie} = 4.186 \text{ joules.}$$

The numbers here are not really important for the SAT Subject Test: Physics, but only the concept that mechanical work and heat are both forms of energy and can be converted from one to the other.

Thermal Expansion of a Solid

When a solid is heated, it typically expands. Different substances expand at different rates, which is why it makes sense to heat the lid of a jar when the lid is too tight. The metal lid will expand more than the glass jar when it is heated, making it easier to loosen. Solids undergo two types of expansion when heated: *linear thermal expansion*, which is the increase in any one dimension of the solid, and *volume thermal expansion*, which results in an increase in the volume of the solid. In the case of linear expansion, the change in length Δl is proportional to the original length and the change in temperature of the solid. The same is true for volume expansion. The change in volume ΔV is proportional to the original volume of the solid and its change in temperature.

Heat Transfer

Three ways of transferring heat are *conduction*, *convection*, and *radiation*.

There are three ways of transferring heat from one place to another:

1. *Conduction.* Conduction is the transfer of heat directly through a material, or by actual contact between two materials. Metals are typically good heat *conductors*.

In fact, materials that are good electrical conductors are usually good heat conductors as well. A material that is not a good heat conductor, like wood or air, is called an *insulator*. If you place an iron skillet on a fire, heat is transferred by conduction to the handle of the skillet. If you grasp the iron handle with your bare hand, you will feel it transfer heat to your hand by conduction.

2. *Convection*. Convection is the transfer of heat by the bulk movement of a fluid (liquid or gas). If the air near the floor of a cool room is heated, it expands and becomes less dense than the air above it, causing it to rise. As it rises, it cools, becomes more dense again, and falls toward the floor. If the air near the floor is continually heated, the cycle will repeat itself. Water heated in a pan is another example of heat transfer by convection, since water near the bottom of the pan near the fire is heated, rises, cools, then falls again. If the temperature gets high enough, the water begins to boil as it cools itself by transferring heat to the air by convection.

3. *Radiation*. Radiation is the process by which heat is transferred by electromagnetic waves. We receive heat from the sun by radiation principally in the form of visible light, infrared, and ultraviolet waves. Microwave ovens use microwaves to transfer heat to food. If you stand near a roaring campfire, you will feel the heat radiating from the fire in the form of light and infrared rays.

SPECIFIC HEAT AND HEAT CAPACITY

Heat is supplied to (or absorbed by) a system to raise its temperature; conversely, heat is released if it cools. The heat absorbed or released by an object as a result of a change in temperature is calculated from the equation

$$Q = mc\Delta T,$$

where Q is the symbol for heat, m is the mass of the object, ΔT is the change in temperature and is equal to the final temperature minus the initial temperature, and c is a quantity known as the *specific heat* of the substance.

The more massive a substance is, the more heat is required to bring about a particular change in temperature. Recall that the temperature of a substance is a measure of the average kinetic energy of the particles in the substance. This applies to all states of matter. In solids, for example, the atoms vibrate about their equilibrium positions; the stronger these vibrations, the higher the temperature of the solid. A small amount of heat supplied to a large number of particles would not increase their average energy by much; however, if there were only a small number of particles in the system, that same amount of heat would not be spread as widely, and thus each particle would gain a larger amount of energy, resulting in a greater increase in temperature.

Yet, not every substance is responsive to heat to the same degree. Even though we expect that raising 2 kg of a substance by 1°C requires more heat than raising 1 kg of the same substance by 1°C (in fact, it requires twice the amount of heat), we would not expect that the same amount of heat is required to raise the temperature of 1 kg of steel versus 1 kg of plastic. The *specific heat c* is a proportionality constant that gives an indication of the ease with which one can raise the temperature of something; the larger it is, the larger the amount of heat required to raise its temperature a certain number of degrees, and also the more heat is released if it cools by a certain number of degrees. Its value is a property of the *nature* of the substance and does not change based on the *amount* of the substance, since that has already been taken into account by the mass variable in the equation. The specific heat is often more formally defined as the heat necessary to raise the temperature of 1 kg or 1 g of a material by 1°C or 1 K. Iron, for example, has a specific heat of about 0.1 kilocalorie/kg°C, while water has a specific heat of 1.0 kcal/kg°C. It is therefore much easier to raise the temperature of 1 kg of iron by 10°C than it is to do the same to 1 kg of water; in fact, you should be able to see that 10 times the amount of heat is needed to heat the water. Specific heat and heat flow are often determined by a device called a *calorimeter*, which isolates objects to measure temperature changes due to heat flow.

The more of a substance there is, the more heat is required to bring about a change in its temperature.

The mass and the specific heat are sometimes lumped together to give a quantity known as the *heat capacity*. This quantity describes the heat needed to raise the temperature of the object as a whole by 1°C or 1 K.

Example: What is the heat necessary to raise the temperature of 2 kg of iron from 40°C to 80°C?

Solution: From our discussion above, we know that the specific heat of iron is 0.1 kcal/kg°C. The heat required is

$$Q = mc\Delta T = mc(T_f - T_i) = (2 \text{ kg})(0.1 \text{ kcal/kg °C})(80 - 40)$$

$$= 8 \text{ kcal or } 8{,}000 \text{ calories.}$$

This is approximately equal to 33,000 J.

PHASE CHANGES

Adding heat can change the temperature of an object or change its phase.

While heat is associated with the change of thermal energy, a system does not necessarily increase in temperature when heat is applied. Heat can also increase the potential (rather than kinetic) energy of the particles in a system; this occurs during a *phase change*. Heat is required to *melt* something (change its phase from a solid to a liquid), or to *vaporize* something (change its phase from a liquid to a gas), or to *sublimate* something (change its phase directly from a solid to a gas). In all these cases, the molecules are overcoming the attractive forces that hold them together. This is where the energy supplied by heating is being put to use. Conversely, heat is released as a substance *freezes* or *condenses*. During such phase changes, the temperature remains constant, and the heat involved in these processes can be expressed as

$$Q = mL,$$

where m is the mass of the substance undergoing the phase change and L is the heat of transformation, the value of which depends on both the substance and the particular process we are talking about: vaporization, sublimation, or fusion (melting).

Example: The heat of fusion L_f of ice is 3.3×10^5 joules/kg°C, and the specific heat of water is 4.2×10^3 joules/kg°C. How much heat is required to completely melt 10 kg of ice (initially at 0°C) and then raise the temperature of the water from 0°C to 30°C?

Solution: The heat required to melt the ice and then raise the temperature of the water is

$$Q = mL_f + mc\Delta T$$

$$Q = (10 \text{ kg})(\ 3.3 \times 10^5 \text{ joules/kg°C})$$
$$+ \ (10 \text{ kg})(4.2 \times 10^3 \text{ joules/kg°C})(30 - 0)$$

$$Q = 4.56 \times 10^6 \text{ joules.}$$

This is approximately 1 million calories.

If we were to continue to heat the water until it boiled and turned to steam at 100°C, and then continued to add heat to the steam to raise its temperature beyond 100°C, the temperature would not change during the phase changes from ice to water and water to steam. The heat added would go into changing the phase of the water, not its temperature.

A graph of temperature vs. heat added for this process is shown below.

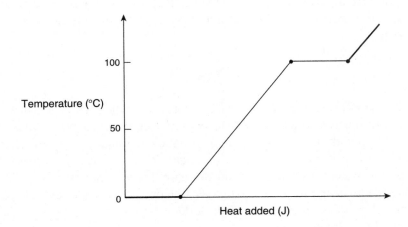

The flat portions of the graph imply that the temperature is not changing, and correspond to the processes of melting and boiling.

THE FIRST AND SECOND LAWS OF THERMODYNAMICS

Thermodynamics is the study of heat transfer. There are actually four laws of thermodynamics, but we will look at the two that are required for the SAT Subject Test: Physics.

In order to understand the laws of thermodynamics, we first need to know the definitions of the three types of *systems*:

Three types of systems: isolated, closed, and open.

1. *Isolated.* A system is said to be isolated when it cannot exchange energy or matter with the surroundings, like a well-insulated thermos flask.

2. *Closed.* A system is said to be closed when it can exchange energy but not matter with the surroundings, like a test tube with a stopper in it.

3. *Open.* A system is said to be open when it can exchange both matter and energy with the surroundings, like a pot of boiling water allowing water vapor to escape into the air.

The First Law of Thermodynamics

As we've discussed in previous chapters, energy can be transformed into many forms but still be conserved; that is, the total amount of energy will remain constant. This is true of a system only if it is isolated; since energy can neither go in nor go out, it must be conserved. If the system is closed or open, however, the amount of energy in the system can certainly change.

The first law of thermodynamics is simply the law of conservation of energy.

A system can exchange energy with its surroundings in two general ways: as heat or as work. *The first law of thermodynamics states that the change in the internal energy ΔU of a system is equal to the heat Q added to the system minus the work W that a system does:*

$$\Delta U = Q - W$$

If work is done ON a system, W is negative. Note that sometimes W is defined as the work done ON, rather than BY, the system, in which case the equation is written as $\Delta U = Q + W$, and the work done BY the system is considered negative. Regardless of which convention is used, if work is done on a system, its energy would increase. If work is done by the system, its energy would decrease. Work is generally associated with movement against some force. For ideal gas systems, for example, expansion against some external pressure means that work is done by the system, while compression implies work being done on the system.

Example: A system has 50 J of heat added to it, resulting in 20 J of work being done BY the system. What is the change in internal energy of the system?

Solution: The change in internal energy is $\Delta U = Q - W = 50 \text{ J} - 20 \text{ J} = 30 \text{ J}$.

Example: A 50 g sample of metal is heated to 100°C and then dropped into a beaker containing 50 g of water at 25°C. If the specific heat capacity of the metal is 0.25 cal/g°C, what is the final temperature of the water?

Solution: Since heat is transferred and no work is done, the heat lost by the metal must equal the heat gained by the water:

$$m_{metal}c_{metal}(T_f - T_i)_{metal} - m_{water}c_{water}(T_f - T_i)_{water} = 0$$

$$(50 \text{ g})(0.25 \text{ cal/g°C})(T_f - 100) - (50 \text{ g})(1 \text{ cal/g°C})(T_f - 25) = 0$$

Since the final equilibrium temperature is the same for the metal and the water, we find that $T_f = 40°C$.

Heat Engine

A *heat engine* is any device that uses heat to perform work. There are three essential features of a heat engine:

1. Heat is supplied to the engine at a high temperature from a hot reservoir.

2. Part of the input heat is used to perform work.

3. The remainder of the input heat that did not do work is exhausted into a cold reservoir, which is at a lower temperature than the hot reservoir.

The *percent efficiency* (%ε) of the heat engine is equal to the ratio of the work done to the amount of input heat.

$$\%\varepsilon = \frac{Work}{Q_{hot}} \times 100$$

Example: A heat engine extracts 100 J of energy from a hot reservoir, does work, then exhausts 40 J of energy into a cold reservoir. What is the work done by the engine, and the percent efficiency of the engine?

Solution: The work done is equal to the difference between the input heat and the output heat:

$$W = 100 \text{ J} - 40 \text{ J} = 60 \text{ J}$$

The percent efficiency is

$$\frac{60 \text{ J}}{100 \text{ J}} = 60\%.$$

The Second Law of Thermodynamics

> The second law of thermo-dynamics is the *law of entropy*.

Entropy is a measure of the disorder, or randomness, of a system. The greater the disorder of a system, the greater the entropy. If a system is highly ordered, like the particles in a solid, we say that the entropy is low. At any given temperature, a solid will have a lower entropy than a gas, because individual molecules in the gaseous state are moving randomly, while individual molecules in a solid are constrained in place.

Entropy is important because it determines whether a process will occur spontaneously. *The second law of thermodynamics states that all spontaneous processes proceeding in an isolated system lead to an increase in entropy.*

In other words, an isolated system will naturally pursue a state of higher disorder. If you watch a magician throw a deck of cards into the air, you would expect the cards to fall to the floor around him in a very disorderly manner, since the system of cards would naturally tend toward a state of higher disorder. If you watched a film of a magician, and his randomly placed cards jumped off the floor and landed neatly stacked in his hand, you would believe the film is running backward, since cards do not seek this state of order by themselves. Thus, the second law of thermodynamics gives us a direction for the passage of time.

The second law of thermodynamics also gives us a direction for the flow of heat. A bowl of ice cream will melt if left out on a hot day. The ice cream would not get colder if left in a hot environment, since heat flows spontaneously from hot to cold. As it relates to heat, the second law can be stated like this: *Heat flows spontaneously from a substance at a higher temperature to a substance at a lower temperature and does not flow spontaneously in the reverse direction.*

Of course, we can *force* heat to flow from a colder object to a hotter object, which is exactly what your refrigerator in your kitchen does. The flow of heat in the refrigerator is not spontaneous, and so the second law of thermodynamics does not apply.

HEAT, TEMPERATURE, AND THERMODYNAMICS REVIEW QUESTIONS

1. The average kinetic energy of the molecules in a substance is most closely associated with

   (A) heat capacity.
   (B) temperature.
   (C) specific heat.
   (D) absolute zero.
   (E) potential energy.

2. The temperature of absolute zero is equal to

   (A) 0°C.
   (B) 100°C.
   (C) 273°C.
   (D) –273°C.
   (E) –100°C.

3. The conversion between mechanical energy and heat energy was first developed by

   (A) Celsius.
   (B) Kelvin.
   (C) Joule.
   (D) Newton.
   (E) Watt.

4. In general, when a solid is heated, it

   (A) expands proportionally to the change in temperature.
   (B) contracts proportionally to the change in temperature.
   (C) expands inversely proportional to the change in temperature.
   (D) contracts inversely proportional to the change in temperature.
   (E) does not expand or contract.

5. A liquid is poured into a pan and heated over a flame. The hot liquid begins rising to the top. This type of heat transfer is called

   (A) conduction.
   (B) convection.
   (C) radiation.
   (D) thermal expansion.
   (E) specific heat.

6. You feel heat as you approach a fire by way of

   (A) conduction.
   (B) convection.
   (C) radiation.
   (D) thermal expansion.
   (E) specific heat.

7. A 3 kg block of aluminum is heated so that its temperature increases by 3 degrees. How much heat would be needed to raise the temperature of a 9 kg block of aluminum by 3 degrees?

   (A) 9 times as much heat as the 3 kg block
   (B) 3 times as much heat as the 3 kg block
   (C) the same amount of heat as the 3 kg block
   (D) one-third as much heat as the 3 kg block
   (E) one-ninth as much heat as the 3 kg block

8. What is the specific heat of a substance that requires 10 J of heat to raise the temperature of a 2 kg sample of the substance from 22°C to 24°C?

   (A) 10 J/kg°C
   (B) 5 J/kg°C
   (C) 4 J/kg°C
   (D) 2.5 J/kg°C
   (E) 2 J/kg°C

9. Heat is added to a block of ice initially at 0°C until the ice changes completely into water. The same amount of heat continues to be added to the liquid water for 15 minutes. Which of the following statements is true?

    (A) The temperature of the ice and water remains constant until the end of the 15-minute time period.
    (B) The temperature of the ice rises steadily until all of the ice has melted into water.
    (C) The temperature of the ice remains constant until all of the ice has melted into water, then the temperature of the water steadily rises for 15 minutes.
    (D) The temperature of the ice rises from 0°C to 32°C, then the temperature of the water rises from 32°C to 100°C.
    (E) The temperature of the ice remains at 0°C until the ice has melted, then the temperature of the water remains constant at 32°C.

10. The first law of thermodynamics is a form of

    (A) the law of conservation of energy.
    (B) the law of specific heat.
    (C) the ideal gas law.
    (D) the law of entropy.
    (E) the law of conservation of temperature.

11. A system has 60 J of heat added to it, resulting in 15 J of work being done by the system, and exhausting the remaining 45 J of heat. What is the efficiency of this process?

    (A) 100%
    (B) 60%
    (C) 45%
    (D) 25%
    (E) 15%

12. The law of entropy states that

    (A) heat always flows spontaneously from a colder body to a hotter one.
    (B) every natural system will tend toward lower entropy.
    (C) heat lost by one object must be gained by another.
    (D) the specific heat of a substance cannot exceed a certain value.
    (E) every natural system will tend toward disorder.

SOLUTIONS TO HEAT, TEMPERATURE, AND THERMODYNAMICS REVIEW QUESTIONS

1. B

The average kinetic energy of the molecules is proportional to the temperature of the substance.

2. D

$$\text{Kelvin} = \text{Celsius} + 273, \text{ so } 0 \text{ K} = -273°C.$$

3. C

Joule first measured the mechanical equivalent of heat.

4. A

The expansion of a substance is proportional to the change in temperature.

5. B

Convection is heat transfer by the rising and falling of a fluid as it heats and cools and changes density.

6. C

The fire radiates heat mostly in the form of infrared electromagnetic waves.

7. B

Three times the mass of the same substance will require three times the heat to raise its temperature by a certain amount according to the equation $Q = mc\Delta T$.

8. D

$$Q = mc\Delta T \text{ implies that } c = \frac{Q}{m\Delta T} =$$
$$\frac{10 \text{ J}}{(2 \text{ kg})(24°C - 22°C)} = 2.5 \text{ J/kg}°C$$

9. C

The heat added to the ice is used only to change the phase of the ice to water, and the heat added to the liquid water is used to change its temperature.

10. A

The first law of thermodynamics states that the heat lost by one object must be gained by another, but the amount of energy in the transfer must remain constant.

11. D

If only 15 J of the 60 J is used to do work, we say that the efficiency of the process is

$$\frac{15 \text{ J}}{60 \text{ J}} \times 100 = 25\%.$$

12. E

Entropy means disorder, and every natural system will tend toward a state of higher disorder. The fact that heat spontaneously flows from a hotter body to a colder body is a consequence of this law.

THINGS TO REMEMBER

- Heat and temperature
  - ○ Mechanical equivalent of heat
  - ○ Thermal expansion of a solid
  - ○ Heat transfer
- Specific heat and heat capacity
- Phase changes
- The first and second laws of thermodynamics
  - ○ The first law of thermodynamics
  - ○ Heat engine
  - ○ The second law of thermodynamics

Chapter 19: **Gases and Kinetic Theory**

- Ideal Gases
- The Kinetic Theory of Gases

Among the different phases of matter, the gaseous phase is the simplest to understand and to model, since all gases display similar behavior and follow similar laws regardless of their identity. The atoms or molecules in a gaseous sample move rapidly and are far apart. In addition, intermolecular forces between gas particles tend to be weak; this results in certain characteristic physical properties, such as the ability to expand to fill any volume and to take on the shape of a container. Furthermore, gases are easily, though not infinitely, compressible.

The state of a gaseous sample is generally defined by four variables: pressure (P), volume (V), temperature (T), and number of moles (n), though as we shall see, these are not all independent. The *pressure* of a gas is the force per unit area that the atoms or molecules exert on the walls of the container through collisions. The SI unit for pressure is the *pascal* (Pa), which is equal to one newton per meter squared. Sometimes gas pressures are expressed in *atmospheres* (atm). One atmosphere is equal to 10^5 Pa, and is approximately equal to the pressure the Earth's atmosphere exerts on us each day. Volume can be expressed in liters (L) or cubic meters (m^3), and temperature is measured in Kelvins (K) for the purpose of the gas laws. Recall that we can find the temperature in K by adding 273 to the temperature in Celsius. Gases are often discussed in terms of *standard temperature and pressure* (STP), which refers to the conditions of 273 K (0°C) and 1 atm.

> The state of a gas can be defined by pressure, volume, temperature, and amount of gas in moles.

IDEAL GASES

When examining the behavior of gases under varying conditions of temperature and pressure, it is most convenient to treat them as ideal gases. An ideal gas represents a hypothetical gas whose molecules have no intermolecular forces; that is, they do not

Most gases can be treated as ideal.

interact with each other and occupy no volume. Although gases in reality deviate from this idealized behavior, at relatively low pressures and high temperatures many gases behave in nearly ideal fashion. Therefore, the assumptions used for ideal gases can be applied to real gases with reasonable accuracy.

The Ideal Gas Law

The *ideal* gas law states that pressure times volume divided by temperature remains constant.

The ideal gas law gives the relationship between the pressure, volume, and temperature of a gas before and after some process. It states that the product of pressure and volume divided by temperature remains constant during any process:

$$\frac{P_1 V_1}{T_1} = \frac{P_2 V_2}{T_2}$$

If temperature remains constant during a process (*isothermic*), the equation becomes

$$P_1 V_1 = P_2 V_2 \text{ (Boyle's law)}.$$

If the volume remains constant during a process (*isochoric*), the equation becomes

$$\frac{P_1}{T_1} = \frac{P_2}{T_2}.$$

If the pressure remains constant during a process (*isobaric*), the equation becomes

$$\frac{V_1}{T_1} = \frac{V_2}{T_2} \text{ (Charles's law)}.$$

Example: Under isothermal conditions, what would be the volume of a 1 liter sample of helium gas after its pressure is changed from 12 atm to 4 atm?

Solution: Isothermal means that the temperature is constant during the process, so the ideal gas law becomes

$$P_1 V_1 = P_2 V_2$$

$$(12 \text{ atm})(1 \text{ L}) = (4 \text{ atm})V_2$$

$$V_2 = 3 \text{ L}.$$

Example: If the temperature of 2 liters of gas is isobarically changed from 10°C to 293°C, what would be the final volume?

Solution: *Isobarically* means that the pressure remains constant during this process. But before we can apply the ideal gas law, or Charles's law in this case, we need to convert Celsius degrees to Kelvins:

$$T_1 = 10°C + 273 = 283 \text{ K and } T_2 = 293°C + 273 = 566 \text{ K}$$

Then,

$$\frac{V_1}{T_1} = \frac{V_2}{T_2}$$

$$\frac{2 \text{ L}}{283 \text{ K}} = \frac{V_2}{566 \text{ K}}$$

$$V_2 = 4 \text{ L}.$$

THE KINETIC THEORY OF GASES

As indicated by the gas laws, all gases show similar physical characteristics and behavior. A theoretical model to explain why gases behave the way they do was developed during the second half of the 19th century. The combined efforts of Boltzmann, Maxwell, and others led to the kinetic theory of gases, which gives us an understanding of gaseous behavior on a microscopic, molecular level. Like the gas laws, this theory was developed in reference to ideal gases, although it can be applied with reasonable accuracy to real gases as well.

The assumptions of the kinetic theory of gases are as follows:

1. Gases are made up of particles whose volumes are negligible compared to the container volume.

2. Gas atoms or molecules exhibit no intermolecular attractions or repulsions.

3. Gas particles are in continuous, random motion, undergoing collisions with other particles and the container walls.

4. Collisions between any two gas particles are elastic, meaning that no energy is dissipated and kinetic energy is conserved.

5. The average kinetic energy of gas particles is proportional to the absolute (Kelvin) temperature of the gas, and is the same for all gases at a given temperature.

GASES AND KINETIC THEORY REVIEW QUESTIONS

1. Which of the following is NOT true of an ideal gas?

    (A) Gas molecules have no intermolecular forces.
    (B) Gas particles are in random motion.
    (C) Gas particles have no volume.
    (D) The collisions between any two gas particles are elastic.
    (E) The average kinetic energy of the gas molecules is proportional to the temperature in Celsius degrees.

2. A sample of argon occupies 50 liters at standard temperature. Assuming constant pressure, what volume will argon occupy if the temperature is doubled?

    (A) 25 liters
    (B) 50 liters
    (C) 100 liters
    (D) 200 liters
    (E) 2,500 liters

3. What is the final pressure of a gas that expands from 1 liter at 10°C to 10 liters at 100°C if the original pressure was 3 atmospheres?

    (A) 0.3 atm
    (B) 0.4 atm
    (C) 3 atm
    (D) 4 atm
    (E) 30 atm

4. Which of the following graphs best represents the relationship between the average kinetic energy of the molecules of a gas and its temperature?

    (A)

    (B)

    (C)

    (D)

    (E)

5. Which of the following pressure vs. volume graphs best represents how pressure and volume change when temperature remains constant (isothermal)?

(A)

(B)

(C)

(D)

(E)

6. Which of the following volume vs. temperature graphs best represents how volume changes with Kelvin temperature if the pressure remains constant (isobaric)?

(A)

(B)

(C)

(D)

(E)

SOLUTIONS TO GASES AND KINETIC THEORY REVIEW QUESTIONS

1. E

The average kinetic energy of the molecules is proportional to the temperature in Kelvins, not Celsius degrees.

2. C

$$\frac{V_1}{T_1} = \frac{V_2}{T_2}$$

$$\frac{50 \text{ L}}{T_1} = \frac{V_2}{2T}$$

$$V_2 = 100 \text{ L}$$

3. B

Don't forget to change Celsius temperature to Kelvin temperature:

$$T_1 = 10°C + 273 = 283 \text{ K and } T_2 = 100°C + 273$$
$$= 373 \text{ K}$$

$$\frac{P_1 V_1}{T_1} = \frac{P_2 V_2}{T_2}$$

$$\frac{(3 \text{ atm})(1 \text{ L})}{283 \text{ K}} = \frac{P_2 (10L)}{373 \text{ K}}$$

Solving for P_2, we get a final pressure of 0.4 atm.

4. B

The average kinetic energy and temperature are proportional to each other, yielding a line with a constant positive slope.

5. A

According to Boyle's law, the product of pressure and volume must remain constant, yielding an inverse relationship.

6. C

According to Charles's law, volume is proportional to Kelvin temperature if pressure is constant, yielding a line with a constant positive slope.

THINGS TO REMEMBER

- Ideal gases
  - The ideal gas law
- The kinetic theory of gases

Chapter 20: **Quantum Phenomena**

- Photons and the Photoelectric Effect
- The Momentum of a Photon and the Heisenberg Uncertainty Principle
- Matter Waves and the de Broglie Wavelength of a Particle

The word *quantum* simply means *the smallest piece of something*. The quantum of American money is one cent; the quantum of negative charge is the electron, since as far as we know there is no smaller negative charge that exists by itself. There are several quantities in physics that are *quantized*, that is, that occur in multiples of some smallest value. Light is one of these quantities.

> A *quantum* is the smallest possible unit of a physical quantity.

PHOTONS AND THE PHOTOELECTRIC EFFECT

In chapters 15 through 17, we treated light as a wave. But there are circumstances when light behaves as though it is made up of individual bundles of energy, separate from each other but sharing a wavelength, frequency, and speed. The quantum of light is called the *photon*. In the late 19th century, an effect was discovered by Heinrich Hertz that could not be explained by the wave model of light. He shined ultraviolet light on a piece of zinc metal, and the metal became positively charged. Although he did not know it at the time, the light was causing the metal to emit electrons. The phenomenon of light causing electrons to be emitted from a metal is called the *photoelectric effect*. According to the theory of light at the time, light was considered a wave, and should not be able to "knock" electrons off of a metal surface. At the turn of the 20th century, Max Planck showed that light could be treated as tiny bundles of energy called photons, and the energy of a photon was proportional to its frequency. Thus, a graph of photon energy E vs. frequency f looks as follows.

> The *photon* is the quantum of light.

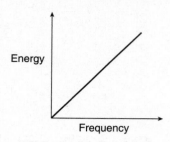

The slope of this line is a constant called *Planck's constant* that appears many times in the study of quantum phenomena. Its symbol is *h*, and its value happens to be 6.63 × 10^{-34} J s. The equation for the energy of a photon is

$$E = hf,$$

$$\text{or, since } f = \frac{c}{\lambda},$$

$$E = \frac{hc}{\lambda}.$$

> The energy of a photon is proportional to its frequency.

So the energy of a photon is proportional to its frequency, but inversely proportional to its wavelength.

Example: List the following photons of light from lowest energy to highest energy:

    (A) green
    (B) violet
    (C) yellow

Solution: Listing these photons from lowest to highest energy is the same as listing them from lowest to highest frequency, or, equivalently, from longest to shortest wavelength: yellow, green, violet.

In 1905, Albert Einstein used Planck's idea of the photon to explain the photoelectric effect: One photon is absorbed by one electron in the metal surface, giving the electron enough energy to be released from the metal. But not just any photon will knock an electron off of a metal surface. The photon must first have enough energy to "dig" the electron out of the metal, and then have some energy left over to give the electron some kinetic energy to escape completely.

> The *photoelectric effect* results when light shined on a metal releases electrons from the surface of the metal.

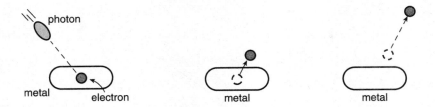

Each metal that can exhibit the photoelectric effect has a minimum energy and frequency called the *threshold frequency* (f_o) that the incoming photon must meet to dig the electron out of the metal and must exceed to give it enough kinetic energy to escape. For example, the metal sodium has a threshold frequency that corresponds to yellow light. If yellow light is shined on a sodium surface, the yellow photons will be absorbed by electrons in the metal, causing them to be released, but there will be no energy left over for the electrons to have any kinetic energy. If we shine green light on the sodium metal, the electrons will be released and have some energy left over to use as kinetic energy, and the electrons will jump off the metal completely, since green light has a higher frequency and energy than yellow light.

> The *threshold frequency* of a metal is the minimum frequency of incoming light necessary to release an electron from a metal surface.

Example: In the case of the yellow light and sodium metal described above, describe what would happen in the following instances:

   (A)   We shine orange light on the sodium metal.

   (B)   We shine very bright red light on the sodium metal.

   (C)   We shine blue light on the sodium metal.

   (D)   We shine very bright blue light on the metal.

   (E)   Sketch a graph of maximum kinetic energy of a photoelectron (an electron emitted in the photoelectric effect) vs. frequency of incident light for this metal.

Solution:

   (A)   Since orange light is below the threshold frequency for sodium, no emission of electrons will take place.

   (B)   The brightness of the light doesn't matter if the threshold frequency (minimum color) is not met, and red photons have less frequency than the necessary yellow photons, so no emission of electrons will occur.

   (C)   Blue light has a higher frequency and energy than yellow, so electrons will be released from the sodium and will have kinetic energy left over to escape the metal.

   (D)   We know that blue light will emit electrons from the sodium, and a brighter blue light means more blue photons. Since one photon can be absorbed by one electron, more electrons will be emitted by a brighter light that exceeds the threshold frequency. If these electrons are funneled into a circuit, we can use them as current in an electrical device.

   (E)   The graph of maximum kinetic energy of a photoelectron vs. frequency of incident light would look as follows.

> For light above the threshold frequency, a brighter light means more photons, and thus more electrons released from the metal.

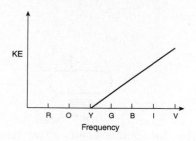

Note that the electrons have no kinetic energy up to the threshold frequency (color), and then their kinetic energy is proportional to the frequency of the incoming light.

THE MOMENTUM OF A PHOTON AND THE HEISENBERG UNCERTAINTY PRINCIPLE

Since a photon has energy, does it follow that it has momentum? Recall that in chapter 6 we defined momentum as the product of mass and velocity. But a photon has no mass. It turns out that in quantum physics, photons do have momentum by virtue of their wavelength. The equation for the momentum of a photon is

$$p = \frac{h}{\lambda}.$$

So the momentum of a photon is inversely proportional to its wavelength. Photons can and do impart momentum to subatomic particles in collisions that follow the law of conservation of momentum. It is difficult to understand how a photon, having only energy and no mass, can collide with a particle such as an electron and change its momentum. But this has been verified experimentally, and we realize that our understanding of quantum phenomena is still catching up with experimental evidence in some cases.

When a policeman wants to measure the speed of your car, he aims his radar gun and shoots a radio wave that bounces off your car and returns to his detector, giving an indication of your speed. One assumption here is that the radio wave reflecting off your car does not significantly add to or take away from the speed of your car. Your car is much too massive to be affected by a radio wave bouncing off of it. But what if you wanted to measure the speed or position of a subatomic particle, like an electron? Even if you shoot a lightweight photon, bounce it off the electron, and measure how quickly the photon returns to you, you have imparted a significant amount of the photon's momentum to the electron in the process, and thus changed the momentum and position of the electron just by trying to measure it. Here we have reached a limit of measurement. Since a photon is the smallest and most unobtrusive measuring device we have available to us, and even a photon is too large to make accurate measurements of the speed and position of subatomic particles, we must admit to an uncertainty that will always exist in quantum measurements. This limit to accuracy at this level was formulated by Werner Heisenberg in 1928 and is called the *Heisenberg uncertainty principle*. It can be stated as follows:

> *There is a limit to the accuracy of the measurement of the speed (or momentum) and position of any subatomic particle. The more accurately we measure the speed of a particular particle, the less accurately we can measure its position, and vice versa.*

> The *Heisenberg uncertainty principle* states that we cannot simultaneously measure the position and speed (or momentum) of a subatomic particle with complete accuracy.

MATTER WAVES AND THE DE BROGLIE WAVELENGTH OF A PARTICLE

In 1924, Louis de Broglie reasoned that if a wave such as light can behave like a particle, having momentum, then why couldn't particles behave like waves? If the momentum of a photon can be found by the equation $\hat{p} = \dfrac{h}{\lambda}$, then the wavelength can be found by $\lambda = \dfrac{h}{p}$. De Broglie suggested that for a particle with mass m and speed v, we could write the equation as $\lambda = \dfrac{h}{mv}$, and the wavelength of a moving particle could be calculated. This hypothesis was initially met with a considerable amount of skepticism until it was shown by Davisson and Germer in 1927 that electrons passing through a nickel crystal were diffracted through the crystal, producing a diffraction pattern on a photographic plate. Thus, de Broglie's hypothesis that particles could behave like waves was experimentally verified. Today, nuclear and particle physicists must take into account the wave behavior of subatomic particles in their experiments. We typically don't notice the wave properties of objects moving around us because the masses are large in comparison to subatomic particles and the value for Planck's constant h is extremely small. But the wavelength of any moving mass is inversely proportional to the momentum of the object.

Example: If an electron, a proton, and an alpha particle (a helium nucleus) are all moving at the same speed, which will have the longest de Broglie wavelength? Which will have the shortest?

Solution: At equal speeds, the particle with the least mass will have the longest wavelength, and the particle with the largest mass will have the shortest wavelength. Listed from longest to shortest wavelength, we have the electron, the proton, and the alpha particle.

QUANTUM PHENOMENA REVIEW QUESTIONS

1. The smallest discrete value of any quantity in physics is called the

   (A) atom.
   (B) molecule.
   (C) proton.
   (D) electron.
   (E) quantum.

2. The smallest discrete value of electromagnetic energy is called the *no mass*

   (A) photon.
   (B) proton.
   (C) electron.
   (D) neutron.
   (E) quark.

3. Which of the following photons has the highest energy?

   (A) X-ray
   (B) ultraviolet light
   (C) green light
   (D) microwave
   (E) radio wave

4. The threshold frequency of zinc for the photoelectric effect is in the ultraviolet range. Which of the following will occur if X-rays are shined on a zinc metal surface?

   (A) No electrons will be emitted from the metal.
   (B) Electrons will be released from the metal but have no kinetic energy.
   (C) Electrons will be released from the metal and have kinetic energy.
   (D) Electrons will be released from the metal but will immediately be recaptured by the zinc atoms.
   (E) Electrons will simply move from one zinc atom in the metal to another zinc atom in the metal.

5. A metal surface has a threshold frequency for the photoelectric effect that corresponds to green light. If blue light is shined on this metal,

   (A) no electrons will be emitted from the metal.
   (B) the number of emitted electrons will be proportional to the brightness (intensity) of the blue light.
   (C) the electrons will have no kinetic energy.
   (D) more electrons will be emitted than if green light were shined on the metal.
   (E) electrons will be emitted from the metal, but since the light is not green, only a few electrons will be released.

6. Light is shined on a metal surface that exhibits the photoelectric effect according to the graph shown.

   What color(s) correspond to the threshold frequency of the metal?

   (A) red only
   (B) red and orange
   (C) red, orange, yellow, and green
   (D) blue only
   (E) blue, indigo, and violet

7. Which of the following is true of the momentum of a photon?

   (A) It is proportional to the wavelength of the photon.
   (B) It is inversely proportional to the wavelength of the photon.
   (C) It is inversely proportional to the square of the wavelength of the photon.
   (D) It is proportional to the mass of the photon.
   (E) It is equal to the energy of the photon.

$$P = \frac{h}{\lambda}$$

$$\lambda = \frac{h}{P}$$

8. The Heisenberg uncertainty principle implies that

   (A) electrons are too small to be studied.

   (B) every photon is exactly the same size.

   (C) the more you know about the momentum of an electron, the less you can know about its position.

   (D) the more you know about the energy of a photon, the less you can know about its frequency.

   (E) you cannot state with accuracy the number of electrons in an atom.

9. Which of the following statements is true for the de Broglie wavelength of a moving particle?

   (A) It is never large enough to measure.

   (B) It is proportional to the speed of the particle.

   (C) It is inversely proportional to the momentum of the particle.

   (D) It is equal to Planck's constant.

   (E) It has no effect on the behavior of electrons.

SOLUTIONS TO QUANTUM PHENOMENA REVIEW QUESTIONS

1. E

The quantum is the smallest discrete value of any quantity, such as the electron for charge and the photon for light.

2. A

A photon is the smallest bundle of light energy.

3. A

The X-ray has the highest frequency of the choices, and since energy is proportional to frequency, it has the highest energy as well.

4. C

Since the frequency of X-rays is higher than the ultraviolet threshold frequency, electrons will be emitted from the metal and have kinetic energy left over.

5. B

After the threshold frequency is met, the number of photons (brightness) dictate how many electrons are emitted, since one photon can release one electron. Thus, a brighter light will release more electrons.

6. D

The electrons begin being released when blue light is shined on the metal, so blue has the threshold (minimum) frequency for this metal.

7. B

Since the equation for the momentum of a photon is $p = \dfrac{h}{\lambda}$, the momentum is inversely proportional to the wavelength of the photon, implying that a photon with a shorter wavelength has a higher momentum than one with a longer wavelength.

8. C

Heisenberg's uncertainty principle states that you have to sacrifice your knowledge of the position of any subatomic particle to know its momentum accurately, and vice versa.

9. C

According to the equations for the de Broglie wavelength, the higher the momentum of the particle, the shorter its wavelength.

THINGS TO REMEMBER

- Photons and the photoelectric effect
- The momentum of a photon and the Heisenberg uncertainty principle
- Matter waves and the de Broglie wavelength of a particle

Chapter 21: **Atomic Physics**

- Rutherford Model of the Atom
- Bohr Model of the Atom

RUTHERFORD MODEL OF THE ATOM

The ancient Greeks were the first to document the concept of the atom. They believed that all matter is made up of tiny indivisible particles. In fact, the word *atom* comes from the Greek word *atomos*, meaning "uncuttable." But a working model of the atom didn't begin to take shape until J. J. Thomson's discovery of the electron in 1897. He found that electrons are tiny, negatively charged particles and that all atoms contain electrons. He also recognized that atoms are naturally neutral, containing equal amounts of positive and negative charge, although he was not correct in his theory of how the charge was arranged.

You may remember studying Thomson's "plum-pudding" model of the atom, with electrons floating around in positive fluid. A significant improvement on this model of the atom was made by Ernest Rutherford around 1911, when he decided to shoot alpha particles at very thin gold foil to probe the inner structure of the atom in an experiment we now refer to as the *Rutherford alpha-scattering experiment*.

Alpha particles are relatively large, positively charged particles that are emitted by certain radioactive elements. Rutherford didn't know at the time that they were actually helium nuclei, consisting of two protons and two neutrons. He aimed a radioactive alpha source at a very thin sheet of gold foil and fully expected the alpha particles to pass straight through the foil, since he believed Thomson's "plum-pudding" model that the atom should not offer any resistance to the alpha particles. As expected, most of the alpha particles passed straight through the foil undeflected; however, some of the particles glanced off at a slight angle. This was a bit surprising to Rutherford, since he didn't know what might cause the alpha particles to change their path as they passed

> All atoms are naturally neutral and contain electrons.

> The *Rutherford alpha-scattering experiment* established that the atom has a nucleus.

through the gold atoms. But the real surprise came when a few of the alpha particles actually bounced back off of the gold foil, and completely reversed their direction.

Rutherford drew the following three conclusions from the results of this experiment:

1. Since most alpha particles passed through undeflected, the atom must be mostly empty space.

2. Since some of the particles deflected at an angle, and a few of them reversed direction, there must be a dense, positively charged central core of the atom that is repelling the positively charged alpha particles as they come near the center of the gold atoms. Rutherford named this core the *nucleus* of the atom.

The Rutherford model of the atom places electrons in orbit around the nucleus.

3. The atom must consist of a dense, positively charged nucleus that contains most of the mass of the atom. The electrons are scattered at a great distance around the nucleus, and orbit the nucleus like the planets orbit the sun. The empty space in the atom is the space between the nucleus and the electrons.

This model of the atom is often called the *Rutherford planetary model of the atom*.

BOHR MODEL OF THE ATOM

Excited, low pressure gases each give off their own bright-line spectrum.

In 1913, Niels Bohr made an important improvement to the Rutherford model of the atom. He observed that excited hydrogen gas gave off a spectrum of colors when viewed through a spectroscope. But the spectrum was not continuous; that is, the colors were bright, sharp lines that were separate from each other. It had long been known that every low pressure, excited gas emitted its own special spectrum in this way, but Bohr was the first to associate the bright-line spectra of these gases, particularly hydrogen, with a model of the atom.

Bohr proposed that the electrons orbiting the nucleus of an atom do not radiate energy in the form of light while they are *in* a particular orbit, but only when they *change* orbits. Furthermore, an electron cannot orbit at just any radius around the nucleus, but only certain selected (quantized) orbits.

The two postulates of the Bohr model of the atom are summarized below.

1. Electrons orbiting the nucleus of an atom can only orbit in certain quantized orbits, and no others. These orbits from the nucleus outward are designated $n = 1, 2, 3...$, and the electron has energy in each of these orbits E_1, E_2, E_3, and so on. The energies of electrons are typically measured in *electron-volts* (*eV*), which is a very small unit of energy. The lowest energy (in the orbit nearest the nucleus) is called the *ground state energy*.

2. Electrons can change orbits when they absorb or emit energy.

   (a) When an electron absorbs *exactly* enough energy to reach a higher energy level—no more, no less—it jumps up to that level. An electron isn't limited to jumping to the level just above it. If it absorbs enough energy, it can jump to a level two, three, or more levels above it. If the energy offered to the electron is not exactly enough to raise it to a higher level, the electron will ignore the energy and let it pass.

   The only exception to this is if an electron absorbs energy equal to or greater than the amount needed to lift it to the highest energy level of its atom. Once it absorbs enough energy to lift it to the highest energy level, it can escape from the atom altogether, and any excess energy is converted to kinetic energy.

   (b) When an electron is in a higher energy level, it can jump down to a lower energy level by releasing energy in the form of a photon of light (see diagram on the next page). The energy of the emitted photon is exactly equal to the difference between the energy levels the electron moves between. As when it absorbs energy, an electron can jump down one, two, or more levels depending on how much energy it releases.

Example: Consider the energy level diagram for a particular atom shown below.

Energy above
ground state

$E_4 = 7$ eV

$E_3 = 6$ eV

$E_2 = 4$ eV

$E_1 = 0$ eV

(A)   An electron begins in the ground state of this atom. How much energy must be absorbed by the electron to reach the fourth energy level?

(B)   How many possible ways can this atom emit a photon if the electron starts in the fourth energy level?

(C)   The electron drops from E_4 to E_2 and emits a photon, then drops from E_2 to E_1 and emits a second photon. Which of these emitted photons has the higher frequency?

Solution:

(A)   Since the energy levels are labeled with the energy of the electron above ground state in each case, the electron would need 7 eV to jump from the ground state energy to E_4.

(B)   If the electron starts at E_4, the possible downward transitions are: 4 to 3, 4 to 2, 4 to 1, then if the electron hesitates at a lower level and then continues to drop, we must also include 3 to 2, 3 to 1, and 2 to 1. There are six possible transitions in all, and thus six possible ways a photon can be emitted.

(C)   When the electron drops from E_4 to E_2, a photon of energy 3 eV is emitted. When the electron drops from E_2 to E_1, a photon of energy 4 eV is emitted. The second transition results in a higher energy photon than the first, and since energy is proportional to frequency, the second photon must also have a higher frequency.

The Bohr model, though an improvement over previous models, is still considered an incomplete and inaccurate description of the atom.

ATOMIC PHYSICS REVIEW QUESTIONS

1. Which of the following was a result of Rutherford's alpha-scattering experiment?

   (A) The electrons in the gold foil absorbed the alpha particles and changed energy levels.

   (B) Most of the alpha particles passed through the foil undeflected.

   (C) A few of the alpha particles knocked the nucleus completely out of the atom.

   (D) A large percentage of alpha particles were turned back when striking the foil.

   (E) The gold foil began to emit a bright-line spectrum.

2. Which of the following is NOT one of the conclusions drawn by Rutherford after his alpha-scattering experiment?

   (A) There is a large space between the nucleus of the atom and the electrons.

   (B) The electrons orbit the nucleus of the atom.

   (C) The nucleus is positively charged.

   (D) The atom is neutral.

   (E) Electrons can change orbits when they absorb or emit energy.

3. An emission spectrum is produced when

   (A) electrons in an excited gas jump up to a higher energy level and release photons.

   (B) electrons in an excited gas jump down to a lower energy level and release photons.

   (C) electrons are released from the outer orbitals of an excited gas.

   (D) an unstable nucleus releases energy.

   (E) light is shined on a metal surface and electrons are released.

4. Consider the electron energy level diagram for a particular atom shown.

   Energy above
   ground state

   ———————— 5 eV
   ———————— 4 eV
   ———————— 3 eV
   ———————— 2 eV

   ———●———— 0

   An electron is in the ground state energy level, and 5 eV is the highest energy level present in the atom. If a photon of energy 6 eV is given to the electron, which of the following will occur?

   (A) The electron will ignore the photon since the photon's energy does not match the energy levels.

   (B) The electron will absorb the photon, jump up to the 5 eV level shown, and convert the remainder of the photon's energy into kinetic energy, but will stay in the 5 eV energy level.

   (C) The electron will absorb the photon, jump out of the atom completely, and convert the remainder of the photon's energy into kinetic energy.

   (D) The electron will absorb the photon, jump up to the 5 eV level, then go back down to the 4 eV level.

   (E) The electron will jump up to the 3 eV level, then immediately go back down the ground state.

5. Consider the electron energy level diagram for hydrogen shown.

   ——————————————— $E_4 = -0.85$ eV
   ——————————————— $E_3 = -1.5$ eV
   ——————————————— $E_2 = -3.4$ eV
   ——————————————— $E_1 = -13.6$ eV

   An electron in the ground state of a hydrogen atom has an energy of -13.6 eV, and 0 eV is the highest energy level present in a hydrogen atom. Which of the following energies is NOT a possible energy for a photon emitted from hydrogen?

   (A) 1.9 eV

   (B) 13.6 eV

   (C) 0.65 eV

   (D) 11.1 eV

   (E) 10.2 eV

SOLUTIONS TO ATOMIC PHYSICS REVIEW QUESTIONS

1. B

Since there is such a large space between the nuclei of adjacent atoms, most of the alpha particles passed through the foil undeflected.

2. E

Rutherford did not yet know that electrons were in energy levels. Bohr's model of the atom placed the electrons in quantized energy levels.

3. B

When electrons jump back to lower energy levels, they emit energy as photons.

4. C

When an electron absorbs enough energy to completely escape the atom, we say that the atom is *ionized*, and the energy remaining, in this case 1 eV, is converted to kinetic energy.

5. D

An electron emits a photon of energy that corresponds exactly to the difference in two energy levels, and 11.1 eV does not correspond to any energy differences in the hydrogen atom.

THINGS TO REMEMBER

- Rutherford model of the atom
- Bohr model of the atom

Chapter 22: **Nuclear and Particle Physics**

- Nuclear Structure
- Nuclear Binding Energy
- Nuclear Reactions

We've established that the atom consists of a positively charged nucleus surrounded by electrons in quantized energy levels. Let's take a look at the nucleus of the atom.

NUCLEAR STRUCTURE

The nucleus is made up of positively charged protons, as well as neutrons, which have no charge. The proton has exactly the same charge as an electron, but is positive. The neutron is actually made up of a proton and an electron bound together to create the neutral particle. A proton is about 1,800 times more massive than an electron, which makes a neutron only very slightly more massive than a proton. We say that a proton has a mass of approximately one *atomic mass unit*, (u). The *atomic number* (Z) of an element is equal to the number of protons found in an atom of that element, and fundamentally is an indication of the charge on the nucleus of that element. All atoms of a given element have the same atomic number. In other words, the number of protons an atom has defines what kind of element it is. The total number of neutrons and protons in an atom is called the *mass number* (A) of that element. The symbol $_Z^A X$ is used to show both the atomic number and the mass number of an X atom, where Z is the atomic number and A is the mass number.

Even though the number of protons must be the same for all atoms of an element, the number of neutrons, and thus the mass number, can be different. Atoms of the same element with different masses are known as isotopes of one another. For example, carbon-12 is a carbon atom with 6 protons and 6 neutrons, while carbon-14 is a carbon

> The nucleus contains protons and neutrons.

> The atomic number Z is the number of protons; the mass number A is the number of protons and neutrons.

> *Isotopes* are atoms containing the same number of protons but different numbers of neutrons.

atom with 6 protons and 8 neutrons. We would write these two isotopes of carbon as $^{12}_{6}C$ and $^{14}_{6}C$.

Table 22.1 below summarizes the basic features of protons, neutrons, and electrons. Notice that we use an H to symbolize the proton, since the proton is a hydrogen nucleus.

Table 22.1: Properties of Subatomic Particles

Particle	Symbol	Relative Mass	Charge	Location
Proton	$^{1}_{1}H$	1	+1	nucleus
Neutron	$^{1}_{0}n$	1	0	nucleus
Electron	$^{0}_{-1}e$ or e^-	0	−1	electron orbitals around the nucleus

Example: Determine the number of protons, neutrons, and electrons in a neutral atom of iron $^{56}_{26}Fe$.

Solution: This isotope of iron has an atomic number of 26 and a mass number of 56. Therefore, it will have 26 protons, 26 electrons, and 56 − 26 = 30 neutrons.

NUCLEAR BINDING ENERGY

Since positive charges repel each other, you might wonder why protons stay together in the nucleus of the atom. There must be a force holding the protons together that is greater than the electrostatic repulsion between them. This force is called the *strong nuclear force*, and is a result of the binding energy of the nucleus. But where does this energy that holds the nucleus together come from?

> Mass is converted into nuclear binding energy to hold the nucleus together.

According to Einstein's famous equation $E = mc^2$, mass and energy can be converted into one another. When a nucleus is assembled, each proton and neutron give up a little of their mass to be converted into binding energy. For example, if you start with two protons and two neutrons, you have a total of 4 atomic mass units. But if these particles are combined into a helium $^{4}_{2}He$ nucleus, the resulting mass of the helium nucleus is less than 4 atomic mass units, since some of the mass of the protons and neutrons has been converted into binding energy to hold the nucleus together. Likewise, when a nucleus is split, it doesn't need all of its original binding energy anymore, and some of that energy is released as heat.

NUCLEAR REACTIONS

Radioactive Decay

At the end of the 19th century, scientists discovered elements that continuously emitted mysterious rays. These elements were identified as being *radioactive*. A radioactive element spontaneously emits particles from its nucleus because the energy of the nucleus is unstable. Examples of naturally occurring radioactive elements are uranium $^{238}_{92}U$, radium $^{226}_{88}Ra$, and carbon $^{14}_{6}C$.

There are four types of particles that can be emitted when an element undergoes radioactive decay:

> Four types of radioactive decay: alpha, beta, gamma, and positron.

1. *Alpha decay.* Uranium, for example, undergoes alpha decay, meaning that it emits an *alpha particle* from its nucleus. An alpha particle is a helium nucleus, consisting of 2 protons and 2 neutrons. When an element emits an alpha particle, its nucleus loses 2 atomic numbers and 4 mass numbers, and thus changes into another element, called the *daughter element*. But what would this element be? We can write the nuclear equation for the radioactive decay of uranium as

    $$^{238}_{92}U \rightarrow\ ^{A}_{Z}X\ +\ ^{4}_{2}He,$$

    where X is the daughter element and $^{4}_{2}He$ is the alpha particle. The atomic number on the left must equal the sum of the atomic numbers on the right, since charge and mass are conserved in this process. The same is true for the mass numbers on the left and right. So, the daughter element has an atomic number $Z = 92 - 2 = 90$ and a mass number $A = 238 - 4 = 234$. Uranium decays into the daughter element $^{234}_{90}Th$, thorium.

2. *Beta decay.* A *beta particle* is the name given to an electron emitted from the nucleus of a radioactive element. But what is an electron doing in the nucleus of an atom? Remember that we described the neutron in the nucleus of an atom as being a proton and an electron bound together. Beta decay is really just a neutron emitting an electron and becoming a proton. Thus, the daughter element resulting from beta decay is one atomic number higher than the parent nucleus, but the mass number essentially does not change. For example, carbon $^{14}_{6}C$ is a radioactive element that undergoes beta decay. The decay equation is

    $$^{14}_{6}C \rightarrow\ ^{A}_{Z}X\ +\ ^{0}_{-1}e\ *.$$

---

*In addition, a small, almost undetectable particle called an *antineutrino* is released in this reaction. You will not need to be familiar with this concept for the purposes of the SAT Subject Test: Physics.

We use the same symbol for a beta particle as we do for an electron. The daughter element must have an atomic number of 6 – (–1) = 7 and a mass number of 14 – 0 = 14. The daughter element is $^{14}_{7}N$, nitrogen.

3. *Gamma decay.* Some radioactive elements emit a gamma ray, a very high energy electromagnetic wave that has no charge or mass. Only the energy of the nucleus changes during gamma ray emission and neither Z nor A changes.

4. *Positron decay (usually considered a form of beta decay).* A positron is exactly like an electron except for the fact that it is positively charged. A positron is not a proton, as their masses and other features are very different. Positron decay equations are typically not included on the SAT Subject Test: Physics.

Radioactive Decay Half-Life

> *Half-life* is the time it takes for half the atoms in a radioactive sample to decay.

The *half-life* of a radioactive sample is the time it takes for half of the atoms in the sample to decay. For example, let's say we begin with one kilogram of the radioactive element radium in a sealed container. The half-life of radium is 1,600 years. After 1,600 years, our descendants could check the container and find only half a kilogram of radium. There would still be one kilogram of substance in the container, but half of it would be radium and the other half would be the daughter of radium, which happens to be radon gas. After 1,600 more years, the container would contain only one-fourth of a kilogram of radium, and so on. We can plot a graph of the amount of radium remaining vs. time on the axes below.

This type of curve is called an *exponential decay curve.*

Example: Cobalt $^{60}_{27}$Co has a half-life of 5 years. If we start with a 100-gram sample of cobalt, how much cobalt remains after 20 years?

Solution: Let's organize our data in a table.

Amount of Co Remaining	Half-Lives	Time (years)
100 g	0	0 (today)
50 g	1	5
25 g	2	10
12.5 g	3	15
6.25 g	4	20

Thus, after 20 years, 4 half-lives have passed, and 6.25 grams of cobalt remain.

Fusion   *more powerful than fission*

Fusion occurs when small nuclei combine into larger nuclei and energy is released. Many stars, including our sun, power themselves by fusing four hydrogen nuclei to make one helium nucleus. The fusion process is "clean," meaning no harmful radioactive products are produced as a result of the reaction, and a large amount of energy is released.

> *Fusion* is the combining of small nuclei into larger ones, releasing energy.

Example: The element tritium $^{3}_{1}$H is combined with another element to form helium $^{4}_{2}$He and a neutron, along with the release of energy. The equation for this fusion reaction is

$$^{3}_{1}H + {}^{A}_{Z}X \rightarrow {}^{4}_{2}He + {}^{1}_{0}n.$$

What is the unknown element X?

Solution: The numbers on the left must equal the numbers on the right, so the atomic number of element X is $Z = 2 + 0 - 1 = 1$, and the mass number for X is $A = 4 + 1 - 3 = 2$. Element X is $^{2}_{1}$H, a hydrogen isotope called *deuterium*.

Fission

Fission is a process in which a large nucleus splits into smaller nuclei. Fission is usually caused artificially by shooting a slow neutron at a large atom, such as uranium, which absorbs the neutron and splits into two smaller atoms, along with the release of more neutrons and some energy.

> *Fission* is the splitting of a large nucleus into smaller ones, with the release of neutrons and energy.

Example: A fission reaction occurs when uranium $^{235}_{92}U$ absorbs a slow neutron and then splits into xenon and strontium, releasing three neutrons and some energy. The equation for this fission reaction is

$$^{235}_{92}U + {}^{1}_{0}n \rightarrow {}^{140}_{54}Xe + {}^{A}_{Z}Sr + 3{}^{1}_{0}n + energy.$$

What are Z and A for strontium?

Solution: Once again, the numbers on the left equal the numbers on the right. Thus, $Z = 92 - 54 = 38$, and $A = 235 + 1 - 140 - 3(1) = 93$.

NUCLEAR AND PARTICLE PHYSICS REVIEW QUESTIONS

1. The neutral element magnesium $^{24}_{12}\text{Mg}$ has

    (A) 12 protons, 12 electrons, and 24 neutrons.

    (B) 12 protons, 12 electrons, and 12 neutrons.

    (C) 24 protons, 24 electrons, and 12 neutrons.

    (D) 24 protons, 12 electrons, and 12 neutrons.

    (E) 12 protons, 24 electrons, and 24 neutrons.

2. All isotopes of uranium have

    (A) the same atomic number and the same mass number.

    (B) different atomic numbers but the same mass number.

    (C) different atomic numbers and different mass numbers.

    (D) the same atomic number but different mass numbers.

    (E) no electrons.

3. Six protons and six neutrons are brought together to form a carbon nucleus, but the mass of the carbon nucleus is less than the sum of the masses of the individual particles that make up the nucleus. This missing mass, called the mass defect, has been

    (A) converted into the binding energy of the nucleus.

    (B) given off in a radioactive decay process.

    (C) converted into electrons.

    (D) converted into energy to hold the electrons in orbit.

    (E) emitted as light.

4. The isotope of thorium $^{234}_{90}\text{Th}$ undergoes alpha decay according to the equation

    $$^{234}_{90}\text{Th} \rightarrow {}^{A}_{Z}\text{X} + {}^{4}_{2}\text{He}.$$

    The element X is

    (A) $^{238}_{92}\text{U}$

    (B) $^{230}_{88}\text{Ra}$

    (C) $^{236}_{94}\text{Pu}$

    (D) $^{238}_{88}\text{Ra}$

    (E) $^{232}_{92}\text{U}$

5. The isotope of cobalt $^{60}_{27}\text{Co}$ undergoes beta decay according to the equation

    $$^{60}_{27}\text{Co} \rightarrow {}^{A}_{Z}\text{X} + {}^{0}_{-1}\text{e}.$$

    The element X is

    (A) $^{60}_{26}\text{Fe}$

    (B) $^{56}_{25}\text{Mn}$

    (C) $^{60}_{28}\text{Ni}$

    (D) $^{60}_{29}\text{Cu}$

    (E) $^{61}_{27}\text{Co}$

6. The half-life of a certain element is 4 years. What fraction of a sample of that isotope will remain after 12 years?

(A) $\dfrac{1}{2}$

(B) $\dfrac{1}{3}$

(C) $\dfrac{1}{4}$

(D) $\dfrac{1}{8}$

(E) $\dfrac{1}{12}$

7. Consider the following nuclear equation:

$$_{92}^{235}U + _{0}^{1}n \rightarrow _{56}^{139}Ba + _{36}^{94}Kr + 3\,_{0}^{1}n$$

This equation describes the process of

(A) radioactivity.

(B) fission.

(C) fusion.

(D) electron energy level transitions.

(E) reduction and oxidation.

SOLUTIONS TO NUCLEAR AND PARTICLE PHYSICS REVIEW QUESTIONS

1. B

The atomic number 12 implies both 12 protons and 12 electrons, and the mass number 24 is the sum of protons and neutrons, giving 12 neutrons.

2. D

All isotopes of a particular element must have the same atomic number (number of protons), since this number identifies the element, but can have a different mass number (number of neutrons).

3. A

Each particle that makes up the nucleus gives up a little mass to be converted into energy by $E = mc^2$ to bind the nucleus together.

4. B

The atomic number Z of element X is found by $90 = Z + 2$, so $Z = 88$, and the mass number A is found by $234 = A + 4$, so $A = 230$. The element X is radium.

5. C

The atomic number Z of element X is found by $27 = Z + (-1)$, so $Z = 28$, and the mass number A is found by $60 = A + 0$, so $A = 60$. The element X is nickel.

6. D

If the half-life is 4 years, then 12 years represents 3 half-lives. If we cut the sample in half three times, we get one-eighth of the sample remaining.

7. B

A neutron is absorbed by a uranium atom, and the atom splits into barium and krypton and three neutrons.

THINGS TO REMEMBER

- Nuclear structure
- Nuclear binding energy
- Nuclear reactions
  - Radioactive decay
  - Radioactive decay half-life
  - Fusion
  - Fission

Chapter 23: **Special Relativity**

- **The Two Postulates in the Theory of Special Relativity**

In the summer of 1905, Albert Einstein submitted to a journal of physics a paper titled "On the Electrodynamics of Moving Bodies" that contained a new theory we now refer to as the *theory of special relativity*. This theory completely challenged our notion of space and time, two concepts we previously believed to be absolute and constant throughout the universe. Yet Einstein clearly showed that it is neither space nor time that is absolute in our universe, but another quantity.

THE TWO POSTULATES IN THE THEORY OF SPECIAL RELATIVITY

To understand special relativity, we must accept two postulates:

⌐ all forces are accounted for

1. The laws of physics are the same in all inertial reference frames.
2. The speed of light is constant in all reference frames, regardless of any relative motion between an observer and the light source.

> There are two postulates in the theory of special relativity.

The first postulate is not difficult to accept. An inertial reference frame is one that is at rest or moving with a constant velocity (constant speed in a straight line). If you throw a ball straight up in the air while you are in a car that is at rest, it comes back down and lands in your hand again. If your car is moving at a constant velocity and you throw the ball straight up, it still comes back down in your hand, since the car, you, and the ball all have the same horizontal velocity. This can be extended to any physics experiment that you can think of. In other words, there is not one special inertial reference frame that is better than or different from any other when it comes to making physical measurements. This leads us to the second postulate, which is a little more difficult for us to accept.

> An inertial reference frame is one that has a constant velocity, including a velocity of zero.

The second postulate of special relativity states that everyone in any reference frame will measure the same value for the speed of light regardless of how fast he or she is moving relative to the light source. If I am at rest relative to your flashlight and you turn it on, I measure the speed of the light as being $c = 3 \times 10^8$ m/s, and so do you. But if you remain at rest, and I begin moving at 100 miles per hour, Newtonian physics says that we would not agree on the speed of the light beam since I am moving and you are not. However, Einstein's second postulate states that we will both still measure the speed of the light beam as $c = 3 \times 10^8$ m/s. Even if I move at half the speed of light (0.5c), the second postulate still holds true; that is, you and I will still agree on the speed of the light beam, $c = 3 \times 10^8$ m/s. This can be difficult for us to accept, since we are used to taking into account the relative motion between reference frames when calculating velocities. This leads us to some interesting effects on length and time.

> The speed of light is constant for all observers.

The basic equation for the speed of an object is

$$v = \frac{\text{distance}}{\text{time}}.$$

The speed of light is written no differently. Substituting the speed of light into the equation, we have

$$c = \frac{\text{distance}}{\text{time}}.$$

We've seen that all observers must agree on the value of the speed of light c, regardless of their frame of reference. This means that all observers must agree on the ratio of the two, but they do not have to agree on the value of distance or the value of time. In other words, if you remain still while I accelerate away from you, the closer I get to the speed of light relative to your position, the more we will disagree on measurements of distance and time. And since we disagree on measurements of distance, we will also disagree on the lengths of objects. This gives rise to the *relativistic effects* on length and time:

> Length contracts in the direction of motion for a moving object.

An observer who measures the length of an object moving relative to the observer will measure the length of the object as being shorter (contracted) in the direction of motion compared to the measurement of its length when it is at rest relative to the observer.

In other words, a moving object is shorter than when it is at rest. In order to keep the ratio of length to time constant (equal to c), time must also change:

A moving clock will run more slowly than a clock that is at rest.

> Moving clocks run more slowly than clocks at rest.

This is called *time dilation*, and has been verified experimentally many times. This means that the ticks of a moving clock are farther apart than the ticks of a clock that is at rest.

Time is simply the duration between two events, and since any two observers must agree on the speed of light, they may not agree on the length of a moving object or how much time has passed between two events. Relativistic effects occur at all speeds, but they only become measurable at speeds above about ten percent the speed of light.

There is one other relativistic effect we should discuss. In his 1905 paper, Einstein suggested that energy and mass are actually different aspects of the same phenomenon. The famous equation that links energy to mass is

$$E = mc^2.$$

This equation tells us that energy and mass can be converted into one another, and that their value is connected by a constant, the speed of light squared. Since the speed of light is a huge number, a little mass can be converted into a lot of energy, as history has witnessed with the release of nuclear binding energy when the nuclei of atoms are split and that energy is released. But not only can mass be converted into energy, energy can be converted into mass.

> Mass and energy can be converted into one another.

A moving object has kinetic energy, and experiments have shown that at high velocities, the kinetic energy of a moving object such as a proton begins turning into mass. As a proton approaches a speed near the speed of light, its mass becomes larger and larger, as verified by momentum measurements. This puts an ultimate speed limit on moving objects, the speed of light. The equations of relativity tell us that if it were possible for an object to achieve a speed equal to the speed of light, it would have zero length, its clock would stop, and it would have infinite mass. Since none of these are possible in our universe as far as we know, achieving the speed of light is impossible.

> Mass increases as speed increases.

Our discussion of special relativity can be summarized as follows:

- *All inertial reference frames are equivalent.*
- *The speed of light is constant for all observers.*
- *An observer watching a moving object will see its length contract in the direction of motion, its clock slow down, and its mass increase by the equation $E = mc^2$.*

Example: Two spaceships pass you at a speed near the speed of light, each containing a meter stick, a clock, and a 1 kg block. For each of the following diagrams, describe the changes in the length of the meter stick, the ticks of the clock, and the mass of the 1 kg block.

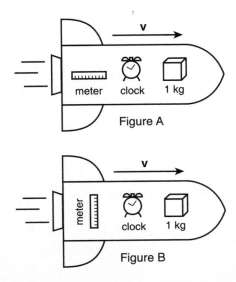

Figure A

Figure B

Solution: In Figure A, the meter stick is aligned in the direction of motion of the ship. Thus, you would measure the meter stick as being shorter than one meter. You would also measure the clock as running slower, that is, more time between ticks, and the mass as larger than one kilogram.

In Figure B, you would still measure the clock as running slower and the mass as larger than one kilogram, but since the meter stick is aligned perpendicular to the motion of the ship, you would still measure it as being one meter long, although a little thinner, since length contraction occurs only in the direction of motion.

If an astronaut in the ship Figure A looked at your reference frame as he was passing you, he would see your meter stick as being shorter than one meter, your clock running slower, and your mass as larger. Since his reference frame is as good as yours in which to make measurements, he should measure the same effects in your reference frame as you measured in his. However, if the astronaut looked at the ship in Figure B, he would see that the length, mass, and time on the other ship would be the same as on his. This is because the two ships are moving at the same speed relative to an outside observer and thus are in the same frame of reference; additionally, their speed relative to one another would be zero.

SPECIAL RELATIVITY REVIEW QUESTIONS

1. A pilot of a spaceship traveling at 90% the speed of light (0.9c) turns on the ship's laser headlights just as it passes a stationary observer. Which of the following statements is true?

   (A) The pilot will measure the speed of the light coming out of the headlights as c, and the observer will measure the speed of the light as 0.9c.

   (B) The pilot will measure the speed of the light coming out of the headlights as c, and the observer will measure the speed of the light as 1.9c.

   (C) The pilot will measure the speed of the light coming out of the headlights as 0.9c, and the observer will measure the speed of the light as 1.9c.

   (D) The pilot will measure the speed of the light coming out of the headlights as 1.9c, and the observer will measure the speed of the light as 0.9c.

   (E) The pilot will measure the speed of the light coming out of the headlights as c, and the observer will measure the speed of the light as c.

2. Which of the following graphs best represents the length L of a horizontal meter stick traveling horizontally with speed v as it approaches the speed of light?

   shortened

   (A)

   (B)

   (C)

   (D)

   (E)

3. Two identical, very precise clocks are started at the same time. One clock is taken on a trip at a very high speed, and the other is left at rest on Earth. When the traveling clock is returned to Earth, it shows that one hour has passed. Which of the following could be the time that has passed on the Earth-bound clock?

   (A) 30 minutes

   (B) 45 minutes

   (C) 59 minutes

   (D) 1 hour

   (E) 2 hours

4. The mass of an object increases as its speed increases. This increase in mass comes from

   (A) nuclear binding energy.

   (B) electron energy in the ground state.

   (C) potential energy being converted into mass by $E = mc^2$.

   (D) kinetic energy being converted into mass by $E = mc^2$.

   (E) the lower pressure on the mass.

SOLUTIONS TO SPECIAL RELATIVITY REVIEW QUESTIONS

1. E

The speed of light is constant to all observers, and thus all observers would measure the speed of the light as c.

2. C

The length gets shorter (contracts) as the speed gets higher, so that the length it approaches zero at $v = c$.

3. E

The traveling clock will have run more slowly than the Earth-bound clock, and thus more time will have passed on the Earth-bound clock than on the traveling clock.

4. D

Some of the kinetic energy converts into mass as the speed of the object approaches the speed of light.

THINGS TO REMEMBER

- The two postulates in the theory of special relativity
  - The laws of physics are the same in all inertial reference frames.
  - The speed of light is constant in all reference frames, regardless of any relative motion between an observer and the light source.

Part Four

Practice Tests

HOW TO TAKE THE PRACTICE TESTS

Before taking a practice test, find a quiet room where you can work uninterrupted for one hour. Make sure you have several No. 2 pencils with erasers.

Use the answer grid provided to record your answers. Guidelines for scoring your test appear on the reverse side of the answer grid. Time yourself. Spend no more than one hour on the 75 questions. Once you start the practice test, don't stop until you've reached the one-hour time limit. You'll find an answer key and complete answer explanations following the test. Be sure to read the explanations for all questions, even those you answered correctly.

Good luck!

HOW TO CALCULATE YOUR SCORE

Step 1: Figure out your raw score. Use the answer key to count the number of questions you answered correctly and the number of questions you answered incorrectly. (Do not count any questions you left blank.) Multiply the number wrong by 0.25 and subtract the result from the number correct. Round the result to the nearest whole number. This is your raw score.

SAT Subject Test: Physics Practice Test 1

Number right	Number wrong	Raw score

$$\boxed{} \; - \; \left(0.25 \times \boxed{}\right) \; = \; \boxed{}$$

Step 2: Find your scaled score. In the Score Conversion Table below, find your raw score (rounded to the nearest whole number) in one of the columns to the left. The score directly to the right of that number will be your scaled score.

A note on your practice test scores: Don't take these scores too literally. Practice test conditions cannot precisely mirror real test conditions. Your actual SAT Subject Test: Physics score will almost certainly vary from your diagnostic and practice test scores. However, your scores on the diagnostic and practice tests will give you a rough idea of your range on the actual exam.

Score Conversion Table

Raw	Scaled	Raw	Scaled	Raw	Scaled	Raw	Scaled	Raw	Scaled	Raw	Scaled
75	800	59	780	43	690	27	590	11	480	−5	380
74	800	58	770	42	680	26	580	10	480	−6	370
73	800	57	770	41	670	25	580	9	470	−7	370
72	800	56	760	40	670	24	570	8	470	−8	360
71	800	55	760	39	660	23	570	7	460	−9	350
70	800	54	750	38	650	22	560	6	450	−10	350
69	800	53	750	37	650	21	550	5	450	−11	340
68	800	52	740	36	640	20	540	4	440	−12	330
67	800	51	730	35	640	19	540	3	430	−13	330
66	800	50	730	34	630	18	530	2	430	−14	320
65	800	49	720	33	630	17	530	1	420	−15	310
64	800	48	720	32	620	16	520	0	410	−16	310
63	800	47	710	31	610	15	510	−1	410	−17	300
62	790	46	700	30	610	14	510	−2	400	−18	290
61	790	45	700	29	600	13	500	−3	390	−19	290
60	780	44	690	28	600	12	490	−4	390		

Practice Test 1
Answer Grid

1. Ⓐ Ⓑ Ⓒ Ⓓ Ⓔ
2. Ⓐ Ⓑ Ⓒ Ⓓ Ⓔ
3. Ⓐ Ⓑ Ⓒ Ⓓ Ⓔ
4. Ⓐ Ⓑ Ⓒ Ⓓ Ⓔ
5. Ⓐ Ⓑ Ⓒ Ⓓ Ⓔ
6. Ⓐ Ⓑ Ⓒ Ⓓ Ⓔ
7. Ⓐ Ⓑ Ⓒ Ⓓ Ⓔ
8. Ⓐ Ⓑ Ⓒ Ⓓ Ⓔ
9. Ⓐ Ⓑ Ⓒ Ⓓ Ⓔ
10. Ⓐ Ⓑ Ⓒ Ⓓ Ⓔ
11. Ⓐ Ⓑ Ⓒ Ⓓ Ⓔ
12. Ⓐ Ⓑ Ⓒ Ⓓ Ⓔ
13. Ⓐ Ⓑ Ⓒ Ⓓ Ⓔ
14. Ⓐ Ⓑ Ⓒ Ⓓ Ⓔ
15. Ⓐ Ⓑ Ⓒ Ⓓ Ⓔ
16. Ⓐ Ⓑ Ⓒ Ⓓ Ⓔ
17. Ⓐ Ⓑ Ⓒ Ⓓ Ⓔ
18. Ⓐ Ⓑ Ⓒ Ⓓ Ⓔ
19. Ⓐ Ⓑ Ⓒ Ⓓ Ⓔ
20. Ⓐ Ⓑ Ⓒ Ⓓ Ⓔ
21. Ⓐ Ⓑ Ⓒ Ⓓ Ⓔ
22. Ⓐ Ⓑ Ⓒ Ⓓ Ⓔ
23. Ⓐ Ⓑ Ⓒ Ⓓ Ⓔ
24. Ⓐ Ⓑ Ⓒ Ⓓ Ⓔ
25. Ⓐ Ⓑ Ⓒ Ⓓ Ⓔ

26. Ⓐ Ⓑ Ⓒ Ⓓ Ⓔ
27. Ⓐ Ⓑ Ⓒ Ⓓ Ⓔ
28. Ⓐ Ⓑ Ⓒ Ⓓ Ⓔ
29. Ⓐ Ⓑ Ⓒ Ⓓ Ⓔ
30. Ⓐ Ⓑ Ⓒ Ⓓ Ⓔ
31. Ⓐ Ⓑ Ⓒ Ⓓ Ⓔ
32. Ⓐ Ⓑ Ⓒ Ⓓ Ⓔ
33. Ⓐ Ⓑ Ⓒ Ⓓ Ⓔ
34. Ⓐ Ⓑ Ⓒ Ⓓ Ⓔ
35. Ⓐ Ⓑ Ⓒ Ⓓ Ⓔ
36. Ⓐ Ⓑ Ⓒ Ⓓ Ⓔ
37. Ⓐ Ⓑ Ⓒ Ⓓ Ⓔ
38. Ⓐ Ⓑ Ⓒ Ⓓ Ⓔ
39. Ⓐ Ⓑ Ⓒ Ⓓ Ⓔ
40. Ⓐ Ⓑ Ⓒ Ⓓ Ⓔ
41. Ⓐ Ⓑ Ⓒ Ⓓ Ⓔ
42. Ⓐ Ⓑ Ⓒ Ⓓ Ⓔ
43. Ⓐ Ⓑ Ⓒ Ⓓ Ⓔ
44. Ⓐ Ⓑ Ⓒ Ⓓ Ⓔ
45. Ⓐ Ⓑ Ⓒ Ⓓ Ⓔ
46. Ⓐ Ⓑ Ⓒ Ⓓ Ⓔ
47. Ⓐ Ⓑ Ⓒ Ⓓ Ⓔ
48. Ⓐ Ⓑ Ⓒ Ⓓ Ⓔ
49. Ⓐ Ⓑ Ⓒ Ⓓ Ⓔ
50. Ⓐ Ⓑ Ⓒ Ⓓ Ⓔ

51. Ⓐ Ⓑ Ⓒ Ⓓ Ⓔ
52. Ⓐ Ⓑ Ⓒ Ⓓ Ⓔ
53. Ⓐ Ⓑ Ⓒ Ⓓ Ⓔ
54. Ⓐ Ⓑ Ⓒ Ⓓ Ⓔ
55. Ⓐ Ⓑ Ⓒ Ⓓ Ⓔ
56. Ⓐ Ⓑ Ⓒ Ⓓ Ⓔ
57. Ⓐ Ⓑ Ⓒ Ⓓ Ⓔ
58. Ⓐ Ⓑ Ⓒ Ⓓ Ⓔ
59. Ⓐ Ⓑ Ⓒ Ⓓ Ⓔ
60. Ⓐ Ⓑ Ⓒ Ⓓ Ⓔ
61. Ⓐ Ⓑ Ⓒ Ⓓ Ⓔ
62. Ⓐ Ⓑ Ⓒ Ⓓ Ⓔ
63. Ⓐ Ⓑ Ⓒ Ⓓ Ⓔ
64. Ⓐ Ⓑ Ⓒ Ⓓ Ⓔ
65. Ⓐ Ⓑ Ⓒ Ⓓ Ⓔ
66. Ⓐ Ⓑ Ⓒ Ⓓ Ⓔ
67. Ⓐ Ⓑ Ⓒ Ⓓ Ⓔ
68. Ⓐ Ⓑ Ⓒ Ⓓ Ⓔ
69. Ⓐ Ⓑ Ⓒ Ⓓ Ⓔ
70. Ⓐ Ⓑ Ⓒ Ⓓ Ⓔ
71. Ⓐ Ⓑ Ⓒ Ⓓ Ⓔ
72. Ⓐ Ⓑ Ⓒ Ⓓ Ⓔ
73. Ⓐ Ⓑ Ⓒ Ⓓ Ⓔ
74. Ⓐ Ⓑ Ⓒ Ⓓ Ⓔ
75. Ⓐ Ⓑ Ⓒ Ⓓ Ⓔ

Practice Test 1

Part A

Directions: Each set of lettered choices below relates to the numbered questions immediately following it. Select the one lettered choice that best answers each question. A choice may be used once, more than once, or not at all in each set.

Questions 1–3 relate to the following graphs of displacement s vs. time t and velocity v vs. time t.

1. In which of the graphs is the velocity of the moving object constant? A

2. In which of the graphs does the moving object reverse its direction? D

3. Which of the graphs is equivalent to the displacement vs. time graph below? C

Questions 4–7 relate to the following nuclear equations.

(A) $^2_1\mathrm{H} + ^2_1\mathrm{H} \rightarrow {}^3_1\mathrm{H} + {}^1_1\mathrm{H} + \text{energy}$

(B) $^{226}_{88}\mathrm{Ra} \rightarrow {}^{222}_{86}\mathrm{Rn} + {}^4_2\mathrm{He}$

(C) $^{209}_{83}\mathrm{Bi} \rightarrow {}^{209}_{84}\mathrm{Po} + {}^0_{-1}\mathrm{e}$

(D) $^{235}_{92}\mathrm{U} + {}^1_0\mathrm{n} \rightarrow {}^{140}_{54}\mathrm{Xe} + {}^{94}_{38}\mathrm{Sr} + {}^1_2\mathrm{n}$

(E) $^4_2\mathrm{He} + {}^{27}_{13}\mathrm{Al} \rightarrow {}^{30}_{15}\mathrm{P} + {}^1_0\mathrm{n}$

4. Which of the above equations represents nuclear <u>fission</u>? D

5. Which of the above equations represents alpha decay? B

6. Which of the above equations represents beta decay? C

7. Which of the above equations represents nuclear fusion? A

GO ON TO THE NEXT PAGE

Questions 8–11 relate to the following equations or physical principles that might be used to solve certain problems.

(A) first law of thermodynamics (conservation of energy)
(B) second law of thermodynamics (law of entropy)
(C) ideal gas law
(D) heat of fusion and heat of vaporization equation
(E) heat engine efficiency

Select the choice that should be used to provide the best and most direct solution to each of the following problems.

8. If the pressure of a gas remains constant and the temperature is doubled, what happens to the volume of the gas? *C*

9. A new soft drink bottle is opened, allowing gas to escape into the atmosphere. As the gas escapes, how does its degree of disorder change? *B*

10. An unknown liquid at a high temperature is safely mixed with water until an equilibrium temperature is reached. How much heat was gained by the water? *A*

11. Heat is added to a block of ice of mass m until the entire block melts into liquid water. How much heat was required to melt the ice?

D

Questions 12–14 relate to the resistance-capacitance circuit and the choices below.

(A) zero
(B) V
(C) R
(D) C
(E) $\dfrac{V}{R}$

$V = I\,R$

$\dfrac{V}{R} = I$

12. Immediately after the switch S is closed, what is the voltage across the resistor R? *B*

13. Immediately after the switch S is closed, what is the current in the circuit? *E*

14. A very long time after the switch S has been closed, what is the current in the circuit?

A

GO ON TO THE NEXT PAGE

Part B

Directions: Each of the questions or incomplete statements below is followed by five answer choices. Select the one that is best in each case.

15. The graph above shows velocity v as a function of time t for a particle moving in a straight line. Graphs of displacement s vs. time t that are consistent with the v vs. t graph above include which of the following?

    (A) I only
    (B) III only
    (C) I and II only
    (D) II and III only
    (E) I, II, and III

16. You are sitting on a seat facing forward on an airplane with its wings parallel to the ground. The window shades of the airplane are closed, and the vibration of the plane is negligible. When you place your class ring on the end of a necklace chain and hold the other end in front of you, you notice that the chain and ring hang vertically and point directly to the floor of the airplane. Which of the following could be true of the airplane?

    I.   The airplane is at rest.
    II. The airplane is moving with a constant velocity.
    III. The airplane is increasing its speed.
    IV. The airplane is decreasing its speed.

    (A) I only
    (B) III only
    (C) I or II, but not III or IV
    (D) III or IV, but not I or II
    (E) IV only

17. If 400 g of water at 40°C is mixed with 100 g of water at 30°C, the resulting temperature of the water is

    (A) 13°C.
    (B) 26°C.
    (C) 36°C.
    (D) 38°C.
    (E) 44°C.

GO ON TO THE NEXT PAGE

18. A 40 Ω resistor in a closed circuit has 20 volts across it. The current flowing through the resistor is

    (A) 0.5 A.
    (B) 2 A.
    (C) 20 A.
    (D) 80 A.
    (E) 800 A.

    $V = IR$
    $20 = (40)(I)$

19. Two blocks each weighing 50 N are connected to the ends of a light string that is passed over a pulley. The tension in the string is

    (A) 25 N.
    (B) 50 N.
    (C) 100 N.
    (D) 200 N.
    (E) 500 N.

50 N

50 N

Questions 20–22 refer to the following.

A horizontal force F acts on a block of mass m that is initially at rest on a floor of negligible friction. The force acts for a time t and moves the block a displacement d.

20. The acceleration of the block is

    (A) Ft.
    (B) Fd.
    (C) $\dfrac{F}{m}$.
    (D) $\dfrac{m}{F}$.
    (E) $\dfrac{d}{t}$.

    $F = ma$
    $\dfrac{F}{m}$

21. The change in momentum of the block is

    (A) $\dfrac{F}{t}$.
    (B) $\dfrac{m}{t}$.
    (C) Fd.
    (D) Ft.
    (E) mt.

    avg.
    force!

22. The change in the kinetic energy of the block is

    (A) Fd.
    (B) $\dfrac{F}{d}$.
    (C) Ft.
    (D) $\dfrac{F}{t}$.
    (E) $\dfrac{d}{t}$.

    $W = Fd$

GO ON TO THE NEXT PAGE

A   B   −q   C   D   −4q   E

23. Two charges $-q$ and $-4q$ are located on a line as shown above. At which point could a positive charge be placed if it is to experience no force?

(A) A
(B) B
(C) C
(D) D
(E) E

24. A charge is placed near a magnetic field. In which of the following cases would the charge experience a force?

   I. The charge is placed inside the magnetic field and is not moving.

   II. The charge is moving and its velocity is perpendicular to the magnetic field lines.

   III. The charge is moving and its velocity is parallel to the magnetic field lines.

(A) I only
(B) I and II only
(C) II and III only
(D) II only
(E) III only

25. A bar magnet is moving through a stationary coil of wire. If the magnet suddenly stops halfway through the coil, which of the following will occur?

(A) The magnet will lose its magnetic field.
(B) The current induced in the coil will continue flowing in the same direction.
(C) The current induced in the coil will stop.
(D) The current induced in the coil will reverse direction.
(E) The magnet will be pushed out of the coil.

26. An ideal gas is enclosed in a container that has a fixed volume. If the temperature of the gas is increased, which of the following will also increase?

   I. The pressure against the walls of the container.

   II. The average kinetic energy of the gas molecules.

   III. The number of moles of gas in the container.

(A) I only
(B) I and II only
(C) II and III only
(D) II only
(E) III only

27. A neutral electroscope is shown above. If a positively charged rod is brought near the knob of the electroscope, which of the following statements is true?

(A) The electroscope can be charged negatively without the positively charged rod touching the knob and using a only grounding wire.
(B) The electroscope can be charged positively without the positively charged rod touching the knob and using only a grounding wire.
(C) The leaves of the electroscope are negatively charged.
(D) The knob of the electroscope is positively charged.
(E) The electroscope has a net positive charge.

GO ON TO THE NEXT PAGE

Questions 28–30 refer to the figure below, which represents a wave propagating along a string with a speed of 320 cm/s.

28. The wave is an example of a(n)

   (A) sound wave.
   (B) transverse wave.
   (C) electromagnetic wave.
   (D) longitudinal wave.
   (E) interference wave.

29. The frequency of the wave is

   (A) 1,280 Hz.
   (B) 640 Hz.
   (C) 320 Hz.
   (D) 80 Hz.
   (E) 40 Hz.

30. The amplitude of the wave is

   (A) 1 cm.
   (B) 2 cm.
   (C) 4 cm.
   (D) 8 cm.
   (E) 16 cm.

31. A generator is constructed by placing a coil of wire in a magnetic field. The coil is rotated in a clockwise direction in the magnetic field at a constant rate to induce a current in the wire. If the coil of wire is rotated in a counter-clockwise direction at the same constant rate, which of the following will occur?

   (A) The current in the coil will reverse its direction.
   (B) The current in the coil will stop flowing.
   (C) The current in the coil will continue to flow in the same direction as before.
   (D) The current in the coil will decrease steadily.
   (E) The current in the coil will increase steadily.

GO ON TO THE NEXT PAGE

Questions 32–33 relate to the positive charge following a circular path in a region of magnetic field in the figure below.

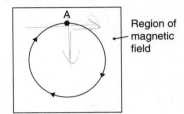

Region of magnetic field

32. At point A, what is the direction of the net force acting on the positive charge?

(A) →
(B) ←
(C) ↑
(D) ↓
(E) There is no net force acting on the charge at point A.

33. The direction of the magnetic field in the region shown is

(A) out of the page and perpendicular to it.
(B) into the page and perpendicular to it.
(C) toward the top of the page.
(D) toward the bottom of the page.
(E) to the right.

Questions 34–35 refer to the following.

A beam of light is incident onto a glass plate. Possible angles for the reflected and refracted rays are drawn in the figure below.

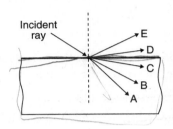

Incident ray

E
D
C
B
A

34. Which of the rays best represents the reflected ray?

(A) A
(B) B
(C) C
(D) D
(E) E

35. Which of the rays best represents the refracted ray?

(A) A
(B) B
(C) C
(D) D
(E) E

$F = \dfrac{C}{V}$

$ohm = \dfrac{V}{amp}$

Questions 36–38 relate to the two masses M_1 and M_2, which have a charge Q_1 and Q_2, respectively. The masses are initially separated by a distance r.

36. If the distance between the masses is doubled, which of the following is true?

   (A) The gravitational force will increase.

   (B) The electric force will increase.

   (C) The gravitational force will decrease, but the electric force will remain the same.

   (D) The electric force will decrease, but the gravitational force will remain the same.

   (E) Both the gravitational and electric forces will decrease.

37. If both masses are doubled, but the charge on each remains the same, which of the following is true?

   (A) The gravitational force will decrease.

   (B) The electric force will increase.

   (C) The gravitational force will increase, but the electric force will remain the same.

   (D) The electric force will increase, but the gravitational force will remain the same.

   (E) Both the gravitational and electric forces will decrease.

38. If the two charged masses are placed in space so that no other forces affect them, and they remain at a distance r apart indefinitely, which of the following must be true?

   (A) Both charges are positive.

   (B) Q_1 is positive and Q_2 is negative.

   (C) Q_1 is negative and Q_2 is positive.

   (D) $Q_1 = Q_2$

   (E) $M_1 = M_2$

39. An ohm is defined as one volt per ampere, and an ampere is a coulomb per second. A farad, the unit for capacitance, is a coulomb per volt. An ohm times a farad is a unit of

   (A) voltage.

   (B) resistance.

   (C) energy.

   (D) time.

   (E) charge.

$amp = \dfrac{S}{s}$

$\dfrac{V}{amp} \cdot \dfrac{C}{V} = \dfrac{C}{amp}$

40. A block of mass m is at rest on a rough inclined plane. Which of the following diagrams best represents the correct directions for the forces acting on the block?

Questions 41–42 refer to the following.

A sealed bottle contains 100 grams of radioactive iodine. After 24 days, the bottle contains only 12.5 grams of radioactive iodine.

41. The half-life of this isotope of iodine is most nearly

   (A) 24 days.

   (B) 16 days.

   (C) 12 days.

   (D) 8 days.

   (E) 3 days.

$\begin{array}{l} 100 \\ 50 \\ 25 \\ 12.5 \end{array}$

GO ON TO THE NEXT PAGE

42. Which of the following graphs best represents the amount of iodine remaining versus time?

Questions 43–44 relate to two waves of equal wavelength and amplitude approaching each other in the same rope as shown.

43. When the waves occupy exactly the same space at the same time, what will the shape of the rope be?

44. After the waves have completely passed each other, what will the shape of the rope be?

45. A converging lens forms an image primarily due to the phenomenon of

  (A) refraction.
  (B) reflection.
  (C) diffraction.
  (D) constructive interference.
  (E) destructive interference.

46. Sound is an example of a(n)

  (A) electromagnetic wave.
  (B) longitudinal wave.
  (C) transverse wave.
  (D) torsional wave.
  (E) circular wave.

47. A car has a speed of 20 m/s and a momentum of 12,000 kg m/s. The mass of the car is

  (A) 240,000 kg.
  (B) 6,000 kg.
  (C) 1,200 kg.
  (D) 600 kg.
  (E) 120 kg.

48. Two metal spheres of equal size are charged and mounted on insulated stands. One sphere has a charge of +8 μC and the second sphere has a charge of –14 μC. The two spheres are touched together and then separated. The charge on the second sphere will now be

  (A) zero.
  (B) +11 μC.
  (C) –6 μC.
  (D) –3 μC.
  (E) +2 μC.

GO ON TO THE NEXT PAGE

Questions 49–50 relate to the diagram below.

A bullet of mass m is fired with a speed v_o into a hanging block of wood of mass M and embeds itself. Consequently, the bullet and block rise to a maximum height h.

49. As the bullet strikes and becomes embedded in the block, which of the following statements is true?

(A) The speed of the bullet immediately before the collision is equal to the speed of the bullet and block immediately after the collision.

(B) The momentum of the bullet immediately before the collision is equal to the momentum of the bullet and block immediately after the collision.

(C) The kinetic energy of the bullet immediately before the collision is equal to the kinetic energy of the bullet and block immediately after the collision.

(D) No energy is lost as the bullet enters the wood block.

(E) The block does not move until the bullet comes to rest inside it.

50. The potential energy of the bullet and block at the maximum height h is equal to the

(A) kinetic energy of the bullet before it strikes the block.

(B) kinetic energy of the bullet and block after the bullet has embedded itself in the block.

(C) momentum of the bullet before it strikes the block.

(D) momentum of the bullet and block after the bullet has embedded itself in the block.

(E) potential energy of the block before it is struck by the bullet.

GO ON TO THE NEXT PAGE

Questions 51–52 relate to the following.

A steel sphere is launched horizontally with a speed v from the edge of a table of height h above a level floor. At the same instant, another steel sphere is dropped from the edge of the same table. Air resistance may be neglected.

51. Which of the following statements is true?

    (A) The two spheres will strike the floor at the same time.

    (B) The sphere that is dropped will strike the floor first.

    (C) The sphere that is launched horizontally will strike the floor first.

    (D) The acceleration of the sphere that is dropped is greater than the acceleration of the other sphere after it is launched.

    (E) The acceleration of the sphere after it is launched is greater than the acceleration of the sphere that is dropped.

52. If the mass of the sphere that is dropped is doubled, and the mass of the launched sphere remains the same, which of the following is true?

    (A) The two spheres will strike the floor at the same time.

    (B) The sphere that is dropped will strike the floor first.

    (C) The sphere that is launched horizontally will strike the floor first.

    (D) The acceleration of the sphere that is dropped is greater than the acceleration of the other sphere after it is launched.

    (E) The acceleration of the sphere after it is launched is greater than the acceleration of the sphere that is dropped.

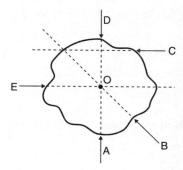

53. The figure above relates to a flat object lying on a table of negligible friction. Five forces are separately applied to the object as shown. The line of action of each force is shown by a dashed line. Which of the five forces will cause the object to rotate about point O?

    (A) A

    (B) B

    (C) C

    (D) D

    (E) E

GO ON TO THE NEXT PAGE

Questions 54–56 relate to the following properties of waves.

I. speed

II. wavelength

III. frequency

54. Which of the properties change when a wave is refracted?

(A) I only

(B) II only

(C) I and II only

(D) II and III only

(E) I, II, and III

55. Which of the properties is equal to the reciprocal of the period?

(A) I only

(B) II only

(C) III only

(D) II and III only

(E) I, II, and III

56. Which one of the three is the product of the other two?

(A) I

(B) II

(C) III

(D) Any one is the product of the other two.

(E) None of the three is the product of the other two.

$v = \lambda \cdot f$

57. A woman standing on a train platform listens to a train as it approaches her at a constant speed. The train engineer blows the whistle of the train that he knows to produce a frequency of 450 Hz. As the train approaches the woman on the platform, she will hear the frequency (pitch) of the whistle as

(A) greater than 450 Hz but constant.

(B) less than 450 Hz but constant.

(C) greater than 450 Hz and steadily increasing.

(D) less than 450 Hz and steadily increasing.

(E) greater than 450 Hz and steadily decreasing.

Lens

58. A light ray passes through a thin lens having a focal point *f* as shown above. Which of the following statements best describes the lens?

(A) The lens is a converging lens.

(B) The lens is thicker in the center than on the edges.

(C) The lens is thinner in the center than on the edges.

(D) The lens will always produce a real image.

(E) The lens will always produce a virtual image.

GO ON TO THE NEXT PAGE

Questions 59–61 refer to the following.

An object's velocity is measured each second and the data is summarized in the table below.

Velocity	Time
0	0
2 m/s	1 s
4 m/s	2 s
6 m/s	3 s
8 m/s	4 s

59. The acceleration of the object is

(A) 1 m/s².

(B) 2 m/s².

(C) 4 m/s².

(D) 6 m/s².

(E) 8 m/s².

60. The distance the object travels during the first four seconds is

(A) 8 m.

(B) 16 m.

(C) 18 m.

(D) 24 m.

(E) 32 m.

$$v_f^2 = v_i^2 + 2ax$$

$$8^2 = 0 + 2(2)(x)$$

$$64 \to 4x$$

61. If the object stops accelerating at 4 s when its speed is 8 m/s, the distance it will travel between 4 s and 7 s is

(A) 8 m.

(B) 16 m.

(C) 18 m.

(D) 24 m.

(E) 32 m.

$$8 \frac{m}{s} \cdot 3s =$$

$$24 m$$

62. A board of negligible mass supports a mass weighing 20 N at a distance of 2 m from the support at point A. How much weight must be placed at point B, which is 5 m from point A, in order for the board to remain horizontal?

(A) 4 N

(B) 8 N

(C) 10 N

(D) 40 N

(E) 60 N

$$20(2) = 5(x)$$

Questions 63–64 relate to the following.

A force of 40 N directed at 30° from the horizontal acts on a block of weight 50 N and pulls it across a level floor through a displacement of 10 meters. (sin 30° = 0.50, cos 30° = 0.87)

63. The work done on the block is most nearly

   (A) 160 J.
   (B) 200 J.
   (C) 350 J.
   (D) 400 J.
   (E) 1,600 J.

64. The normal force between the floor and the block while the block is being pulled is most nearly

   (A) 50 N.
   (B) 44 N.
   (C) 30 N.
   (D) 25 N.
   (E) 5 N.

65. Which of the following diagrams best represents the electric field around a positive charge?

(A)   (B)   (C)   (D)   (E)

66. Two ammeters are placed in the circuit above with the two resistors shown. If A_1 is the reading on ammeter 1 and A_2 is the reading on ammeter 2, which of the following statements is true?

   (A) $A_1 = A_2$.
   (B) $A_1 > A_2$.
   (C) $A_1 < A_2$.
   (D) $A_1 = 0$.
   (E) $A_2 = 0$.

67. If electrons are added or removed from an atom, the atom is said to be

   (A) polarized.
   (B) ionized.
   (C) neutralized.
   (D) an isotope.
   (E) a molecule.

68. Which of the following are emitted from a metal surface in the photoelectric effect?

   (A) electrons
   (B) protons
   (C) neutrons
   (D) photons
   (E) atoms

69. Which of the following particles has the largest mass?

   (A) electron
   (B) proton
   (C) neutron
   (D) alpha particle
   (E) beta particle

GO ON TO THE NEXT PAGE

70. The graph above shows position x as a function of time t for a particle moving along the x-axis. Which of the following graphs of velocity v as a function of time t describes the motion of this particle?

71. A stone of mass 1 kg and weight 10 N falls through the air. The air resistance acting on the stone is 2 N. What is the acceleration of the stone?

   (A) 12 m/s²
   (B) 9.8 m/s²
   (C) 8 m/s²
   (D) 5 m/s²
   (E) 2 m/s²

72. If the volume of a gas is decreased while its temperature is held constant, which of the following will occur?

   (A) The average kinetic energy of the molecules of the gas will increase.
   (B) The average kinetic energy of the molecules of the gas will decrease.
   (C) The mass of the gas will decrease.
   (D) The pressure of the gas will increase.
   (E) The pressure of the gas will decrease.

73. A satellite is orbiting the Earth in an elliptical orbit. Which of the following must be true if the satellite's speed is increasing?

   (A) The satellite's distance from the Earth is increasing.
   (B) The satellite's distance from the Earth is decreasing.
   (C) The kinetic energy of the satellite is decreasing.
   (D) The momentum of the satellite is decreasing.
   (E) The gravitational force acting on the satellite is decreasing.

74. The angle above which total internal reflection will occur is called the

   (A) critical angle.
   (B) refracted angle.
   (C) diffracted angle.
   (D) incident angle.
   (E) normal angle.

75. A wire on the x-axis of a coordinate system has a current I in the $+x$ direction as shown above. What is the direction of the magnetic field due to the wire at point P?

   (A) to the left
   (B) to the right
   (C) into the page and perpendicular to the page
   (D) out of the page and perpendicular to the page
   (E) toward the bottom of the page

STOP!

**If you finish before time is up,
you may check your work.**

Answer Key
Practice Test 1

1. A	20. C	39. D	58. C
2. D	21. D	40. A	59. B
3. C	22. A	41. D	60. B
4. D	23. C	42. B	61. D
5. B	24. D	43. D	62. B
6. C	25. C	44. A	63. C
7. A	26. B	45. A	64. C
8. C	27. A	46. B	65. B
9. B	28. B	47. D	66. C
10. A	29. D	48. D	67. B
11. D	30. A	49. B	68. A
12. B	31. A	50. B	69. D
13. E	32. D	51. A	70. E
14. A	33. A	52. A	71. C
15. C	34. E	53. C	72. D
16. C	35. A	54. C	73. B
17. D	36. E	55. C	74. A
18. A	37. C	56. A	75. D
19. B	38. A	57. A	

ANSWERS AND EXPLANATIONS

1. A

The slope of a displacement vs. time graph is velocity, and the slope is constant; thus the velocity is constant.

2. D

The object begins with a high velocity, then slows down until its velocity is zero, then begins speeding up again in the negative direction.

3. C

Both graphs imply that the velocity starts out as zero; then the slope of the *s* vs. *t* graph begins getting steeper and more negative, indicating that the velocity is increasing and negative.

4. D

Fission occurs when a large atom, such as uranium, splits into two smaller ones, such as xenon and strontium.

5. B

Radium is a radioactive element that emits an alpha particle ($_2^4$He), leaving radon gas.

6. C

A beta particle is an electron ($_{-1}^0$e) produced in this radioactive decay process where bismuth decays into polonium.

7. A

Fusion is the process in which two lighter atoms, such as two atoms of deuterium ($_1^2$H), fuse to form a heavier atom, such as tritium ($_1^3$H).

8. C

The ideal gas law relates the pressure, volume, and temperature of a gas.

9. B

The second law of thermodynamics, or the law of entropy, states that all natural systems tend toward a state of higher disorder. As the gas escapes from the bottle, it is becoming more disordered.

10. A

The first law of thermodynamics states that the heat lost by one liquid must be gained by the other liquid, as long as no work is done.

11. D

The heat of fusion or vaporization equation allows us to calculate the heat required to change the state of a substance from a solid to a liquid or a liquid to a gas.

12. B

The voltage across the resistor is equal to the voltage in the battery, since when the switch is first closed, the capacitor has no charge on it and therefore no voltage across it.

13. E

Immediately after the switch is closed, the capacitor has no charge on it and therefore provides no resistance to the current, and so the current is simply V/R by Ohm's law.

14. A

A very long time after the switch is closed, the capacitor is full of charge and the voltage across the capacitor is equal and opposite to the voltage provided by the battery. Thus, the capacitor will not allow any current to flow through the circuit.

15. C

The velocity vs. time graph implies that the velocity is not changing. Graphs I and II both have a constant slope, which also implies a constant velocity, even though one graph begins at a different position than the other graph.

16. C

The plane must be at rest or moving at a constant velocity for the chain to hang vertically. A reference frame that has a constant velocity (including rest) is called an inertial reference frame. If the airplane were accelerating, the chain would angle forward or backward, depending on the direction of the acceleration.

17. D

The heat lost by the warmer water must be gained by the cooler water until all of the water reaches a final equilibrium temperature T_f.

$$Q_{lost} = Q_{gained}$$
$$m_1 c \Delta T = -m_2 c \Delta T$$
$$m_1 c(T_f - T_i) = -m_2 c(T_f - T_i).$$

Since the specific heat is the same for water on both sides of the equation, we have

$$m_1(T_f - T_i) = -m_2(T_f - T_i)$$
$$(400 \text{ g})(T_f - 40°) = (-100 \text{ g})(T_f - 30°)$$
$$T_f = 38°.$$

18. A

$$I = \frac{V}{R} = \frac{20 \text{ V}}{40 \text{ Ω}} = 0.5 \text{ } A$$

19. B

If we draw the free-body force diagram for each block, we see that each block has a weight force of 50 N pulling downward that is balanced by the tension force pulling upward. Thus, the tension in the string must be 50 N.

20. C

Newton's second law states that $F = ma$, so $a = F/m$.

21. D

The change in momentum of the block is equal to the impulse imparted to the block. The impulse is the product of the force and the time during which it acts, Ft.

22. A

The work-energy theorem states that the work (Fd) done on the block is equal to the change in kinetic energy of the block, since net work done on an object always changes the energy of the object.

23. C

If the charge is to feel no force, it must be closer to the smaller charge, $-q$, and farther away from the larger charge, $-4q$. In other words, the charge must be at the "center of charge," similar to the center of mass of two objects. If the charge were placed at points A, B, or E, it would be repelled and accelerate away from the two negative charges. The forces acting on the charge at point C balance each other out, since electric force is proportional to the product of the charges and inversely proportional to the square of the distance between the charges.

24. D

For a charge to experience a force in a magnetic field, its velocity must have a component that is perpendicular to the magnetic field lines, which implies that it is crossing the magnetic field lines.

25. C

For a current to be induced in a coil of wire by electromagnetic induction, there must be relative motion between the magnetic field of the coil. If the magnet stops, so does the current in the coil.

26. B

If the temperature is increased but the volume remains constant, the pressure inside the container will become greater since there will be more collisions between the molecules of the gas and the walls of the container. Since temperature is proportional to the average kinetic energy of the gas molecules, a higher temperature would imply a higher average kinetic energy of the molecules of the gas.

27. A

In the process of charging by induction, a positively charged rod is brought near the knob of the electroscope, and the electroscope is grounded so that more electrons that are attracted to the positively charged rod can come up from the ground and be deposited on the electroscope, giving it a net negative charge.

28. B

A transverse wave vibrates in a direction perpendicular to the direction of motion of the wave, as this wave does.

29. D

The wavelength of the wave is 4 cm, being the length of one full vibration of the wave. The frequency of the wave is

$$f = \frac{v}{\lambda} = \frac{320 \text{ cm/s}}{4 \text{ cm}} = 80 \text{ Hz.}$$

30. A

The amplitude is the maximum displacement from the base line to the crest of the wave (or, equivalently, to the trough of the wave), which is 1 cm in this case.

31. A

The amount of current will be the same, since the coil is turned at the same constant rate, but since it is rotated in the opposite direction, the current is induced in the opposite direction.

32. D

The magnetic force acting on a charge in the magnetic field is a centripetal force causing the charge to turn its path downward in the magnetic field and point to the center of the circle, which is toward the bottom of the page from point A.

33. A

Since the charge is positive, we can use the right-hand rule to find the direction of the magnetic field. At point A, if you point your thumb in the direction of the velocity of the charge (to the right), and your palm faces the direction of the force on the charge at A (toward the bottom of the page), then your fingers point out of the page in the direction of the magnetic field.

34. E

The angle of incidence is equal to the angle of reflection, and ray E is reflected at an angle most similar to the incident angle.

35. A

Since the ray is passing from a less dense medium (air) to a more dense medium (glass), the refracted ray must bend toward the normal, causing the refracted angle to be smaller than the incident angle.

36. E

Since both the electric and gravitational forces are inverse-square laws, the farther apart the charged masses are, the smaller the forces between them.

37. C

The gravitational force is proportional to the product of the masses, so the gravitational force will be doubled. But the electric force is not related to the masses and so it will not change.

38. A

If they remain the same distance apart, then the gravitational force (attractive) is equal and opposite to the electric force, which must be repulsive in this case. Thus, the only answer choice that will produce a repulsive electric force is A, both charges are positive.

39. D

$$\Omega F = \left(\frac{V}{A}\right)\left(\frac{C}{V}\right) = \frac{C}{A} = \frac{C}{C/s} = \text{second, which is a}$$
unit of time.

40. A

The weight vector always points straight down, the normal force is perpendicular to the plane, and the frictional force is acting up the plane to keep the block from sliding down the plane.

41. D

The 100 g sample of iodine is cut in half three times (50 g, 25 g, 12.5 g), which took 24 days. Thus, the time for the iodine sample to be cut in half one time is $\frac{24}{3} = 8$ days.

42. B

The amount of iodine starts off at 100 g, and is reduced exponentially over time.

43. D

When the two waves meet, the crest of one wave is superposed onto the trough of the other, creating destructive interference, and the waves cancel each other out for the instant they occupy the same space at the same time.

44. A

After the waves completely pass each other, they behave exactly as they did before they met. They've just switched places.

45. A

As a ray of light passes through a lens, it is refracted and changes its direction.

46. B

Sound waves vibrate in a direction that is parallel to the direction of motion of the wave, and are thus longitudinal.

47. D

Momentum is mass times velocity, so

$$m = \frac{p}{v} = \frac{12,000 \text{ kg m/s}}{20 \text{ m/s}} = 600 \text{ kg.}$$

48. D

When the two spheres are touched, they exchange charge until they both have the same charge. Since the total charge is $-6 \ \mu C$, they will each retain $-3 \ \mu C$ when they are again separated.

49. B

The bullet collides with and sticks to the block in an inelastic collision. Momentum is conserved in an inelastic collision, but kinetic energy is not conserved, since some of the energy is lost to heat and deformation of the wood and bullet.

50. B

After the bullet embeds itself in the block, the bullet and block have a new kinetic energy (since the collision is not elastic), which is converted into potential energy at the height h.

51. A

The two spheres will strike the floor at the same time since they have the same initial vertical velocity (zero) and the same vertical acceleration (10 m/s^2).

52. A

Once again, the spheres will strike the floor at the same time, since mass has no effect on the acceleration of a falling object.

53. C

The force applied at C is the only force whose line of action does not pass through the point of rotation A, and thus it is the only force that can cause a torque and a rotation about point A.

54. C

When a wave passes from one medium to another, it is refracted, changing its speed and wavelength. The frequency does not depend on the medium, and therefore it is not changed when the wave is refracted.

55. C

Frequency (cycles/second) is the reciprocal of period (seconds/cycle).

56. A

The speed is the product of frequency and wavelength.

57. A

As the train approaches the stationary woman on the platform, she hears a higher pitch (frequency) than the pitch associated with 450 Hz since the waves appear to be reaching her more often due to the Doppler effect. The pitch she hears will be constant, since the train is not accelerating.

58. C

Since the parallel rays diverge as they exit the lens, this lens is a diverging (concave) lens, which is thinner in the center and thicker on the edges.

59. B

The speed of the object is increasing by 2 m/s for each second it moves.

60. B

$$s = v_i t + \frac{1}{2} a t^2 = (0) + \frac{1}{2} (2 \text{ m/s})^2 (4 \text{ s})^2 = 16 \text{ m}$$

61. D

The distance traveled at a constant speed between 4 s and 7 s is $d = vt = (8 \text{ m/s})(3 \text{ s}) = 24 \text{ m}$.

62. B

The torque on the left must equal the torque on the right for the board to be balanced.

$$(F_{left})(r_{left}) = (F_{right})(r_{right})$$
$$(20N)(2m) = (F_{right})(5m)$$
$$F_{right} = 8N.$$

63. C

$$W = Fs \cos\theta = (40 \ N)(10 \ m)\cos 30° = 350 \ J.$$

64. C

The normal force is equal to the difference between the weight of the block and the vertical component of the applied force.

$$F_N = W - F \sin\theta = 50 \ N - (40 \ N)\sin 30° = 30 \ N.$$

65. B

Electric field lines are always drawn in the direction a small positive test charge would experience a force, which is radially outward anywhere around a positive source charge.

66. C

Ammeter 2 will read twice as much current as ammeter 1, since ammeter 2 is in series with a resistor with only half the ohms as the resistor on the parallel branch with ammeter 1.

67. B

An atom with extra electrons is a negative ion, and an atom with a deficiency of electrons is a positive ion.

68. A

Photons above the threshold frequency "dig out" electrons from the metal, which in turn are emitted by the metal.

69. D

An alpha particle is equivalent to a helium nucleus, and is composed of two protons and two neutrons.

70. E

The x vs. t graph and the v vs. t graph both imply that the object is initially moving at a constant positive velocity, then remains at rest for a time, then accelerates positively.

71. C

The net force acting on the falling stone is 10 N – 2 N = 8 N. The stone's acceleration, then, is

$$a = \frac{F_{net}}{m} = \frac{8\,\text{N}}{1\,\text{kg}} = 8\,\text{m/s}^2.$$

72. D

The ideal gas law states that if temperature is held constant, pressure and volume are inversely proportional to each other. Thus, if volume is decreased, this will cause an increase in pressure. This relationship is sometimes referred to as Boyle's law.

73. B

Conservation of angular momentum states that speed and orbital distance are inversely proportional to each other. Thus, the satellite moves faster as its orbital distance gets smaller (closer to the Earth).

74. A

A ray directed at an angle greater than the critical angle as measured from the normal line will not exit the medium, but will be reflected internally.

75. D

By the first right-hand rule, place your thumb in the direction of the current, and your fingers will curl around the wire in the direction of the magnetic field the current produces, which is out of the page at point A.

HOW TO CALCULATE YOUR SCORE

Step 1: Figure out your raw score. Use the answer key to count the number of questions you answered correctly and the number of questions you answered incorrectly. (Do not count any questions you left blank.) Multiply the number wrong by 0.25 and subtract the result from the number correct. Round the result to the nearest whole number. This is your raw score.

SAT Subject Test: Physics Practice Test 2

Number right		Number wrong		Raw score
☐	−	(0.25 × ☐)	=	☐

Step 2: Find your scaled score. In the Score Conversion Table below, find your raw score (rounded to the nearest whole number) in one of the columns to the left. The score directly to the right of that number will be your scaled score.

A note on your practice test scores: Don't take these scores too literally. Practice test conditions cannot precisely mirror real test conditions. Your actual SAT Subject Test: Physics score will almost certainly vary from your diagnostic and practice test scores. However, your scores on the diagnostic and practice tests will give you a rough idea of your range on the actual exam.

Score Conversion Table

Raw	Scaled	Raw	Scaled	Raw	Scaled	Raw	Scaled	Raw	Scaled	Raw	Scaled
75	800	59	780	43	690	27	590	11	480	−5	380
74	800	58	770	42	680	26	580	10	480	−6	370
73	800	57	770	41	670	25	580	9	470	−7	370
72	800	56	760	40	670	24	570	8	470	−8	360
71	800	55	760	39	660	23	570	7	460	−9	350
70	800	54	750	38	650	22	560	6	450	−10	350
69	800	53	750	37	650	21	550	5	450	−11	340
68	800	52	740	36	640	20	540	4	440	−12	330
67	800	51	730	35	640	19	540	3	430	−13	330
66	800	50	730	34	630	18	530	2	430	−14	320
65	800	49	720	33	630	17	530	1	420	−15	310
64	800	48	720	32	620	16	520	0	410	−16	310
63	800	47	710	31	610	15	510	−1	410	−17	300
62	790	46	700	30	610	14	510	−2	400	−18	290
61	790	45	700	29	600	13	500	−3	390	−19	290
60	780	44	690	28	600	12	490	−4	390		

Practice Test 2
Answer Grid

1. Ⓐ Ⓑ Ⓒ Ⓓ Ⓔ
2. Ⓐ Ⓑ Ⓒ Ⓓ Ⓔ
3. Ⓐ Ⓑ Ⓒ Ⓓ Ⓔ
4. Ⓐ Ⓑ Ⓒ Ⓓ Ⓔ
5. Ⓐ Ⓑ Ⓒ Ⓓ Ⓔ
6. Ⓐ Ⓑ Ⓒ Ⓓ Ⓔ
7. Ⓐ Ⓑ Ⓒ Ⓓ Ⓔ
8. Ⓐ Ⓑ Ⓒ Ⓓ Ⓔ
9. Ⓐ Ⓑ Ⓒ Ⓓ Ⓔ
10. Ⓐ Ⓑ Ⓒ Ⓓ Ⓔ
11. Ⓐ Ⓑ Ⓒ Ⓓ Ⓔ
12. Ⓐ Ⓑ Ⓒ Ⓓ Ⓔ
13. Ⓐ Ⓑ Ⓒ Ⓓ Ⓔ
14. Ⓐ Ⓑ Ⓒ Ⓓ Ⓔ
15. Ⓐ Ⓑ Ⓒ Ⓓ Ⓔ
16. Ⓐ Ⓑ Ⓒ Ⓓ Ⓔ
17. Ⓐ Ⓑ Ⓒ Ⓓ Ⓔ
18. Ⓐ Ⓑ Ⓒ Ⓓ Ⓔ
19. Ⓐ Ⓑ Ⓒ Ⓓ Ⓔ
20. Ⓐ Ⓑ Ⓒ Ⓓ Ⓔ
21. Ⓐ Ⓑ Ⓒ Ⓓ Ⓔ
22. Ⓐ Ⓑ Ⓒ Ⓓ Ⓔ
23. Ⓐ Ⓑ Ⓒ Ⓓ Ⓔ
24. Ⓐ Ⓑ Ⓒ Ⓓ Ⓔ
25. Ⓐ Ⓑ Ⓒ Ⓓ Ⓔ

26. Ⓐ Ⓑ Ⓒ Ⓓ Ⓔ
27. Ⓐ Ⓑ Ⓒ Ⓓ Ⓔ
28. Ⓐ Ⓑ Ⓒ Ⓓ Ⓔ
29. Ⓐ Ⓑ Ⓒ Ⓓ Ⓔ
30. Ⓐ Ⓑ Ⓒ Ⓓ Ⓔ
31. Ⓐ Ⓑ Ⓒ Ⓓ Ⓔ
32. Ⓐ Ⓑ Ⓒ Ⓓ Ⓔ
33. Ⓐ Ⓑ Ⓒ Ⓓ Ⓔ
34. Ⓐ Ⓑ Ⓒ Ⓓ Ⓔ
35. Ⓐ Ⓑ Ⓒ Ⓓ Ⓔ
36. Ⓐ Ⓑ Ⓒ Ⓓ Ⓔ
37. Ⓐ Ⓑ Ⓒ Ⓓ Ⓔ
38. Ⓐ Ⓑ Ⓒ Ⓓ Ⓔ
39. Ⓐ Ⓑ Ⓒ Ⓓ Ⓔ
40. Ⓐ Ⓑ Ⓒ Ⓓ Ⓔ
41. Ⓐ Ⓑ Ⓒ Ⓓ Ⓔ
42. Ⓐ Ⓑ Ⓒ Ⓓ Ⓔ
43. Ⓐ Ⓑ Ⓒ Ⓓ Ⓔ
44. Ⓐ Ⓑ Ⓒ Ⓓ Ⓔ
45. Ⓐ Ⓑ Ⓒ Ⓓ Ⓔ
46. Ⓐ Ⓑ Ⓒ Ⓓ Ⓔ
47. Ⓐ Ⓑ Ⓒ Ⓓ Ⓔ
48. Ⓐ Ⓑ Ⓒ Ⓓ Ⓔ
49. Ⓐ Ⓑ Ⓒ Ⓓ Ⓔ
50. Ⓐ Ⓑ Ⓒ Ⓓ Ⓔ

51. Ⓐ Ⓑ Ⓒ Ⓓ Ⓔ
52. Ⓐ Ⓑ Ⓒ Ⓓ Ⓔ
53. Ⓐ Ⓑ Ⓒ Ⓓ Ⓔ
54. Ⓐ Ⓑ Ⓒ Ⓓ Ⓔ
55. Ⓐ Ⓑ Ⓒ Ⓓ Ⓔ
56. Ⓐ Ⓑ Ⓒ Ⓓ Ⓔ
57. Ⓐ Ⓑ Ⓒ Ⓓ Ⓔ
58. Ⓐ Ⓑ Ⓒ Ⓓ Ⓔ
59. Ⓐ Ⓑ Ⓒ Ⓓ Ⓔ
60. Ⓐ Ⓑ Ⓒ Ⓓ Ⓔ
61. Ⓐ Ⓑ Ⓒ Ⓓ Ⓔ
62. Ⓐ Ⓑ Ⓒ Ⓓ Ⓔ
63. Ⓐ Ⓑ Ⓒ Ⓓ Ⓔ
64. Ⓐ Ⓑ Ⓒ Ⓓ Ⓔ
65. Ⓐ Ⓑ Ⓒ Ⓓ Ⓔ
66. Ⓐ Ⓑ Ⓒ Ⓓ Ⓔ
67. Ⓐ Ⓑ Ⓒ Ⓓ Ⓔ
68. Ⓐ Ⓑ Ⓒ Ⓓ Ⓔ
69. Ⓐ Ⓑ Ⓒ Ⓓ Ⓔ
70. Ⓐ Ⓑ Ⓒ Ⓓ Ⓔ
71. Ⓐ Ⓑ Ⓒ Ⓓ Ⓔ
72. Ⓐ Ⓑ Ⓒ Ⓓ Ⓔ
73. Ⓐ Ⓑ Ⓒ Ⓓ Ⓔ
74. Ⓐ Ⓑ Ⓒ Ⓓ Ⓔ
75. Ⓐ Ⓑ Ⓒ Ⓓ Ⓔ

Practice Test 2

Part A

Directions: Each set of lettered choices below relates to the numbered questions immediately following it. Select the one lettered choice that best answers each question. A choice may be used once, more than once, or not at all in each set.

Questions 1–3 relate to the following.

A ball of mass *m* on the end of a string is swung clockwise in a horizontal circle at a constant radius *r*. When the ball is a point P as shown below, some of the choices that follow represent the directions of the vectors associated with the motion of the ball.

(A) →   (B) ←   (C) ↓   (D) ↑   (E) ↔

1. What is the direction of the velocity of the ball at point P?   *B*

2. What is the direction of the acceleration of the ball at point P?   *D*

3. What is the direction of the net force acting on the ball at point P?   *D*

Questions 4–7 relate to the following series of images of a moving ball below.

Each image represents a time interval of one second, and the motion of the ball is not necessarily horizontal.

4. In which of the choices above is the ball increasing its speed?   *B*

5. In which of the choices above is the ball moving at a constant velocity?   *A*

6. Which of the choices above could represent the ball being thrown upward before it begins falling back down?   *C*

7. Which of the choices above could represent the ball being rolled up an incline and then allowed to roll back down again?   *E*

Questions 8–10 relate to the following diagram of two charges, +Q and –4 Q.

8. The net electric field is zero nearest which point? A

9. At which point does the net electric field vector point to the left? E

10. At which point would a small positive charge q feel the greatest force? D

Questions 11–13 relate to the following graphs.

11. Which of the graphs above represents the energy of a photon vs. its frequency? B

12. Which of the graphs above represents the maximum kinetic energy of electrons emitted in the photoelectric effect vs. frequency of incoming light? A

13. Which of the graphs above represents the mass of a relativistic particle vs. its speed? D

GO ON TO THE NEXT PAGE

Part B

Directions: Each of the questions or incomplete statements below is followed by five answer choices. Select the one that is best in each case.

Questions 14–15 refer to the following.

A red car and a blue car have the same mass and are moving on the highway. The red car is traveling at 60 miles per hour and the blue car is traveling at 30 miles per hour.

14. The ratio of the red car's momentum to the blue car's momentum is

    (A) 4.

    (B) 2.

    (C) 1.

    (D) $\frac{1}{2}$.

    (E) $\frac{1}{4}$.

15. The ratio of the red car's kinetic energy to the blue car's kinetic energy is

    (A) 4.

    (B) 2.

    (C) 1.

    (D) $\frac{1}{2}$.

    (E) $\frac{1}{4}$.

16. The waves on a lake cause a buoy to oscillate up and down 90 times per minute. The frequency of the waves in hertz is

    (A) 90 Hz.

    (B) 60 Hz.

    (C) 1.5 Hz.

    (D) 0.6 Hz.

    (E) 0.67 Hz.

17. A ray of light passes through a piece of glass at the angle of incidence shown above. As the light passes through the glass and exits the glass into the air, the path of the ray is represented by which of the rays above?

    (A) A

    (B) B

    (C) C

    (D) D

    (E) E

GO ON TO THE NEXT PAGE

Questions 18–19 refer to the following.

A block falls onto a vertical spring from a height h and compresses the spring a distance y. Air resistance and friction may be neglected.

18. At the point of maximum compression, which of the following must be true?

(A) The speed of the block is maximum.
(B) The acceleration of the block is not zero.
(C) The potential energy of the block is zero.
(D) The kinetic energy of the block is maximum.
(E) The potential energy of the spring is zero.

19. The spring expands upward and throws the block vertically back into the air. Which of the following is true after the block leaves the spring?

(A) The block has no kinetic energy.
(B) The block has no potential energy.
(C) The block will rise to exactly half the height from which it was dropped.
(D) The block reaches its maximum acceleration just after leaving the spring.
(E) The block will rise to the height from which it was dropped.

Questions 20–21 relate to the following.

The velocity and acceleration vectors associated with the motion of three particles are shown below.

$F = ma$

20. Which of the above could represent the velocity and acceleration vectors for an object in uniform circular motion?

(A) I only
(B) II only
(C) III only
(D) I and II only
(E) II and III only

21. Which of the above could represent the velocity and acceleration vectors for a projectile following a parabolic path?

(A) I only
(B) II only
(C) III only
(D) I and II only
(E) II and III only

22. Two stars are separated by a distance r and are moving away from each other. Which of the graphs below best represents the gravitational force between the stars as a function of r, the distance between them?

$\dfrac{gM_1M_2}{r^2}$

GO ON TO THE NEXT PAGE

Questions 23–24 refer to the following.

A 15 kg block rests on a surface of negligible friction and is pulled by a string that is passed over a pulley of negligible mass and connected to a hanging 5 kg block.

15 kg

5 kg

23. The net force acting on the 15 kg block is equal to

(A) the weight of the 5 kg block.

(B) the tension in the string.

(C) the difference between the weight of the 15 kg block and the 5 kg block.

(D) the sum of the weight of the 15 kg block and the 5 kg block.

(E) the weight of the 15 kg block.

24. In terms of the acceleration due to gravity g, the acceleration of the system is

(A) $\frac{g}{5}$.

(B) $\frac{g}{4}$.

(C) $\frac{g}{3}$.

(D) g.

(E) $3g$.

Energy above ground state

$n = 3$ —————— 6 eV

$n = 2$ —————— 4 eV

$n = 1$ —————— 0 eV

25. The energy levels above ground state for a hypothetical atom are shown above. What is the energy of a photon emitted as a result of an electron in this atom making a transition from the third energy level to the second energy level?

(A) 10 eV

(B) 6 eV

(C) 4 eV

(D) 2 eV

(E) 1 eV

26. Consider the three statements below.

I. The atom is mostly empty space.

II. Electrons orbit the nucleus of the atom.

III. The atom has a dense, positively charged nucleus.

Which of the above statements were conclusions drawn by Rutherford about the structure of the atom after studying the results of his alpha-scattering experiment?

(A) I only

(B) II only

(C) I and II only

(D) II and III only

(E) I, II, and III

GO ON TO THE NEXT PAGE

27. Which of the following colors of light has the lowest frequency?

    (A) violet
    (B) blue
    (C) green
    (D) yellow
    (E) orange

28. A heat pump warms a house by absorbing 90 J of heat and doing 60 J of work on the pump. The heat then delivered to the house is

    (A) 5,400 J.
    (B) 150 J.
    (C) 30 J.
    (D) 1.5 J.
    (E) 0.67 J.

Questions 29–30 relate to the following.

A resistor in a closed circuit has 2 A of current flowing through it and 12 volts across it.

29. The value of the resistor is

    (A) 6 Ω.
    (B) 10 Ω.
    (C) 14 Ω.
    (D) 24 Ω.
    (E) 144 Ω.

30. The power dissipated in the resistor is

    (A) 6 watts.
    (B) 10 watts.
    (C) 14 watts.
    (D) 24 watts.
    (E) 144 watts.

31. Which of the following is NOT a unit for energy?

    (A) joule
    (B) kilowatt-hour
    (C) calorie
    (D) watt
    (E) eV

32. A pendulum is dropped from a height of 4 m as shown above. The speed of the pendulum at the lowest point in the swing is most nearly

    (A) 6 m/s.
    (B) 7 m/s.
    (C) 8 m/s.
    (D) 9 m/s.
    (E) 10 m/s.

33. Consider the acceleration graph shown above and the following choices below.

    I.   A stone is falling toward the Earth.
    II. A car is decreasing its speed.
    III. A bicycle is rolling up a hill.

Which of the choices above could be represented by the acceleration vs. time graph?

    (A) I only
    (B) II only
    (C) II and III only
    (D) I and III only
    (E) I, II, and III

GO ON TO THE NEXT PAGE

$$\frac{20}{3} \qquad \frac{20}{3} \qquad F = ma$$
$$40 = (3)\, m$$

34. Two blocks of equal mass are connected by a string. Block 2 is pulled by a force of 40 N, which accelerates both blocks at 3 m/s² along a surface of negligible friction. The tension in the string connecting the blocks is

   (A) 120 N.
   (B) 80 N.
   (C) 40 N.
   (D) 20 N.
   (E) 13 N.

35. A ball dropped from a tower will strike the ground below in 3 s. If the ball is launched horizontally from the tower at a speed of 10 m/s, how far horizontally from the base of the tower will the ball land on the level ground?

   (A) 100 m
   (B) 45 m
   (C) 30 m
   (D) 10 m
   (E) 3.3 m

$$t = 3s$$
$$x = x_{vi}\, t$$
$$= (10)(3)$$

36. A cluster of magnetically aligned atoms in a magnetic material is called a

   (A) domain.
   (B) molecule.
   (C) pole.
   (D) charge.
   (E) electron cloud.

37. On the microscopic scale, friction is caused by which of the following fundamental forces?

   (A) gravitational
   (B) electrostatic
   (C) strong nuclear
   (D) weak nuclear
   (E) proton and neutron

38. The time for one complete swing of a pendulum is called its period. The period of a pendulum for small swings near the Earth depends on its

   (A) length and amplitude of swing only.
   (B) amplitude of swing and mass only.
   (C) length only.
   (D) amplitude only.
   (E) length, mass, and amplitude of swing.

$$F - T = \left(\frac{20}{3}\right)(3)$$
$$40 - T = 20$$

GO ON TO THE NEXT PAGE

bulb 1   bulb 2

50 V

Questions 39–41 refer to the circuit shown above.

A 50-volt battery supplies 100 w of power to each of the two identical light bulbs. The current passing through bulb 1 is 4 A.

39. The voltmeter across bulb 1 will read

   (A) 100 V.
   (B) 50 V.
   (C) 25 V.
   (D) 4 V.
   (E) zero.

$V = IR$
$P = IV$
$100 = (4)(V)$

40. The current through bulb 2 is

   (A) 2 A.
   (B) 4 A.
   (C) 8 A.
   (D) 100 A.
   (E) zero.

41. The resistance of each bulb is most nearly

   (A) 25 Ω.
   (B) 20 Ω.
   (C) 6 Ω.
   (D) 4 Ω.
   (E) 2 Ω.

$V = IR$
$25 = 4(R)$
$\dfrac{25}{4}$

Red

Blue

higher energy

42. Two beams of light, red and blue, enter a prism as shown above. Which of the following statements is true concerning the light as it passes through the prism?

   (A) The blue light will bend more than the red light, since the blue light has a longer wavelength.
   (B) The red light will bend more than the blue light, since the red light has a longer wavelength.
   (C) The blue light will bend more than the red light, since the blue light has a shorter wavelength.
   (D) The red light will bend more than the blue light, since the red light has a shorter wavelength.
   (E) The red and blue light will bend by the same amount, since all colors of light refract equally.

43. Green light is passed through two narrow slits and forms a pattern of bright and dark lines on a screen. The phenomena primarily responsible for this pattern is

   (A) refraction.
   (B) reflection.
   (C) polarization.
   (D) interference.
   (E) intensity.

GO ON TO THE NEXT PAGE

44. An ultraviolet photon has twice the frequency of a red photon. The ratio of the energy of the ultraviolet photon to the energy of the red photon is

(A) 4.

(B) 2.

(C) 1.

(D) $\frac{1}{2}$.

(E) $\frac{1}{4}$.

review types of waves

Questions 45–47 refer to the figure below, which represents a longitudinal wave moving through water in a glass tank of length 9 meters. The frequency of the wave is 500 Hz.

45. This wave could be which of the following types of waves?

(A) visible light
(B) radio wave
(C) microwave
(D) sound wave
(E) X-ray

46. What is the wavelength of the longitudinal wave?

$f = 500$ Hz

(A) 1.5 m
(B) 3 m
(C) 4.5 m
(D) 9 m
(E) 18 m

47. The speed of the wave is most nearly

(A) 500 m/s.
(B) 750 m/s.
(C) 1,500 m/s.
(D) 3,000 m/s.
(E) 4,500 m/s.

$c = (500)(3)$

48. A ball is moving downward with a velocity **v** as shown in the figure above, with a force **F** directed to the right acting on the ball. Which of the statements is true?

(A) The ball is moving with a constant velocity.
(B) The ball is moving with a constant speed.
(C) The force **F** is doing work on the ball.
(D) The force **F** is changing the kinetic energy of the ball.
(E) The velocity and the acceleration of the ball are in the same direction.

49. The bar of negligible mass shown above is marked in eight equal parts. The bar has a 2 kg mass attached to one end and a 6 kg mass attached to the other end. The center of mass of the two masses is most nearly at which point?

$6(x) = (2)(4)$

(A) A
(B) B
(C) C
(D) D
(E) E

GO ON TO THE NEXT PAGE

Questions 50–51 refer to the diagram below.

A block of mass m is pushed against a rough, fixed wall by a force **P**. The frictional force between the block and the surface is **f**, and the normal force is F_N.

50. Which of the following diagrams correctly shows all of the forces acting on the block?

51. If the block is not moving, the magnitude of the force of friction acting on the block is equal to the magnitude of the force

   (A) **P**.
   (B) mg.
   (C) F_N.
   (D) $F_N + P$.
   (E) $F_N - P$.

$\Sigma F = ma$

52. Which of the following is NOT a vector quantity?

   (A) kinetic energy $\frac{1}{2}mv^2$
   (B) force
   (C) displacement
   (D) velocity
   (E) momentum mv

53. The molecules of an ideal gas are increasing their collisions per unit time with the walls of a sealed container of constant volume. Which of the three choices below must also be increasing?

   I.   pressure
   II. temperature
   III. number of moles of gas

   (A) I only
   (B) II only
   (C) I and II only
   (D) II and III only
   (E) I and III only

GO ON TO THE NEXT PAGE

Questions 54–55 relate to the diagram below.

A battery of voltage V is connected to two parallel conducting plates, 1 and 2.

54. The device connected to the battery is generally called a

(A) generator.
(B) capacitor.
(C) motor.
(D) charger.
(E) resistor.

55. An electron is placed in the center of the space between the plates. The subsequent motion of the electron is described by which of the following?

(A) The electron accelerates toward plate 1.
(B) The electron accelerates toward plate 2.
(C) The electron moves with constant velocity toward plate 1.
(D) The electron moves with constant velocity toward plate 2.
(E) The electron remains at rest halfway between the plates.

56. The current in a wire is directed out of the page and perpendicular to the page. Which of the following best represents the magnetic field produced by the current in the wire?

Questions 57–58 refer to a candle burning inside the metal container shown below.

Three types of heat transfer are listed below.

I. radiation
II. conduction
III. convection

57. Heat can be transferred to the inside surface of the walls of the container by which of the above?

(A) I only
(B) I and II only
(C) I and III only
(D) II only
(E) I, II, and III only

58. If you touch the outside surface of the metal container, your hand will become warmer directly by which of the above choices?

(A) I only
(B) I and II only
(C) I and III only
(D) II only
(E) III only

GO ON TO THE NEXT PAGE

59. Let g be the acceleration due to gravity at the surface of the Earth. What would be the acceleration due to gravity at a distance of four Earth radii from the center of the Earth?

(A) 16 g

(B) 4 g

(C) 2 g

(D) $\frac{1}{4} g$

(E) $\frac{1}{16} g$

Rate $\left(\frac{kg}{hr}\right)$

time (hr)

60. The graph above shows the number of kilograms of sand that falls into a truck per hour as a function of time in hours. The shaded area under the curve has units of

(A) volume.

(B) mass.

(C) mass per hour.

(D) volume per hour.

(E) inverse hours.

Questions 61–62 relate to the following.

An object starts with a speed of 10 m/s and accelerates at –2 m/s².

61. How much time will pass until it comes to rest?

(A) 2 s

(B) 4 s

(C) 5 s

(D) 12 s

(E) 20 s

$V_F = 0$

$V_F = V_i + at$

$0 = 10 + (-2)(t)$

62. How far does the object travel before coming to rest?

(A) 10 m

(B) 25 m

(C) 50 m

(D) 75 m

(E) 100 m

$V_F^2 = V_i^2 + 2a\Delta$

$0 = 100 + 2(-2) x$

GO ON TO THE NEXT PAGE

Questions 63–65 relate to the graph of the net force **F** exerted on a 2 kg block as a function of time in seconds, shown above.

63. The acceleration of the block between 0 and 2 seconds is

(A) 1.5 m/s².
(B) 3 m/s².
(C) 4 m/s².
(D) 6 m/s².
(E) 9 m/s².

64. The speed of the block is greatest at

(A) 2 s.
(B) 3 s.
(C) 4 s.
(D) 5 s.
(E) The speed is constant at all times.

65. If the block starts from rest, its momentum at 5 seconds is

(A) 1 kg m/s.
(B) 3 kg m/s.
(C) 6 kg m/s.
(D) 8 kg m/s.
(E) 10 kg m/s.

Questions 66–67 refer to a positive charge moving in a straight line through space.

66. A person who is at rest as the charge moves by him will measure

(A) a magnetic field and an electric field due to the moving charge.
(B) a magnetic field, but not an electric field due to the moving charge.
(C) an electric field, but not a magnetic field due to the moving charge.
(D) neither an electric field nor a magnetic field due to the moving charge.
(E) a decrease in the amount of charge.

67. A person who is moving parallel to the charge and at the same velocity as the charge will measure

(A) a magnetic field and an electric field due to the moving charge.
(B) a magnetic field, but not an electric field due to the moving charge.
(C) an electric field, but not a magnetic field due to the moving charge.
(D) neither an electric field nor a magnetic field due to the moving charge.
(E) a decrease in the amount of charge.

68. In 1887, Heinrich Hertz discovered the photoelectric effect. When ultraviolet light is shined on a zinc metal surface, he found that the metal

(A) emitted protons.
(B) emitted neutrons.
(C) became negatively charged.
(D) became positively charged.
(E) emitted photons.

GO ON TO THE NEXT PAGE

69. Which of the following is NOT a postulate or result of Bohr's model of the hydrogen atom?

    (A) Excited gases emit a bright-line emission spectrum.
    (B) The electron in the hydrogen atom can be found at any radius around the nucleus of the atom.
    (C) When the electron makes a transition to a higher energy level, it has absorbed energy.
    (D) When the electron makes a transition to a lower energy level, it has emitted energy.
    (E) The energy levels of the electron are quantized.

70. The Heisenberg uncertainty principle states that

    (A) we can measure the position of an electron only if we know its momentum.
    (B) we can measure the momentum of an electron only if we know its position.
    (C) only one electron can exist in the lowest energy level of an atom.
    (D) light can behave like a wave or a photon.
    (E) there is a limit to the accuracy of the measurement of subatomic particles.

71. If electricity costs $0.12 per kilowatt-hour, how much does it cost for electricity to operate a 150-watt light bulb for 5 hours?

    (A) $0.009
    (B) $0.09
    (C) $0.90
    (D) $9.00
    (E) $90.00

Questions 72–74 relate to the temperature vs. time graph below for 2 kg of a particular substance. Heat is being applied to the system for the entire time interval that is graphed. The substance is in the solid state at a temperature of 20°C.

72. The interval during which the substance is changing from the liquid phase to the gas phase is

    (A) AB.
    (B) AC.
    (C) BC.
    (D) CD.
    (E) DE.

73. If 100 J of heat is needed to completely change the substance from a solid to a liquid state, what is the heat of fusion for the substance?

    (A) 1,000 J/kg
    (B) 100 J/kg
    (C) 50 J/kg
    (D) 20 J/kg
    (E) 5 J/kg

GO ON TO THE NEXT PAGE

74. If 200 J of heat is added during the time interval from B to C, the specific heat of the substance is

(A) 200 J/kg°C.
(B) 100 J/kg°C.
(C) 60 J/kg°C.
(D) 17 J/kg°C.
(E) 1.67 J/kg°C.

$$\frac{\overset{100}{\cancel{200}} \text{ J}}{2kg \cdot 60C} = \frac{10}{6} \frac{J}{C} = \frac{5}{3} \frac{J}{C}$$

$$1\frac{2}{3}$$

$$1.67 \frac{J}{C}$$

75. The diagram above best represents the ray diagram for a

(A) converging lens.
(B) diverging lens.
(C) converging mirror.
(D) diverging mirror.
(E) plane mirror.

STOP!

**If you finish before time is up,
you may check your work.**

Answer Key
Practice Test 2

1.	B	20.	A	39.	C	58.	D
2.	D	21.	D	40.	B	59.	E
3.	D	22.	B	41.	C	60.	B
4.	B	23.	B	42.	C	61.	C
5.	A	24.	B	43.	D	62.	B
6.	C	25.	D	44.	B	63.	A
7.	E	26.	E	45.	D	64.	D
8.	A	27.	E	46.	B	65.	E
9.	E	28.	C	47.	C	66.	A
10.	D	29.	A	48.	B	67.	C
11.	B	30.	D	49.	B	68.	D
12.	A	31.	D	50.	D	69.	B
13.	D	32.	D	51.	B	70.	E
14.	B	33.	E	52.	A	71.	B
15	A	34.	D	53.	C	72.	D
16.	C	35.	C	54.	B	73.	C
17.	D	36.	A	55.	A	74.	E
18.	B	37.	B	56.	D	75.	C
19.	E	38.	C	57.	C		

ANSWERS AND EXPLANATIONS

1. B

The velocity vector is tangent to the path of the circle and in the direction the ball is moving at the instant the ball is at point P.

2. D

The ball is constantly accelerating toward the center of the circle as it accelerates away from a straight-line path. We say that the acceleration is centripetal.

3. D

The net force and the acceleration must be in the same direction according to Newton's second law. The string is always pulling the ball toward the center of the circle.

4. B

Since the distance between the constant time intervals is increasing, the ball is covering more distance per second each second, which is an increase in speed (acceleration).

5. A

The distance covered per one second time interval is constant; therefore, the velocity is constant.

6. C

When a ball is thrown upward, the acceleration is in the opposite direction of the velocity, and so the speed of the ball decreases. This means that the distance covered per time interval decreases.

7. E

The dots represent a ball that starts out at a high velocity (large distance per unit time), slowing down to a small velocity (small distance per unit time), and then the speed increases again as the ball rolls down the incline.

8. A

The electric field is defined as the force per unit charge acting on a positive charge. If we place a small positive charge at point A to test the electric field, it would be repelled from +Q and attracted by −4 Q. The electric force is proportional to the product of the charges and inversely proportional to the square of the distance between the charges (Coulomb's law), and since the negative charge is four times greater than +Q, the positive test charge must be farther from −4 Q than from +Q for the forces from each to cancel each other out and produce a net electric field of zero at point A.

9. E

Even though the electric field at point E due to +Q points to the right, +Q is very far away, and −4 Q applies a greater force to a charge placed at E. Therefore, the electric field due to −4 Q points to the left at E.

10. D

A small charge placed at point D would experience a strong attractive force (to the right) from −4 Q and a repulsive force (to the right) from +Q. The force on the small charge is greatest at the closest distance from the large charge.

11. B

The energy of a photon is proportional to its frequency.

12. A

The emissions of electrons in the photoelectric effect does not occur until a minimum frequency is met, indicated by the graph starting at a particular frequency called the threshold frequency.

13. D

When the object is at rest, the mass has a value that increases as the object begins to move with a velocity. As the object moves closer to the speed of light, the mass gets larger and larger, but can't quite achieve the speed of light c.

14. B

Momentum is mass times velocity. Since the masses are the same but the red car has twice the velocity of the blue car, the red car has twice the momentum.

15. A

Kinetic energy is proportional to the square of the speed ($KE = \frac{1}{2}mv^2$), so the car with twice the speed will have four times the kinetic energy.

16. C

A hertz is a cycle per second. The waves oscillate at 90 cycles per minute, or 90 cycles/60 s = 1.5 cycles/sec or 1.5 Hz.

17. D

As the ray passes from a less dense medium (air) to a more dense medium (glass), the ray bends toward the normal line. As the ray exits the glass back into the air, it must bend back to the original angle in the air.

18. B

The block is momentarily at rest, but it will not stay at rest because the spring is accelerating the block upward with a spring force. This is similar to a ball thrown up into the air when it comes to rest at the top of the flight; it has no velocity but does have an acceleration at that point.

19. E

As long as there is no energy lost to friction, the gravitational potential energy of the block at height h will be converted into spring potential energy at compression distance y and then back to gravitational potential energy at the maximum height again.

20. A

For an object in uniform circular motion, the force (toward the center of the circle) is perpendicular to the velocity (tangent to the circular path).

21. D

Figure I could represent the velocity and acceleration vectors of the projectile when it is at the top of the trajectory, and figure II could represent the velocity and acceleration vectors when the projectile is rising during the first half of its flight.

22. B

The force between the stars is inversely proportional to the square of the distance r between them, so a small r would produce a large force, and a large r would produce a small force.

23. B

The weight of the 15 kg block and the normal force the table exerts on the block are equal and opposite, so the only force that can accelerate the 15 kg block is the tension in the string.

24. B

If we look at the entire system as a whole, then the weight of the 5 kg block, which is 50 N, is the force that accelerates both the 5 kg block and the 15 kg block. In other words, the weight of one block is accelerating the equivalent of four 5 kg blocks, giving only one-fourth as much acceleration as the block would have if it were falling freely.

25. D

The energy of the emitted photon is equal to the difference in the two energy levels, so 6 eV – 4 eV = 2 eV.

26. E

All three of the statements describe the conclusions reached by Rutherford as a result of his alpha-scattering experiment.

27. E

The color with the lowest frequency corresponds to the longest wavelength, which is orange in this case.

28. C

Since 60 of the 90 joules of heat are used to do work, there are only 30 joules of heat left to deliver to the house, 90 J – 60 J = 30 J.

29. A
$$R = \frac{V}{I} = \frac{12\ V}{2\ A} = 6\ \Omega.$$

30. D
$$P = IV = (2\ A)(12\ V) = 24\ W.$$

31. D

A watt is a unit for power, which is energy per unit time.

32. D

By conservation of energy, the pendulum's initial potential energy is equal to the kinetic energy at the bottom of the swing:

$$mgh = \frac{1}{2}mv^2$$

$$v = \sqrt{2\,gh} = \sqrt{2(10\ \text{m/s}^2)(4\ \text{m})}$$

$$= 9\ \text{m/s (approximately)}.$$

33. E

All three choices could be represented by the graph, which depicts constant negative acceleration.

34. D

The string between the blocks has to accelerate only half the mass (block 1) as the 40 N force at an acceleration of 3 m/s², so the tension in the string between the blocks is half of 40 N, or 20 N.

35. C

The horizontal distance $x = vt = (10\ \text{m/s})(3\ \text{s}) = 30$ m.

36. A

Each atom has its own magnetic field, and if a group of atoms can align their magnetic fields, this group or cluster of atoms is called a magnetic domain.

37. B

Friction is caused by the electrons in two surfaces repelling each other.

38. C

The period of a pendulum does not depend on the mass of the pendulum or the amplitude of swing (for small swings). The period is proportional to the square root of the length of the pendulum.

39. C

The identical bulbs have equal resistance, so they will divide the total voltage equally, each bulb having 25 V across it. Another way to calculate the voltage across bulb 1 is power divided by current, also yielding 25 V.

40. B

Since the two bulbs are in series with each other, the same current passes through both of them.

41. C
$$R = \frac{V}{I} = \frac{25\ V}{4\ A} = 6\ \Omega \text{ (approximately)}.$$

42. C

Blue light has a shorter wavelength than red light, and shorter wavelengths refract more than longer wavelengths in the glass.

43. D

The waves pass through the double-slit and interfere with each other, creating nodes and antinodes on the screen, which we see as alternating bright and dark lines.

44. B

Since the energy of a photon is proportional to its frequency, twice the frequency will give twice the energy.

45. D

Sound is the only longitudinal wave listed. All of the other waves listed are transverse.

46. B

The wavelength is the length of one compression and one expansion. Since there are three wavelengths shown in the 9 m tank, each wavelength must be 3 m.

47. C

The speed of the wave is the frequency times the wavelength, so (500 Hz)(3 m) = 1,500 m/s.

48. B

The ball is moving with constant speed because the force is perpendicular to the velocity and cannot change the magnitude of the velocity (speed) but only its direction, like we would see in uniform circular motion. The force does no work on the ball and therefore cannot change its kinetic energy.

49. B

The product of mass and distance from the center of mass on the left must equal the product of mass and distance from the center of mass on the right, thus, (6 kg)(2) = (2 kg)(6).

50. D

The normal force is equal and opposite to the push P, and the weight is equal and opposite to the frictional force.

51. B

The frictional force must be equal and opposite to the weight (mg) of the block, since the block is not sliding up or down the wall.

52. A

Kinetic energy is not a vector, since it has no direction associated with it. Work and energy are scalars.

53. C

If there are more collisions between the molecules and the walls of the container, there must be more pressure against the walls. If there are more collisions, the molecules must have a higher average kinetic energy, and since kinetic energy is proportional to temperature, the temperature is also increasing.

54. B

Two conductors that are oppositely but equally charged are the capacitor.

55. A

The negatively charged electron will be attracted to plate I since it is the positive plate (connected to the positive terminal of the battery). The electron will accelerate, since the electric force acts on it until it reaches the top plate.

56. D

By the first right-hand rule, your thumb points out of the page in the direction of the current, and your fingers curl around in the direction of the magnetic field produced by the wire.

57. C

As the candle is burning, it radiates heat in the form of infrared radiation, and also heats the air around it, creating convection currents that reach the inner walls of the container.

58. D

Heat is conducted through the metal to your hand.

59. E

Like the gravitational force, the gravitational acceleration depends on the inverse square of the distance from the center of the Earth, so four times the distance gives $\frac{1}{16}$ of the force and acceleration.

60. B

The area under the curve is $\left(\frac{\text{kg}}{\text{hr}}\right)(\text{hr}) = \text{kg}$, the unit for mass.

61. C

$v_f = 0 = v_i + at = 10 \text{ m/s} + (-2 \text{ m/s}^2)(t)$
gives $t = 5$ s.

62. B

$s = v_i t + \frac{1}{2} at^2 =$
$(10 \text{ m/s})(5 \text{ s}) + \frac{1}{2}(-2 \text{ m/s}^2)(5 s^2) = 25$ m.

63. A

$a = \frac{F}{m} = \frac{3 \text{ N}}{2 \text{ kg}} = 1.5 \text{ m/s}^2$

64. D

Since there is a force acting on the block at all times up to 5 s, the block continues accelerating up to 5 s, where its speed is the greatest.

65. E

The change in momentum is equal to the impulse ($F\Delta t$), which is the area under the curve. The change in momentum is equal to the final momentum, since the initial momentum is zero, and the area under the curve is 10 kg m/s.

66. A

All charges produce an electric field whether they are moving or not, and magnetic fields are created by moving charges, so the person would measure both.

67. C

The person will measure an electric field, but since the charge is at rest relative to the person making the measurement, no magnetic field will be detected.

68. D

Hertz found that the metal became positively charged when ultraviolet light was shined on it, and it was later discovered that the metal was emitting electrons.

69. B

Bohr showed that the electron in the hydrogen atom could only be found in certain selected (quantized) orbits, and no others.

70. E

The more we know about the momentum of a subatomic particle, the less we can be certain of its position, and vice versa.

71. B

$\text{cost} = (0.150 \text{ kWh})(5 \text{ hr})\left(12 \frac{\text{cents}}{\text{kWh}}\right) = 9 \text{ cents}$
$= \$0.09$.

72. D

The temperature does not change during a phase change, since the heat is used to change the state of the substance and not its temperature. Since the substance is in the solid state at 20°C, it is changing from a solid to a liquid during interval AB and a liquid to a gas during the interval CD.

73. C

$Q = mL_f$ implies that

$$L_f = \frac{Q}{m} = \frac{100 \text{ J}}{2 \text{ kg}} = 50 \frac{\text{J}}{\text{kg}}.$$

74. E

$Q = mc\Delta T$ implies that

$$c = \frac{Q}{m\Delta T} = \frac{200 \text{ J}}{(2 \text{ kg})(80°\text{C} - 20°\text{C})} = 1.67 \frac{\text{J}}{\text{kg}°\text{C}}.$$

75. C

The rays strike the concave side of the mirror and converge at the focal point.

HOW TO CALCULATE YOUR SCORE

Step 1: Figure out your raw score. Use the answer key to count the number of questions you answered correctly and the number of questions you answered incorrectly. (Do not count any questions you left blank.) Multiply the number wrong by 0.25 and subtract the result from the number correct. Round the result to the nearest whole number. This is your raw score.

SAT Subject Test: Physics Practice Test 3

Number right		Number wrong		Raw score
☐	−	$\left(0.25 \times \right.$ ☐ $\left.\right)$	=	☐

Step 2: Find your scaled score. In the Score Conversion Table below, find your raw score (rounded to the nearest whole number) in one of the columns to the left. The score directly to the right of that number will be your scaled score.

A note on your practice test scores: Don't take these scores too literally. Practice test conditions cannot precisely mirror real test conditions. Your actual SAT Subject Test: Physics score will almost certainly vary from your diagnostic and practice test scores. However, your scores on the diagnostic and practice tests will give you a rough idea of your range on the actual exam.

Score Conversion Table

Raw	Scaled	Raw	Scaled	Raw	Scaled	Raw	Scaled	Raw	Scaled	Raw	Scaled
75	800	59	780	43	690	27	590	11	480	−5	380
74	800	58	770	42	680	26	580	10	480	−6	370
73	800	57	770	41	670	25	580	9	470	−7	370
72	800	56	760	40	670	24	570	8	470	−8	360
71	800	55	760	39	660	23	570	7	460	−9	350
70	800	54	750	38	650	22	560	6	450	−10	350
69	800	53	750	37	650	21	550	5	450	−11	340
68	800	52	740	36	640	20	540	4	440	−12	330
67	800	51	730	35	640	19	540	3	430	−13	330
66	800	50	730	34	630	18	530	2	430	−14	320
65	800	49	720	33	630	17	530	1	420	−15	310
64	800	48	720	32	620	16	520	0	410	−16	310
63	800	47	710	31	610	15	510	−1	410	−17	300
62	790	46	700	30	610	14	510	−2	400	−18	290
61	790	45	700	29	600	13	500	−3	390	−19	290
60	780	44	690	28	600	12	490	−4	390		

Practice Test 3
Answer Grid

1. Ⓐ Ⓑ Ⓒ Ⓓ Ⓔ
2. Ⓐ Ⓑ Ⓒ Ⓓ Ⓔ
3. Ⓐ Ⓑ Ⓒ Ⓓ Ⓔ
4. Ⓐ Ⓑ Ⓒ Ⓓ Ⓔ
5. Ⓐ Ⓑ Ⓒ Ⓓ Ⓔ
6. Ⓐ Ⓑ Ⓒ Ⓓ Ⓔ
7. Ⓐ Ⓑ Ⓒ Ⓓ Ⓔ
8. Ⓐ Ⓑ Ⓒ Ⓓ Ⓔ
9. Ⓐ Ⓑ Ⓒ Ⓓ Ⓔ
10. Ⓐ Ⓑ Ⓒ Ⓓ Ⓔ
11. Ⓐ Ⓑ Ⓒ Ⓓ Ⓔ
12. Ⓐ Ⓑ Ⓒ Ⓓ Ⓔ
13. Ⓐ Ⓑ Ⓒ Ⓓ Ⓔ
14. Ⓐ Ⓑ Ⓒ Ⓓ Ⓔ
15. Ⓐ Ⓑ Ⓒ Ⓓ Ⓔ
16. Ⓐ Ⓑ Ⓒ Ⓓ Ⓔ
17. Ⓐ Ⓑ Ⓒ Ⓓ Ⓔ
18. Ⓐ Ⓑ Ⓒ Ⓓ Ⓔ
19. Ⓐ Ⓑ Ⓒ Ⓓ Ⓔ
20. Ⓐ Ⓑ Ⓒ Ⓓ Ⓔ
21. Ⓐ Ⓑ Ⓒ Ⓓ Ⓔ
22. Ⓐ Ⓑ Ⓒ Ⓓ Ⓔ
23. Ⓐ Ⓑ Ⓒ Ⓓ Ⓔ
24. Ⓐ Ⓑ Ⓒ Ⓓ Ⓔ
25. Ⓐ Ⓑ Ⓒ Ⓓ Ⓔ

26. Ⓐ Ⓑ Ⓒ Ⓓ Ⓔ
27. Ⓐ Ⓑ Ⓒ Ⓓ Ⓔ
28. Ⓐ Ⓑ Ⓒ Ⓓ Ⓔ
29. Ⓐ Ⓑ Ⓒ Ⓓ Ⓔ
30. Ⓐ Ⓑ Ⓒ Ⓓ Ⓔ
31. Ⓐ Ⓑ Ⓒ Ⓓ Ⓔ
32. Ⓐ Ⓑ Ⓒ Ⓓ Ⓔ
33. Ⓐ Ⓑ Ⓒ Ⓓ Ⓔ
34. Ⓐ Ⓑ Ⓒ Ⓓ Ⓔ
35. Ⓐ Ⓑ Ⓒ Ⓓ Ⓔ
36. Ⓐ Ⓑ Ⓒ Ⓓ Ⓔ
37. Ⓐ Ⓑ Ⓒ Ⓓ Ⓔ
38. Ⓐ Ⓑ Ⓒ Ⓓ Ⓔ
39. Ⓐ Ⓑ Ⓒ Ⓓ Ⓔ
40. Ⓐ Ⓑ Ⓒ Ⓓ Ⓔ
41. Ⓐ Ⓑ Ⓒ Ⓓ Ⓔ
42. Ⓐ Ⓑ Ⓒ Ⓓ Ⓔ
43. Ⓐ Ⓑ Ⓒ Ⓓ Ⓔ
44. Ⓐ Ⓑ Ⓒ Ⓓ Ⓔ
45. Ⓐ Ⓑ Ⓒ Ⓓ Ⓔ
46. Ⓐ Ⓑ Ⓒ Ⓓ Ⓔ
47. Ⓐ Ⓑ Ⓒ Ⓓ Ⓔ
48. Ⓐ Ⓑ Ⓒ Ⓓ Ⓔ
49. Ⓐ Ⓑ Ⓒ Ⓓ Ⓔ
50. Ⓐ Ⓑ Ⓒ Ⓓ Ⓔ

51. Ⓐ Ⓑ Ⓒ Ⓓ Ⓔ
52. Ⓐ Ⓑ Ⓒ Ⓓ Ⓔ
53. Ⓐ Ⓑ Ⓒ Ⓓ Ⓔ
54. Ⓐ Ⓑ Ⓒ Ⓓ Ⓔ
55. Ⓐ Ⓑ Ⓒ Ⓓ Ⓔ
56. Ⓐ Ⓑ Ⓒ Ⓓ Ⓔ
57. Ⓐ Ⓑ Ⓒ Ⓓ Ⓔ
58. Ⓐ Ⓑ Ⓒ Ⓓ Ⓔ
59. Ⓐ Ⓑ Ⓒ Ⓓ Ⓔ
60. Ⓐ Ⓑ Ⓒ Ⓓ Ⓔ
61. Ⓐ Ⓑ Ⓒ Ⓓ Ⓔ
62. Ⓐ Ⓑ Ⓒ Ⓓ Ⓔ
63. Ⓐ Ⓑ Ⓒ Ⓓ Ⓔ
64. Ⓐ Ⓑ Ⓒ Ⓓ Ⓔ
65. Ⓐ Ⓑ Ⓒ Ⓓ Ⓔ
66. Ⓐ Ⓑ Ⓒ Ⓓ Ⓔ
67. Ⓐ Ⓑ Ⓒ Ⓓ Ⓔ
68. Ⓐ Ⓑ Ⓒ Ⓓ Ⓔ
69. Ⓐ Ⓑ Ⓒ Ⓓ Ⓔ
70. Ⓐ Ⓑ Ⓒ Ⓓ Ⓔ
71. Ⓐ Ⓑ Ⓒ Ⓓ Ⓔ
72. Ⓐ Ⓑ Ⓒ Ⓓ Ⓔ
73. Ⓐ Ⓑ Ⓒ Ⓓ Ⓔ
74. Ⓐ Ⓑ Ⓒ Ⓓ Ⓔ
75. Ⓐ Ⓑ Ⓒ Ⓓ Ⓔ

Practice Test 3

Part A

Directions: Each set of lettered choices below relates to the numbered questions immediately following it. Select the one lettered choice that best answers each question. A choice may be used once, more than once, or not at all in each set.

Questions 1–3 relate to the following.

Two masses m_1 and m_2 are separated by a distance R so that there is a gravitational force F between them. The following choices refer to the gravitational force on m_1 due to m_2.

    (A) It is quadrupled.
    (B) It is doubled.
    (C) It remains the same.
    (D) It is halved.
    (E) It is quartered.

1. What happens to the magnitude of the force on m_1 if the mass of m_2 is doubled?   *B*

2. What happens to the magnitude of the force on m_1 if the distance between the centers of the masses is doubled?   *E*

3. What happens to the magnitude of the force on m_1 if the distance between the centers of the masses is halved?   *A*

Questions 4–6 relate to the following circuit and the choices that follow. The resistors R_1, R_2, and R_3 each have a different value.

    (A) R_1, R_2, and R_3
    (B) R_1 only
    (C) R_2 only
    (D) R_3 only
    (E) R_2 and R_3 only

4. Through which resistor(s) will the total current in the circuit pass?   *B*

5. Through which resistor(s) will the ammeter read the current?   *C*

6. Across which resistor(s) will the voltmeter correctly read the voltage?   *E*

GO ON TO THE NEXT PAGE

Questions 7–9 relate to the following.

Five objects are moving in straight-line paths. The objects all cross a starting line at the instant a clock is started. The distances from the starting line in meters after 1, 2, 3, 4, and 5 equal time units are as follows.

	Time (units)				
Object	1	2	3	4	5
(A)	1 m	4 m	9 m	16 m	25 m
(B)	2 m	2 m	4 m	4 m	6 m
(C)	2 m	4 m	6 m	8 m	10 m
(D)	6 m	11 m	15 m	18 m	20 m
(E)	4 m	9 m	15 m	22 m	29 m

7. Which object is moving with a constant velocity?

8. Which object could be in free fall, neglecting air resistance?

9. Which object's acceleration is opposite to its velocity?

Questions 10–12 relate to the converging lens and principal axis shown and the choices that follow.

The focal length *f* and twice the focal length *2f* are marked on either side of the lens.

(A) position 1
(B) position 2
(C) position 3
(D) position 4
(E) position 5

10. At which position could a candle be placed so that a virtual image would be formed?

11. At which position could a candle be placed so that an image smaller than the candle would be formed?

12. At which position could a candle be placed so that neither a real nor a virtual image would be formed?

GO ON TO THE NEXT PAGE

Part B

Directions: Each of the questions or incomplete statements below is followed by five answer choices. Select the one that is best in each case.

# of protons

13. Which of the following radioactive processes, when occurring separately, must alter the atomic number of the radioactive nucleus?

    I.   alpha decay   *helium nucleus*
    II. beta decay   *electron shift*
    III. gamma decay

    (A) I only
    (B) II only
    (C) III only
    (D) I and II only
    (E) I, II, and III

    pure energy O—O

14. The diagram above shows an isolated positive charge Q. Point Y is three times as far away from Q as point X. The ratio of the electric force that would act on a small charge placed at point Y compared to the charge placed at point X is

    $F = \dfrac{kq_1q_2}{r^2}$

    (A) 1 to 9.
    (B) 1 to 3.
    (C) 1 to 1.
    (D) 3 to 1.
    (E) 9 to 1.

15. Which of the following particles would experience the greatest electric force in the same uniform electric field?

    (A) proton
    (B) electron
    (C) alpha particle
    (D) neutron
    (E) photon

Questions 16–18 refer to the figure below.

A ball is projected and follows a parabolic path. Point Y is the highest point on the path, and air resistance is negligible.

16. Which of the following is true of how the speeds of the ball at the three points compare?

    (A) $v_X > v_Y > v_Z$
    (B) $v_X > v_Z > v_Y$
    (C) $v_Y > v_X > v_Z$
    (D) $v_Z > v_X = v_Y$
    (E) $v_Y > v_X = v_Z$

17. Which of the following best shows the direction of the acceleration of the ball at point Z?

18. What is the direction of the net force acting on the ball at point Y?

19. Neutral isotopes of the same element may have different numbers of

    (A) protons.
    (B) neutrons.
    (C) electrons.
    (D) alpha particles.
    (E) positrons.

GO ON TO THE NEXT PAGE

Questions 20–21 refer to the standing wave in a vibrating string 3 meters long as shown below. The frequency of the wave is 60 Hz.

20. The wavelength of the wave is

    (A) 1 m.
    (B) 2 m.
    (C) 3 m.
    (D) 6 m.
    (E) 9 m.

21. The speed of the wave is

    (A) 180 m/s.
    (B) 120 m/s.
    (C) 60 m/s.
    (D) 30 m/s.
    (E) 6 m/s.

$$c = f\lambda$$
$$= (2)(60)$$

22. A candle is placed near a plane mirror as shown above. At which point above is the image of the candle formed?

    (A) A
    (B) B
    (C) C
    (D) D
    (E) E

$$y = \frac{mg}{\sin\theta} \cdot \frac{1}{2}$$

23. Which of the following was one of the two basic postulates of special relativity formulated by Albert Einstein?

    (A) Accelerating reference frames are equivalent to reference frames that are moving with a constant velocity.
    (B) The speed of light has the same constant value in all inertial reference frames.
    (C) Photons move slightly faster than light waves.
    (D) When moving the speed of light, mass will be converted to pure energy.
    (E) All physical laws are relative.

24. A space traveler is moving relative to the Earth at 0.6 times the speed of light, as measured in the Earth's frame of reference. In one year as measured in the Earth's frame of reference, the space traveler will

    (A) age more than one year.
    (B) age less than one year.
    (C) age exactly one year.
    (D) not age at all.
    (E) become younger.

$$\sin\theta = \frac{mg}{y}$$

25. A mass m is hung from two light strings as shown above. The tension in each string is

    (A) $mg\cos\theta$
    (B) $2\,mg\cos\theta$
    (C) $mg\sin\theta$
    (D) $\frac{1}{2}\,mg\sin\theta$
    (E) $\frac{mg}{2\sin\theta}$

GO ON TO THE NEXT PAGE

Handwritten: $V_f = V_i + at$

Handwritten: $V_f = 0 + (5)(4)$

Questions 26–27 refer to the energy level diagram for a hypothetical atom shown below. The energy for each level is given above ground state.

Energy above
ground state

$n = 4$ ——————— $E_4 = 7$ eV

$n = 3$ ——————— $E_3 = 6$ eV

$n = 2$ ——————— $E_2 = 4$ eV

$n = 1$ ——————— $E_1 = 0$

26. Which of the following photon energies could NOT be emitted from this atom after it has been excited to the 4th energy level?

    (A) 1 eV
    (B) 2 eV
    (C) 3 eV
    (D) 4 eV
    (E) 5 eV

27. Which of the following transitions will produce the photon with the highest frequency?

    (A) $n = 2$ to $n = 1$
    (B) $n = 3$ to $n = 1$
    (C) $n = 3$ to $n = 2$
    (D) $n = 4$ to $n = 1$
    (E) $n = 4$ to $n = 3$

    Handwritten: energy = freq

28. If the mass of an object is doubled, and the net force acting on the object is quadrupled, the acceleration of the object is

    (A) quartered.
    (B) halved.
    (C) unchanged.
    (D) doubled.
    (E) quadrupled.

    Handwritten: $F = ma$

    Handwritten: $(4F) = (2m)$

29. An object starts from rest and accelerates at 5 m/s^2. How far will it travel during the first 4 seconds?

    (A) 20 m
    (B) 40 m
    (C) 80 m
    (D) 120 m
    (E) 160 m

    Handwritten: $V_f^2 = V_i^2 + 2ax$

    Handwritten: $400 = 0 + 2(5)(x)$

30. Light passes from medium 1 to medium 2 and bends along the path between points A and B as shown above. Which of the following statements is correct?

    (A) Medium 1 is more dense than medium 2.
    (B) Medium 1 is less dense than medium 2.
    (C) The speed of the light in medium 1 is greater than the speed of the light in medium 2.
    (D) The frequency of the light in medium 1 is greater than the frequency of the light in medium 2.
    (E) The wavelength is the same in medium 1 and medium 2.

GO ON TO THE NEXT PAGE

31. Consider the three lenses below.

 I. II. III.

Which of the above will cause light rays to diverge?

(A) I only
(B) II only
(C) I and II only
(D) III only
(F) I, II, and III

M   6 kg

32. A meter stick of negligible mass is hung from a rope attached to its center, as shown above. A 6 kg mass is hung from one end of the meter stick, and another mass M is hung at a distance of 30 cm from the center of the meter stick, but on the opposite side of the 6 kg mass. What is the value of M?

(A) 3 kg
(B) 5 kg
(C) 6 kg
(D) 10 kg
(E) 30 kg

33. A wire in the plane of the page carries a current I directed toward the right, as shown. If the wire is located in a uniform magnetic field that is directed into the page, the force on the wire resulting from the magnetic field is

(A) zero.
(B) directed out of the page.
(C) directed to the bottom of the page.
(D) directed to the left.
(E) directed to the top of the page.

34. An ideal gas in a closed container initially has a volume V, a pressure P, and Kelvin temperature T. If the temperature is changed to 4 T, which of the following pairs of pressure and volume is possible?

(A) P and V

(B) P and $\frac{1}{2}$ V

(C) 4 P and 4 V

(D) 4 P and V

(E) $\frac{1}{4}$ P and V

35. A gas in a container absorbs 300 J of heat, then has 100 J of work done on it, then does 50 J of work. The increase in the internal energy of the gas is

(A) 450 J.
(B) 400 J.
(C) 350 J.
(D) 200 J.
(E) 100 J.

GO ON TO THE NEXT PAGE

Questions 36–37 refer to the following.

Two large parallel conducting plates are connected to a battery of voltage *V*, as shown below. Point I is halfway between the plates. Edge effects may be neglected.

36. If a proton is placed at one of the three points above, which of the following statements is true?

    (A) The proton will experience a greater force at point I than at point II.

    (B) The proton will experience a greater force at point II than at point I.

    (C) The proton will experience a greater force at point III than at point II.

    (D) The proton will experience the same force at points I, II, and III.

    (E) The proton will experience no force at point I.

37. If an electron is placed at one of the three points above, which of the following statements is true?

    (A) The electron will experience a greater upward acceleration at point I than at point II.

    (B) The electron will experience a greater downward acceleration at point II than at point I.

    (C) The electron will experience the same upward acceleration at points I, II, and III.

    (D) The electron will experience the same downward acceleration at points I, II, and III.

    (E) The electron will experience no acceleration at points I, II, or III.

38. The direction of the magnetic field at point A caused by the current I in the wire shown above is

    (A) to the right.
    (B) to the left.
    (C) toward the wire.
    (D) into the page.
    (E) out of the page.

39. Two long parallel wires are separated by a distance *d* as shown above. One wire carries a steady current *I* into the plane of the page, and the other wire carries an equal steady current *I* that is out of the page. The net magnetic field at a point halfway between the wires points in which of the following directions?

    (A) →   (B) ←   (C) ↑   (D) ↓   (E) zero

GO ON TO THE NEXT PAGE

Questions 40–42 refer to the following.

A block of weight 180 N is pulled along a horizontal surface at a constant speed by a force of 80 N. The force acts at an angle of 30° with the horizontal, as shown below. (sin 30° = 0.50, cos 30° = 0.87)

40. The normal force by the surface on the block is most nearly

    (A) 20 N.
    (B) 40 N.
    (C) 60 N.
    (D) 80 N.
    (E) 140 N.

41. The frictional force acting between the block and the surface is most nearly

    (A) 20 N.
    (B) 40 N.
    (C) 70 N.
    (D) 80 N.
    (E) 92 N.

42. The coefficient of friction between the block and the surface is most nearly

    (A) 5.
    (B) 2.
    (C) 0.87.
    (D) 0.50.
    (E) 0.13.

Questions 43–45 refer to the diagram of a mass on a spring below.

The mass is oscillating about point O on a surface of negligible friction, and the maximum distances on either side of point O are labeled A_1 and A_2. The graphs below can represent quantities associated with the oscillation as a function of length x of the spring.

43. Which graph(s) can represent the potential energy of the spring and mass as a function of distance x?

    (A) I only
    (B) I and II only
    (C) II only
    (D) III only
    (E) II and III only

44. Which graph(s) can represent the kinetic energy of the spring and mass as a function of distance x?

    (A) I only
    (B) I and II only
    (C) II only
    (D) III only
    (E) II and III only

$$PE = \frac{1}{2}kx^2$$

GO ON TO THE NEXT PAGE

$F = kx$

45. Which graph(s) can represent the magnitude of the net force acting on the mass as a function of distance x?

(A) I only

(B) I and II only

$F^2 = kx$

(C) II only

(D) III only

(E) II and III only

Questions 46–47 refer to the following.

Two moons orbit a planet in circular orbits. The first moon orbits at a radius R from the center of the planet, and the second moon orbits at a radius 2R.

46. The ratio of the gravitational force between the planet and the first moon to the gravitational force to the second moon is equal to

R

$(2R$

(A) $\dfrac{1}{4}$.

(B) $\dfrac{1}{2}$.

(C) 1.

$\dfrac{1}{r}$ $\dfrac{1}{4r}$

(D) 2.

(E) 4.

47. Which of the following statements is true?

(A) The closer moon has a shorter period than the farther moon.

(B) The farther moon has a shorter period than the closer moon.

(C) The two moons must have the same period.

(D) The two moons must have the same linear speed.

(E) The two moons must have the same period and the same linear speed.

$V_B = V_A \rightarrow 0 = V_i + (-9.8)(3)$

$V_F = V_i + at$

Questions 48–50 relate to a ball thrown straight up, reaching its maximum height in 3 s.

Air resistance may be neglected.

48. The initial velocity of the ball is most nearly

(A) 10 m/s.

(B) 15 m/s.

(C) 30 m/s.

(D) 45 m/s.

(E) 60 m/s.

49. The magnitude of the acceleration of the ball at the instant it reaches its maximum height is most nearly

(A) zero.

(B) 5 m/s².

(C) 10 m/s².

(D) 12 m/s².

(E) 20 m/s².

50. The maximum height of the ball is most nearly

(A) 10 m.

(B) 15 m.

(C) 30 m.

(D) 45 m.

(E) 60 m.

$v^2 = (30)^2 + 2(-9.8)(x)$

$= 900 + (-20)(x)$

GO ON TO THE NEXT PAGE

51. The half-life of thorium is 24 days. If you start with a 60 µg sample of thorium, approximately how many micrograms of thorium remain after 120 days?

    (A) zero
    (B) 2 µg
    (C) 4 µg
    (D) 8 µg
    (E) 15 µg

52. The three statements below relate to ammeters and voltmeters used in an electrical circuit.

    I.   An ammeter must be placed in series with a resistor to correctly measure the current.

    II. A voltmeter must be placed in series with a resistor to correctly measure the voltage across the resistor.

    III. A voltmeter must have a high resistance.

    Which of the above statements are true?

    (A) I only
    (B) II only
    (C) I and II only
    (D) II and III only
    (E) I and III only

Questions 53–54 relate to the circuit shown below.

53. What is the value of the resistor R?

    (A) 1 Ω
    (B) 2 Ω
    (C) 4 Ω
    (D) 6 Ω
    (E) 12 Ω

54. What is the power dissipated through one of the 4 Ω resistors?

    (A) 4 W
    (B) 8 W
    (C) 16 W
    (D) 32 W
    (E) 36 W

GO ON TO THE NEXT PAGE

Questions 55–56 relate to the following.

A piece of metal with a mass of 2 kg and specific heat of 200 J/kg°C is initially at a temperature of 120°C. The metal is placed into an insulated container that contains a liquid of mass 4 kg, a specific heat of 600 J/kg°C, and an initial temperature of 20°C.

55. After a long time, the final equilibrium temperature of the metal and liquid is

    (A) 24°C.
    (B) 34°C.
    (C) 48°C.
    (D) 68°C.
    (E) 100°C.

56. In actuality, some of the heat is lost to the surroundings during the heat transfer from the metal to the liquid. This heat loss would result in

    (A) a lower equilibrium temperature.
    (B) a higher equilibrium temperature.
    (C) a lower specific heat for the liquid.
    (D) a lower specific heat for the metal.
    (E) more heat gained by the liquid.

Questions 57–58 refer to the velocity vs. time graph below.

57. The acceleration of the object between t = 0 and t = 4 s is

    (A) zero.
    (B) 1 m/s².
    (C) 2 m/s².
    (D) 4 m/s².
    (E) 8 m/s².

58. The displacement of the object between t = 0 and t = 8 s is

    (A) 64 m.
    (B) 32 m.
    (C) 24 m.
    (D) 16 m.
    (E) 8 m.

GO ON TO THE NEXT PAGE

59. Two identical metal spheres are equally but oppositely charged. If the spheres are brought into contact with each other for a long time and then separated, which of the following statements is true?

    (A) The charge on each sphere is the same as it was before the spheres were brought into contact.
    (B) The spheres will be equally charged and positive.
    (C) The spheres will be equally charged and negative.
    (D) The spheres will both be neutral.
    (E) The positive sphere must have more charge than the negative sphere.

60. A pencil is placed in a beaker of water and appears to be bent or broken. The property of light responsible for the pencil appearing to be bent is

    (A) refraction.
    (B) reflection.
    (C) diffraction.
    (D) interference.
    (E) polarization.

61. The second law of thermodynamics (law of entropy) explains which of the following?

    (A) The heat lost by one object must be gained by another object.
    (B) Heat flows naturally from a hotter body to a cooler body.
    (C) Celsius degrees and Kelvin degrees are equivalent.
    (D) Heat can be transformed into work.
    (E) The average kinetic energy of molecules is proportional to temperature.

62. Three forces that are in the same plane act on the same point above. Which of the following diagrams best represents the resultant of the forces?

63. Two electrons, each with a charge of magnitude 10^{-19} C, are separated by a distance of magnitude 10^{-10} m. If the Coulomb constant is 10^{10} N m^2/C^2, the magnitude of the force between the electrons is most nearly

    (A) 10^{-8} N.
    (B) 10^{-28} N.
    (C) 10^{-38} N.
    (D) 10^{-48} N.
    (E) 10^{-58} N.

64. A toy railroad car of mass 3 kg moving east collides with a 6 kg railroad car at rest, and the two cars lock together on impact and move away together toward the east at 2 m/s. The speed of the first car before the collision is

    (A) 2 m/s.
    (B) 3 m/s.
    (C) 4 m/s.
    (D) 6 m/s.
    (E) 9 m/s.

GO ON TO THE NEXT PAGE

65. A machine can lift a 500 N weight up to a height of 2 m in 20 seconds. The power developed by this machine is

(A) 10,000 W.
(B) 1,000 W.
(C) 50 W.
(D) 40 W.
(E) 25 W.

66. One end of a horizontal string is fixed to a wall, as shown above. A transverse wave pulse is generated at the other end, moves toward the wall, and is reflected at the wall. Which of the diagrams below best represents the pulse after it is reflected from the wall?

67. Electromagnetic induction is the basic principle for

(A) a resistor.
(B) an electric generator.
(C) a capacitor.
(D) a battery.
(E) an electroscope.

68. In a radioactive decay process, the parent atom undergoes the following radioactive decays: alpha, alpha, beta. The atomic number of the final daughter element is how many atomic mass units less than the parent atom?

(A) 2
(B) 3
(C) 4
(D) 5
(E) 7

Questions 69–70 refer to the diagram below.

A pattern of alternating bright and dark lines is produced on the screen when light is passed through the two narrow slits.

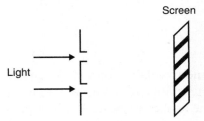

69. The property of light that is responsible for the bright and dark lines on the screen is

(A) refraction.
(B) reflection.
(C) polarization.
(D) frequency.
(E) interference.

70. If the screen is moved a greater distance from the slits, the center bright band of light will

(A) become wider.
(B) become narrower.
(C) remain unchanged.
(D) disappear completely.
(E) rotate 90°.

GO ON TO THE NEXT PAGE

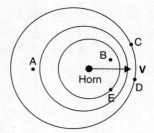

71. Sound waves of a constant frequency are being emitted by a horn as it moves to the right, as shown above. At which point would a listener hear a pitch that is lower than she would hear if the horn were at rest?

   (A) A
   (B) B
   (C) C
   (D) D
   (E) E

72. In a photoelectric effect experiment, light of a particular frequency is shined on a metal surface, and as a result electrons are emitted from the metal surface. Which of the following actions would produce more electrons per second?

   (A) Increase the frequency of the light.
   (B) Decrease the frequency of the light.
   (C) Increase the intensity (brightness) of the light.
   (D) Decrease the intensity (brightness) of the light.
   (E) Increase the wavelength of the light.

73. Which of the following statements is NOT a correct assumption of the model of an ideal monatomic gas?

   (A) The atoms are constantly moving.
   (B) The atoms' collisions with one another create pressure directly on the container of the gas.
   (C) The collisions between atoms are elastic.
   (D) The only significant forces acting on the atoms are those that are applied as a result of collisions.
   (E) The volume of each atom can be neglected.

74. An astronaut floating in space throws a small hand tool away from his space shuttle. Which of the following statements is true?

   (A) The velocity of the astronaut is equal and opposite to the velocity of the tool.
   (B) The impulse applied to the astronaut is equal and opposite to the impulse applied to the tool.
   (C) The mass of the astronaut is equal to the mass of the tool.
   (D) The momentum of the astronaut is greater than the momentum of the tool.
   (E) The force applied to the tool is greater than the force applied to the astronaut.

momentum is conserved

GO ON TO THE NEXT PAGE

Displacement

1 s   2 s   3 s   t

75. A pendulum oscillates in simple harmonic
    motion as represented by the figure above.
    The frequency of the pendulum is

    (A) 3 Hz.

    (B) 2 Hz.

    (C) 1 Hz.

    (D) $\frac{1}{2}$ Hz.

    (E) $\frac{1}{3}$ Hz.

STOP!

**If you finish before time is up,
you may check your work.**

Answer Key
Practice Test 3

1. B	20. B	39. D	58. C
2. E	21. B	40. E	59. D
3. A	22. C	41. C	60. A
4. B	23. B	42. D	61. B
5. C	24. B	43. A	62. C
6. E	25. E	44. C	63. A
7. C	26. E	45. D	64. D
8. A	27. D	46. E	65. C
9. D	28. D	47. A	66. A
10. E	29. B	48. C	67. B
11. A	30. A	49. C	68. B
12. D	31. D	50. D	69. E
13. D	32. D	51. B	70. A
14. A	33. E	52. E	71. A
15. C	34. D	53. B	72. C
16. B	35. C	54. C	73. B
17. A	36. D	55. B	74. B
18. B	37. C	56. A	75. D
19. B	38. D	57. B	

ANSWERS AND EXPLANATIONS

1. B

The gravitational force is proportional to the product of the masses, so doubling one of the masses would double the force. Thus,

$$\frac{G(m)(2\,m)}{r^2} = 2\,F.$$

2. E

The force is inversely proportional to the square of the distance between the two masses, so twice the distance would result in one-quarter the force. Thus,

$$\frac{Gm_1m_2}{(2\,r)^2} = \frac{1}{4}\,F.$$

3. A

If the masses are brought closer together, the force between them will be greater. Since the force is inversely proportional to the square of the distance between the masses, cutting the distance between them in half would increase the force by four times.

4. B

The total current will pass through R_1 since the current from the battery has not split up into any branches.

5. C

The ammeter is in series only with R_2, so the same current will pass through the ammeter and R_2.

6. E

The voltmeter, R_2, and R_3 are all in parallel with each other, and thus will have the same voltage across them.

7. C

The distance covered during each equal time unit is the same, 2 m. Thus, the object must be moving at a constant velocity.

8. A

For an object in free fall, the distance fallen is proportional to the square of the time.

9. D

If the change in distance between time intervals is decreasing, the object is slowing down, and thus the acceleration is opposite to the velocity.

10. E

An enlarged virtual image is formed when an object is placed inside the focal length of a converging lens. This is the principle behind a magnifying glass.

11. A

When the candle is placed at a distance greater than twice the focal length, the image is smaller than the object and is real and inverted.

12. D

When an object is placed at the focal length of a converging lens, the rays pass through the lens parallel to each other, and no image is formed.

13. D

Alpha decay reduces the atomic number of the parent atom by 2 atomic mass units, and beta decay increases the atomic number by one atomic mass unit. The gamma ray is an electromagnetic wave that has no mass.

14. A

Coulomb's law states that the force between two charges is inversely proportional to the square of the distance between the charges, and thus a charge placed at three times the distance will experience one-ninth as much force.

15. C

The alpha particle is made up of two protons and two neutrons, and therefore has twice the charge of either a proton or an electron and will experience twice the force in the same electric field.

16. B

The velocity is greatest at point X, and although the horizontal component of the velocity remains constant, the vertical component of the velocity decreases on the way up and increases on the way down. Thus, the velocity is greater at Z than at Y.

17. A

The only acceleration the ball has after it is launched is the acceleration due to gravity, which points straight downward.

18. B

The net force acting on the ball at point Y is the gravitational force, which points straight downward.

19. B

Isotopes of a particular element have the same number of protons but may have a different number of neutrons, which do not change the charge on the nucleus.

20. B

The wavelength is the length of one full cycle of the wave, which includes two loops of the standing wave, and is two-thirds of the length of the string in this case, or 2 m.

21. B

$v = f\lambda = (60 \text{ Hz})(2 \text{ m}) = 120 \text{ m/s}.$

22. C

Someone looking into the mirror would see an image of the candle at point C, the same distance behind the mirror as the candle is in front of the mirror. The reflected rays from the light of the candle appear to originate at point C.

23. B

The two postulates are: (1) All inertial reference frames are equivalent; and (2) All observers will measure the same value for the speed of light regardless of any relative motion between the observer and the light source.

24. B

The astronaut's moving clock will run more slowly according to the Earth's frame of reference, and the astronaut will age more slowly as well.

25. E

If we break the tensions in the strings into their x- and y-components, we see that the x-components cancel each other out, and the sum of the two y-components of the tension must equal the weight of the block.

Thus, $2T \sin\theta = mg$, and $T = \dfrac{mg}{2 \sin\theta}$.

26. E

The energy of the emitted photon must equal the difference between two levels, whether the electron jumps down from the 4th level to a lower level and emits a photon, or jumps down from the 4th level to a lower level and emits a photon and then jumps to an even lower level, emitting another photon. None of the energy differences in the diagram correspond to 5 eV.

27. D

Since the energy of the emitted photon is proportional to its frequency, the highest energy difference corresponds to the highest frequency photon.

28. D

By Newton's second law, the acceleration is proportional to the force, and inversely proportional to the mass. Thus,

$$\frac{4\,F}{2\,m} = 2\,a.$$

29. B

$$s = v_i t + \frac{1}{2}\,at^2 = (0) + \frac{1}{2}\,(5\text{ m/s}^2)(4\text{ s})^2 = 40\text{ m}.$$

30. A

Light bends away from the normal when it passes into a less dense medium, or, equivalently, the angle of refraction is greater than the angle of incidence when light enters a less dense medium.

31. D

Lens III is a diverging (concave) lens, which will diverge parallel rays passing through it. The other two lenses will converge parallel rays passing through them.

32. D

For the meter stick to remain horizontal, the torque on the left of the string must equal the torque on the right of the string.

$$Mgr_1 = mgr_2$$
$$(M)(30\text{ cm}) = (6\text{ kg})(50\text{ cm})$$

Thus, $M = 10$ kg.

33. E

By the second right-hand rule, if you put your fingers in the direction of the magnetic field (into the page), and your thumb in the direction of the current, the force on the wire comes out of your palm, toward the top of the page.

34. D

By the ideal gas law,

$$\frac{PV}{T} = \frac{4\,PV}{4\,T}.$$

35. C

The internal energy of the gas rises to 400 J when 100 J of work is done on it, then loses internal energy when the gas itself does 50 J of work, leaving an increase in internal energy of 350 J.

36. D

Since the electric field is uniform everywhere between the plates, the proton will experience the same force (downward) everywhere between the plates.

37. C

Since the electric field is uniform everywhere between the plates, the electron will experience the same force (upward) everywhere between the plates.

38. D

Using the first right-hand rule, we place our thumb in the direction of the current and our fingers curl around the wire in the direction of the magnetic field, which is out of the page above the wire and into the page at point A below the wire.

39. D

Once again, applying the first right-hand rule, the wire on the left creates a magnetic field halfway between the wires that points down toward the bottom of the page, as does the current on the right. Thus, the net magnetic field at that point is downward.

40. E

The free-body force diagram for the block looks like this:

The forces in the y-direction must balance each other, and so $F_N + F \sin\theta = W$, or $F_N = 180\ \text{N} - 40\ \text{N} = 140\ \text{N}$

41. C

Since the block is moving with a constant velocity in the horizontal direction, the forces in the horizontal direction must balance each other. Thus,

friction = $F\cos\theta = (80\ \text{N})(0.87) = 70\ \text{N}$.

42. D

The coefficient of friction is the ratio of the frictional force to the normal force. Thus,

$$\mu = \frac{f}{F_N} = \frac{70\ \text{N}}{140\ \text{N}} = 0.5.$$

43. A

The potential energy is maximum at the amplitudes A_1 and A_2, and decreases parabolically to zero at the equilibrium position O.

44. C

The kinetic energy is always doing the opposite of the potential energy. When the potential energy is maximum, the kinetic energy is minimum, and vice-versa, with the maximum kinetic energy occurring at the equilibrium position O.

45. D

For an ideal spring, the spring force acting on the mass is proportional to the stretch of the spring x (Hooke's law), and therefore a force vs. distance graph for this spring would be linear. The force is maximum at the amplitudes, and zero at the equilibrium position.

46. E

The gravitational force is inversely proportional to the square of the distance between the moons and the planet, so the closer moon, being twice as close to the planet, will experience four times the force as the farther moon, which is twice as far away.

47. A

The shorter the orbital radius, the more quickly a satellite will complete an orbit.

48. C

At the ball's maximum height, its speed is zero.
$$v = 0 = v_i - gt$$
$$v_i = gt = (10\ \text{m/s}^2)(3\text{s}) = 30\ \text{m/s}$$

49. C

Since gravity causes the acceleration of the ball, and gravity is still acting on the ball at the top of its flight, the acceleration is still $10\ \text{m/s}^2$. If there were no acceleration of the ball at the top, the ball would never come back down.

50. D

The maximum height of the ball is the same distance as if we dropped the ball from its maximum height and let it fall for 3 seconds:
$$s = \frac{1}{2}gt^2 = \frac{1}{2}(10\ \text{m/s}^2)(3\ \text{s})^2 = 45\ \text{m}.$$

51. B

The 60 μg sample is cut in half five times in 120 days: 60 μg, 30 μg, 15 μg, 7.5 μg, 3.75 μg, and 1.88 μg, rounded to 2 μg of thorium remaining after 120 days.

52. E

An ammeter must be placed in series with the resistor through which it is measuring the current, so that the same current passes through the ammeter and the resistor. A voltmeter is placed in parallel with a resistor, so that the voltmeter and resistor will have the same voltage across them, but the resistance of the voltmeter should be high, so that very little current will flow through it.

53. B

Since the three resistors are in series, the total resistance is the sum of the resistances. By Ohm's law,

$$R + 4\,\Omega + 4\,\Omega = \frac{20\ V}{2\ A}\ \text{implies that}\ R = 2\,\Omega.$$

54. C

Power dissipated is equal to the product of the current squared and the resistance:

$$P = I^2 R = (2\ A)^2 (4\ \Omega) = 16\ \text{W}.$$

55. B

The heat lost by the metal equals the heat gained by the liquid:

$$m_{metal}\,c_{metal}(T_f - T_i) = m_{liquid}\,c_{liquid}\,(T_f - T_i),$$

$$(2\ \text{kg})(200\ \text{J/kg°C})(T_f - 120°C) =$$
$$(4\ \text{kg})(600\ \text{J/kg°C})(T_f - 20°C),$$

$$T_f = 34°C.$$

56. A

Since heat is lost to the surroundings, the water is not gaining as much heat as it would in a totally insulated container, so the final temperature would be lower than our previous calculation.

57. B

The acceleration is the slope of the graph from a time of zero to 4 s, which is 1 m/s^2.

58. C

The displacement of the object is the area under the graph from a time of zero to 8 s, which is 24 m.

59. D

If the spheres begin by being equally and oppositely charged, the total charge on both together is zero. When they come into contact with each other, they will exchange charge in such a way as to keep a total charge of zero, but each must end up with the same amount of charge, which would have to be zero. Thus, each sphere will be neutral.

60. A

Light enters the water, bends, reflects off of the pencil, and then comes back out of the water to your eye. Because the light changes media, it refracts, and you see a distorted image of the pencil.

61. B

The law of entropy states that all natural systems tend toward a state of higher disorder. Heat leaving a hotter body implies a move to higher disorder, because the vibrating molecules in the hot body impart momentum and energy to the molecules in the cold body, causing them to be in a state of higher disorder.

62. C

The forces F_1 and F_3 are equal and opposite and therefore cancel each other out, leaving only F_2 as the resultant.

63. A

Coulomb's law gives $F = \dfrac{Kq_1 q_2}{r^2} =$

$$\frac{(10^{10}\ Nm^2/C^2)(10^{-19}\ C)(10^{-19}\ C)}{(10^{-10}\ m)^2} = 10^{-8}\ N.$$

64. D

Conservation of momentum:

$$m_1v_1 = (m_1 + m_2)v'$$
$$(3 \text{ kg})v_1 = (3 \text{ kg} + 6 \text{ kg})(2 \text{ m/s})$$
$$v_1 = 6 \text{ m/s.}$$

65. C

$$\text{Power} = \frac{\text{Work}}{\text{time}} = \frac{Fs}{t} = \frac{(500 \text{ N})(2 \text{ m})}{20 \text{ s}} = 50 \text{ W.}$$

66. A

A wave pulse, when reflected off a fixed end, will invert and return on the opposite side of the string with the same amplitude.

67. B

A coil of wire is rotated in a magnetic field, inducing a current in the wire by electromagnetic induction.

68. B

The atomic number of an element is the number of protons it has in its nucleus. When an element emits an alpha particle, it loses two protons (and two neutrons), and therefore loses 2 atomic mass units. When an element emits a beta particle, a neutron in the nucleus has ejected an electron, leaving one more proton in the nucleus and increasing the atomic number by one. Thus, this element loses 4 protons and then gains one, leaving the nucleus 3 atomic mass units less than before.

69. E

The bright and dark lines are called an interference pattern, and are created by the interference of the light waves after they have passed through the double-slit.

70. A

If the screen is moved back away from the slits, the bright band will become wider, because the light waves will have a little more space to spread out before striking the screen.

71. A

The waves trailing the sound source appear to the listener to have a lower frequency, and thus a lower pitch, since the waves reach the listener's ears less often.

72. C

A more intense (brighter) light would contain more photons, which can eject more electrons.

73. B

The gas atoms create pressure on the container by striking the container walls, not each other.

74. B

By Newton's third law, the law of action and reaction, both the astronaut and the tool experience the same force during the same time interval, and thus the same impulse acts on each of them. According to the law of conservation of momentum, they each have different accelerations and resulting velocities, since their masses are different.

75. D

The period for one oscillation of the pendulum is 2 s, and the frequency is the inverse of its period, $\frac{1}{2}$ cycle per second, or $\frac{1}{2}$ Hz.

Glossary

A

absolute zero
the lowest possible temperature, at which all molecular motion would cease and a gas would have no volume

acceleration
the rate of change in velocity

action-reaction forces
the pair of forces that are equal in magnitude and opposite in direction; these forces are involved in the same interaction, but act on different objects

adiabatic
the expansion or compression of a gas without a gain or loss of heat

air resistance
the opposing force the air exerts on an object moving through it

alpha decay
the process by which a radioactive element emits an alpha particle

alpha particle
positively charged particle consisting of two protons and two neutrons

alternating current
electric current that rapidly reverses its direction

ammeter
device used to measure electrical current

ampere
unit of electrical current equal to one coulomb per second

amplitude
maximum displacement from equilibrium position; the distance from the midpoint of a wave to its crest or trough

angle of incidence
the angle between the normal line to a surface and the incident ray or wave

angle of reflection
the angle between the normal line to a surface and the reflected ray or wave

angle of refraction
the angle between the normal line to a surface and the refracted ray or wave at the boundary between two media

angular momentum
the conserved rotational quantity that is equal to the product of the mass, velocity, and radius of motion

antinode
point of maximum displacement of two or more waves constructively interfering

atom
the smallest particle of an element that can be identified with that element; consists of protons and neutrons in the nucleus, and electrons in motion around the nucleus

atomic mass unit
the unit of mass equal to $\frac{1}{12}$ the mass of a carbon-12 nucleus

atomic number
the number of protons in the nucleus of an atom

average acceleration
the acceleration of an object measured over a time interval; the total change in velocity divided by the total time taken to achieve that velocity

average velocity
the velocity of an object measured over a time interval; the total change in displacement divided by the total time taken to achieve that displacement

B

battery
device that converts chemical energy into electrical energy, creating a potential difference (voltage)

beta decay
the emission of an electron from the nucleus of a radioactive element as a result of a neutron decaying into a proton

beta particle
high speed electron emitted from a radioactive element when a neutron decays into a proton

binding energy
the nuclear energy that binds protons and neutrons in the nucleus of the atom

boiling point
temperature at which a substance boils at normal atmospheric pressure, changing from a liquid to a vapor state

C

calorie
the amount of heat required to raise the temperature of one gram of water by one degree Celsius

calorimeter
device that isolates objects to measure temperature changes due to heat flow

capacitance
ratio of the charge stored on a conductor per unit voltage

capacitor
electrical device used to store charge and energy in an electric field

Carnot efficiency
the ideal efficiency of a heat engine or refrigerator working between two constant temperatures

center of mass
the point that represents the average location of all the mass in a system; for a rigid object, it is the point at which all of the mass of an object can be considered concentrated

centripetal acceleration
for an object moving in circular motion, the acceleration that is directed toward the center of the circular path

centripetal force
the central force causing an object to move in a circular path

chain reaction
nuclear process producing more neutrons, which in turn can create more nuclear processes, usually applied to fission

charge
the fundamental quantity that underlies all electrical phenomena

charging by conduction
transfer of charge by actual contact between two objects

charging by induction
transfer of charge by bringing a charged object near a conductor, then grounding the conductor

circular motion
motion of an object moving at a constant radius in a circular path

closed system
a system that can exchange energy but cannot exchange matter with the surroundings

coefficient of friction
ratio of the frictional force between two surfaces and the normal force between the surfaces

component
the shadow or projection of a vector on a particular coordinate axis

compound
chemical substance consisting of two or more different elements combined in a fixed proportion

concave lens
a lens that is thinner in the center than at the edges; also known as a diverging lens

concave mirror
a mirror that converges light rays to a focal point; also known as a converging mirror

conductor
a material through which heat or electric current can easily flow

conservation of charge
law stating that the total charge in a system must remain constant during any process

conserved properties
any properties that remain constant during a process

constant acceleration
acceleration that does not change during a time interval

constant velocity
velocity that does not change during a time interval

constructive interference
addition of two or more waves that are in phase, resulting in a wave of increased amplitude

convection
heat transfer by the movement of a heated substance, such as currents in a fluid

conventional current
the movement of positive charges through a conductor

converging lens
a lens that converges light rays to a focal point; also known as a convex lens

convex lens
a lens that is thicker in the center than at the edges; also known as a converging lens

convex mirror
a mirror that diverges light rays; also known as a diverging mirror

cosine
the ratio of the adjacent side of an angle in a right triangle to the hypotenuse

coulomb
the unit for electric charge

Coulomb's law
the electric force between two charges is proportional to the product of the charges and inversely proportional to the square of the distance between them

crest of a wave
the highest point on a wave

critical angle
the minimum angle for light entering a different medium at which total internal reflection will occur

critical mass
the minimum amount of mass of fissionable material necessary to sustain a nuclear chain reaction

D

de Broglie wavelength
the wavelength associated with a moving particle with a momentum mv

density
the ratio of the mass to the volume of a substance

destructive interference
addition of two or more waves that are out of phase, resulting in a wave of decreased amplitude

diffraction
the spreading of a wave beyond the edge of a barrier or through an opening

diffraction grating
material containing many parallel lines that are very closely spaced so that when light is passed through the lines, an interference pattern is produced

diffuse reflection
reflection of light in many directions by a rough surface

direct current
electric current whose flow of charges is in one direction only

dispersion of light
the separation of light into its component colors using a prism or diffraction grating

displacement
change in position in a particular direction (vector)

distance
the length moved between two points (scalar)

diverging lens
a lens that is thinner in the middle than at the edges that diverges light rays passing through it; also known as a concave lens

Doppler effect
the apparent change in frequency of a sound or light source due to relative motion between the source and the observer

dynamics
the study of the causes of motion (forces)

E

elastic collision
a collision in which both momentum and kinetic energy are conserved

electric circuit
a continuous closed path in which electric charges can flow

electric current
flow of charged particles; conventionally, the flow of positive charges

electric field
the space around a charge in which another charge will experience a force; electric field lines always point from positive charge to negative charge

electric generator
a device that uses electromagnetic induction to convert mechanical energy into electrical energy

electric potential
the amount of work per unit charge to move a charge from a very distant point to another point in an electric field

electric potential difference
the difference in potential between two points in an electric field; also known as voltage

electromagnet
a magnet with a magnetic field produced by an electric current

electromagnetic induction
inducing a voltage in a conductor by changing the magnetic field around the conductor

electromagnetic wave
a wave produced by the vibration of an electric field and a magnetic field, which propagates itself through space at a very high speed

electron
the smallest negatively charged particle

electrostatics
the study of electric charge, field, and potential at rest

element
a substance made of only one kind of atom

elementary charge
the smallest existing charge; the charge on one electron or one proton (1.6×10^{-19} C)

ellipse
an oval-shaped curve that is the path taken by a point that moves such that the sum of its distances from two fixed points (foci) is constant; the planets move in elliptical orbits around the Sun

emf
electromotive force; another name for voltage, particularly voltage induced in a conductor by electromagnetic induction

energy
the nonmaterial quantity that is the ability to do work on a system

energy level
amount of energy an electron has while in a particular orbit around the nucleus of an atom

entropy
the measure of the amount of disorder in a system

equilibrant
the vector that can balance a resultant vector; the force that can put a system in equilibrium

equilibrium
condition of a system in which the vector sum of the forces and torques is equal to zero

equivalent resistance
the single resistance that could replace the individual resistances in a circuit and produce the same result

evaporation
the process by which a liquid changes into a gas

excited state
the energy level of an electron in an atom after the electron has absorbed energy

external force
force exerted from outside the defined system

F

farad
the unit for capacitance equal to one coulomb per volt

Faraday's law of induction
law stating that a voltage can be induced in a conductor by changing the magnetic field around the conductor

first law of thermodynamics
the heat lost by a system is equal to the heat gained by the system minus any work done by the system; conservation of energy

fission
the splitting of a large nucleus into two smaller ones

fluid
any substance that flows, typically a liquid or a gas

focal length
the distance between the center of a lens or mirror to the point at which the incoming parallel rays converge at the focal point

focal point
the point at which incoming parallel light rays converge or appear to originate

force
any influence that tends to accelerate an object; a push or a pull

frame of reference
point of view or coordinate system used to study motion

free fall
motion under the influence of gravity

frequency
the number of vibrations or revolutions per unit of time

friction
the force that acts to resist the relative motion between two rough surfaces that are in contact with each other

fundamental overtone
lowest frequency sound produced by a musical instrument

fundamental particles
the particles (quarks and leptons) of which all matter is composed

fusion
the combining of two light nuclei into a heavier one with a release of energy

G

galvanometer
device used to measure small electrical currents

gamma decay
process by which a radioactive element emits a gamma ray

gamma ray
high energy electromagnetic wave emitted by a radioactive nucleus

gas
a state of matter that expands to fill a container

gravitational field
space around a mass in which another mass will experience a force

gravitational force
the force of attraction between two objects due to their masses

gravitational potential energy
the energy a mass has because of its position in a gravitational field

grounding
the process of connecting a charged object to the earth or a large conductor to remove its excess charge

ground state
the lowest energy state of an electron in an atom

H

half-life
the time it takes for half the atoms in a radioactive sample to decay

heat
the energy that is transferred from one body to another because of a temperature difference

heat engine
device that changes internal energy into mechanical work

heat of fusion
energy needed to change a unit mass of a substance from a solid to a liquid state at the melting point

heat of vaporization
energy needed to change a unit mass of a substance from a liquid to a gaseous state at the boiling point

Heisenberg uncertainty principle
the more accurately one determines the position of a subatomic particle, the less accurately its momentum is known, and vice versa

hertz
the unit for frequency equal to one cycle or vibration per second

Hooke's law
the displacement (stretch) of a spring is proportional to the force applied to it

hypotenuse
the side opposite to the right angle in a right triangle

I

image
reproduction of an object using lenses or mirrors

impulse
the product of the force acting on an object and the time over which it acts

impulse-momentum theorem
the impulse imparted to an object is equal to the change in momentum it produces

incandescent body
an object that emits light because of its high temperature

index of refraction
the ratio of the speed of light in a vacuum to the speed of light in another medium

inelastic collision
a collision in which only momentum is conserved, and not kinetic energy

inertia
the tendency of an object to not change its state of rest or motion at a constant velocity; mass is a measure of inertia

inertial reference frame
a reference frame that is at rest or moving with a constant velocity; Newton's laws are valid within any inertial reference frame

infrared
electromagnetic waves of frequencies just below those of red visible light

initial velocity
the velocity at which an object starts at the beginning of a time interval

in phase
term applied to two or more waves whose crests and troughs arrive at a place at the same time in such a way as to produce constructive interference

instantaneous acceleration
the acceleration of an object at a particular instant of time

instantaneous position
the position of an object at a particular instant of time

instantaneous velocity
the velocity of an object at a particular instant of time

insulator
a material that is a poor conductor of heat or electric current due to a poor supply of free electrons

interference of waves
displacements of two or more waves in the same medium at the same time, producing either larger or smaller waves

internal forces
forces between objects in the same system

inverse relationship
relationship between two variables that change in opposite directions, so that if one is doubled the other is reduced to one-half

inverse square law
situation where one physical quantity varies as the inverse square of the distance from its source

isolated system
a collection of objects not acted upon by any external forces and which energy neither enters or exits

isotope
a form of an element that has a particular number of neutrons; has the same atomic number but a different mass number than the other isotopes that occupy the same place on the periodic table

J

joule
the unit for energy equal to one Newton-meter

joule heating
the increase in temperature in an electrical conductor due to the conversion of electrical energy into heat energy

Joule's law of heating
the heating power of an electric current through a resistance is equal to the product of the current and the voltage across the resistor

K

Kelvin (absolute) temperature scale
scale in which zero Kelvins is defined as absolute zero, the temperature at which all molecular motion ceases

Kepler's laws
the three laws of motion for objects, such as the planets and the Sun, attracted to each other by the gravitational force

kilogram
the fundamental unit of mass

kilowatt-hour
amount of energy equal to 3.6×10^6 joules, usually used in electrical measurement

kinematics
the study of how motion occurs, including distance, displacement, speed, velocity, acceleration, and time

kinetic energy
the energy a mass has by virtue of its motion

kinetic molecular theory
the description of matter as being made up of extremely small particles that are in constant motion

L

laser
light amplification by stimulated emission of radiation; laser light is coherent and monochromatic (i.e., all the waves are of the same wavelength and are in phase with each other)

law of conservation of energy
the total energy of a system remains constant during a process

law of conservation of momentum
the total momentum of a system remains constant during a process

law of inertia
see *Newton's first law*

law of reflection
the angle of incidence of an incoming wave is equal to the angle of reflection measured from a line normal (perpendicular) to the surface

law of universal gravitation
the gravitational force between two masses is proportional to the product of the masses and inversely proportional to the square of the distance between them

lens
a piece of transparent material that can bend light rays to converge or diverge

lever arm
perpendicular distance from the axis of rotation to a line of force producing or potentially producing the rotation

light
the range of electromagnetic waves that is visible to the human eye; alternately used by physicists to refer to the entire range of electromagnetic radiation

linear accelerator
device used to accelerate subatomic particles to high energies so that they may be more easily studied

linear relationship
relationship between two variables that are proportional to each other

linear restoring force
a force such as a spring force in which the force is proportional to the displacement (stretch) and opposite to the direction of the displacement

line spectrum
discrete lines emitted by a cool excited gas

liquid
substance that has a fixed volume, but assumes the shape of its container

lodestone
a naturally occurring magnetic rock made principally of iron

longitudinal wave
wave in which the vibration of the medium is parallel to the direction of motion of the wave

loudness
the quality of a sound wave that is measured by its amplitude

M

magnetic domain
cluster of magnetically aligned atoms

magnetic field
the space around a magnet in which another magnet or moving charge will experience a force

magnification
ratio of the size of an optical image to the size of the object

mass defect
the mass equivalent of the binding energy in the nucleus of an atom by $E = mc^2$

mass number
the total number of protons and neutrons in the nucleus of a particular atom

matter wave
the wave associated with a mass having a momentum according to the de Broglie hypothesis

mechanical energy
the sum of the potential and kinetic energies in a system

mechanical resonance
condition in which natural oscillation frequency equals frequency of driving force

mechanical wave
a wave that needs a medium through which to travel

melting point
the temperature at which a substance changes from a solid to a liquid state

meter
the SI unit of length

molecule
two or more atoms joined to form a larger particle

momentum
the product of the mass of an object and its velocity

monochromatic light
light having a single color or frequency

N

net force
the vector sum of the forces acting on an object

neutral
having no net charge

neutron
an electrically neutral subatomic particle found in the nucleus of an atom

newton
the SI unit for force equal to the force needed to accelerate one kilogram of mass by one meter per second squared

Newton's first law of motion
every body continues in its state of rest or at a constant velocity unless acted on by an unbalanced force; also known as the law of inertia

Newton's second law of motion
a net force acting on a mass causes an acceleration that is proportional to and in the direction of the force and inversely proportional to the mass of the object

Newton's third law of motion
for every action force there is an equal and opposite reaction force

node
the point of minimum displacement in a standing wave

noninertial reference frame
a reference frame that is accelerating; Newton's laws are not valid within a noninertial reference frame

normal
a line that is perpendicular to a surface

normal force
the reaction force of a surface on an object when an object is in contact with the surface; always acts perpendicularly to the surface

nuclear fission
the splitting of a heavy nucleus into smaller fragments with the release of energy

nuclear fusion
the combining of two light nuclei into one larger one with the release of energy

nuclear reaction
any process in the nucleus of an atom that causes the number of protons and/or neutrons to change

nuclear reactor
device in which nuclear fission or fusion is used to generate electricity

nucleon
either a proton or a neutron in the nucleus of an atom

O

object (optics)
the source of diverging light rays

ohm
the SI unit for resistance equal to one volt per ampere

Ohm's law
the ratio of voltage to current in a circuit is a constant called resistance

opaque
material that will not transmit light

open system
a system that can exchange both matter and energy with the surroundings

out of phase
term applied to two or more waves when the crest of one wave arrives at a point at the same time as the trough of a second wave arrives, producing destructive interference

P

parallel circuit
an electric circuit that has two or more paths for the current to follow, allowing each branch to function independently of the others

Pascal
the SI unit for pressure equal to one newton of force per square meter of area

period
the time for one complete cycle or revolution

periodic motion
motion that repeats itself at regular intervals of time

photoelectric effect
the ejection of electrons from certain metals when exposed to light of a minimum frequency

photon
the smallest particle (quantum) of light

physics
the study of matter and energy and all their relationships

pitch
the perceived characteristic of a sound that is equivalent to its frequency

Planck's constant
the quantity that results when the energy of a photon is divided by its frequency

plane mirror
smooth, flat surface that reflects light regularly

polarized light
light in which the electric fields are all in the same plane

position
the distance between an object and a reference point

position-time graph
the graph of the motion of an object that shows how its position varies with time

power
the rate at which work is done or energy is dissipated

pressure
force per unit area

primary light colors
red, green, or blue light

principal axis
the line connecting the center of curvature of a curved mirror with its geometrical vertex; the line perpendicular to the plane of a lens passing through its center

principle of superposition
the displacement due to two or more interfering waves is equal to the sum of the displacement of the individual waves

projectile
any object that is projected by a force and continues to move by its own inertia in a gravitational field

proton
subatomic particle with positive charge that is the nucleus of a hydrogen atom

Q

quantized
occuring in multiples of some smallest possible increment (quantum); refers to quantities

quantum mechanics
the study of the properties of matter using its wave properties

quantum model of the atom
atomic model in which only the probability of locating an electron is known

quark
one of the elementary particles of which all protons and neutrons are made

R

radiation
the transmission of energy by electromagnetic waves, or the particles given off by radioactive atoms

radioactive decay
the spontaneous change of unstable nuclei into other nuclei

range of a projectile
the horizontal distance between the launch point of a projectile and where it returns to its launch height

ray model of light
light may be represented by a straight line along the direction of motion

ray optics
study of light using the ray model

real image
an image that can be projected onto a screen

reference point
zero location in a coordinate system

refraction
the bending of a wave due to a change in medium

resistance
the ratio of the voltage across a device to the current running through it

resistor
device designed to have a specific resistance to electric current

resultant
the vector sum of two or more vectors

right-hand rules
used to find the magnetic field around a current-carrying wire or the force acting on a wire or charge in a magnetic field

Rutherford's model of the atom
the first nuclear model of the atom (1911)

S

scalar
a quantity in physics, such as mass, that can be completely described by its magnitude or size, without regard to direction

schematic diagram
a diagram using special symbols to represent a circuit

scientific notation
numbers represented as a mantissa times a power of ten, such as 3×10^8

second
the SI unit of time

second law of thermodynamics
heat flows naturally from a region of higher temperature to a lower temperature; all natural systems tend toward a state of higher disorder

series circuit
an electric circuit in which devices are arranged so that charge flows through each equally

SI
Systeme Internationale; agreed-upon method of using the metric system of measurement

simple harmonic motion
periodic motion in which the restoring force is proportional to the displacement of the oscillating object, and this force is directed toward the point of equilibrium

sine
the ratio of the opposite side of an angle in a right triangle to its hypotenuse

sliding (or kinetic) friction
resistive force between two surfaces that are moving relative to each other

slope
on a graph, the ratio of the vertical separation (rise) to the horizontal separation (run)

solid
state of matter with fixed volume and shape

special relativity
theory that describes how mass, length, and time are related, and the equivalence of matter and energy

specific heat capacity
the quantity of heat required to raise the temperature of one gram of water by one degree Celsius

spectrum
the range of electromagnetic waves from low frequency to high frequency, or colors when white light is passed through a prism

speed
the ratio of distance to time

speed of light
3×10^8 m/s in a vacuum; represented by the constant c

standing wave
wave with stationary nodes produced by two identical waves traveling in opposite directions in the same medium at the same time

static friction
the resistive force that opposes the start of motion between two surfaces in contact

strong nuclear force
the force that binds protons and neutrons together in the nucleus of an atom

superconductor
material that has practically no resistance to the flow of current at low temperatures

symmetry
property that is not changed when the reference frame is changed

system
defined collection of objects

T

tangent
touching at only one point on a curve; in a right triangle, the ratio of the opposite side to an adjacent side for either of the acute angles

tangential velocity
the velocity tangent to the path of an object moving in a curved path

temperature
the property of a body that indicates how hot or cold a substance is with respect to a standard, or a measure of the average internal kinetic energies of the molecules in an object

terminal velocity
the constant velocity of a falling object when the force of air resistance equals the object's weight

test charge
the very small charge used to test the strength of an electric field

thermal energy
the sum of the internal potential and kinetic energies of the random motion of the molecules making up an object

thermal equilibrium
state between two or more objects or systems in which temperature doesn't vary

thermal expansion
increase in length or volume of a material due to an increase in temperature

thermodynamics
the study of heat transfer

torque
the tendency of a force to cause rotation about an axis; the product of the force and the lever arm length

total internal reflection
the complete reflection of light that strikes the boundary between two media at an angle greater than the critical angle

trajectory
the path followed by a projectile

transformer
device that uses electromagnetic induction to transfer energy from one circuit to another

translucent
a material that passes light but distorts its path

transparent
material through which light can pass without distorting the direction of the rays

transverse wave
a wave in which the vibration is perpendicular to the velocity of the wave

trigonometry
the study of the relationships among the angles and sides of triangles

trough of a wave
the low point of wave motion

U

ultraviolet
electromagnetic waves of frequencies higher than those of violet light

uniform acceleration
constant acceleration

uniform circular motion
motion in a circular path of constant radius at a constant speed

uniform velocity
constant velocity

V

vector quantity
a quantity, such as displacement, having both magnitude and direction

velocity
ratio of the displacement of an object to a time interval

velocity-time graph
plot of the velocity of an object as a function of time, the slope of which is acceleration

virtual image
an image that cannot be projected onto a screen; point at which diverging light rays appear to originate

volt
the SI unit of potential or potential difference

voltage
amount of electric potential or potential difference

W

watt
the SI unit for power equal to one joule of energy per second

wavelength
the distance between successive identical parts of a wave

weight
the result of a gravitational force acting on a mass; the product of mass and the acceleration due to gravity at a location

weightlessness
the state of free fall where an object experiences only the force of gravity

white light
visible light consisting of all colors

work
the scalar product of force and displacement

work-energy theorem
the work done on a system is equal to the change in energy of the system

work function
the minimum energy required to release an electron from a metal

X

X-ray
high-frequency, high-energy electromagnetic waves or photons

Index

NOTES

NOTES

NOTES

NOTES